FRENCH CANADA
IN TRANSITION

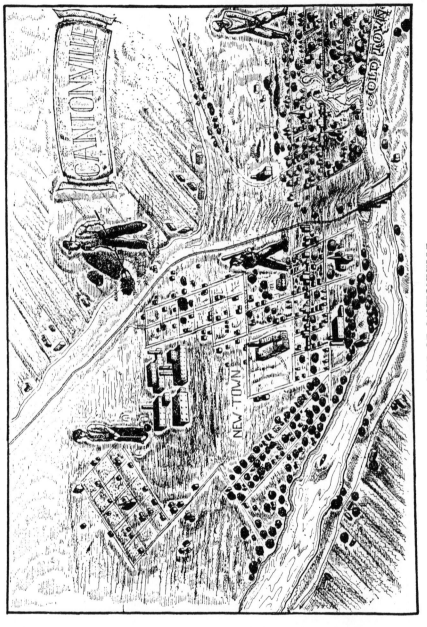

MAP OF CANTONVILLE

FRENCH CANADA
IN TRANSITION

EVERETT C. HUGHES

Phoenix Books

THE UNIVERSITY OF CHICAGO PRESS

CHICAGO AND LONDON

THE UNIVERSITY OF CHICAGO PRESS, CHICAGO & LONDON
The University of Toronto Press, Toronto 5, Canada

FOREWORD

FRENCH CANADA STILL IN TRANSITION

IN QUEBEC, as wherever the industrial revolution starts and continues, people move from the countryside to the cities; but English and French have not moved at the same pace and time. Montreal is said to have been predominantly English at the beginning of the nineteenth century; in the first national census taken in 1871 it showed 48,000 persons of English, Irish, and Scottish origins against 57,000 of French origin. With the passage of time the ratio of French to English has steadily increased. The 1931 census, whose figures were the latest available for the first printing of this book, showed 620,000 of French against 265,000 of British ancestry. The 1961 census shows the French to have climbed to 1,353,000, the British to 378,000. Aside from the steadily rising ratio of French to British origin, we note the rapid increase of other origins, which by 1961 were approximately equal to British and which reflect the post–World War II immigration.

In the countryside French population has increased very slowly: from 745,000 in 1871 to 921,000 in 1921, at which date, for the first time, more French were classified as urban than as rural. The crossing of the lines of rural and urban population undoubtedly took place as an immediate result of the industrial development of World War I. Since then the divergence has been considerable and is probably underestimated by the census, since with the overflowing of the city boundaries many people are classified as rural for census purposes who are economically a part of the city. The 1961 census, whose definition takes this into account to some extent, shows for the French 3,009,000 urban against 1,232,000 rural.

More precise than residence is the classification by occupation, though this too has some elements of incomparability from census to census. In 1931 the Quebec male labor force was 27 per cent agricultural, a proportion identical to that of Ontario and somewhat lower than that of Canada (34 per cent). The 1961 census shows that the proportion for Quebec has gone down to 9 per cent, as has that for Ontario, and both are again lower than Canada as a whole which stands at 12 per cent. Ontario and Quebec have thus arrived at about the same point, but in a process of evolution by which the figure for

Ontario fell considerably earlier. Thus Quebec increased its agricultural labor force during the 1930's when that of Ontario had already
started to fall; Ontario's biggest drop came in the 1940's, while that
of Quebec came in the 1950's.

The generalization that comes out of all this is that the industrialization and urbanization of French Canada have been retarded:
Quebec as a whole became urbanized later than Ontario, and within
Quebec the French became urbanized later than the English. The
1961 census shows the French not only to have caught up in these
respects but to be in a position of accelerating urbanization. Montreal's growth was 18.6 per cent in 1951–56, and 20.9 per cent in
1956–61. Almost all the cities of English Canada grew by smaller percentages in the second period than in the first.

The sentiment which has gone along with this growth has been
crystallized governmentally in the *politique de grandeur*, which has its
roots in these demographic facts and draws on French-Canadian history and aspirations. It is reflected in the pride of Montrealers in the
accomplishments of Hydro-Québec, in the *métro* which is being built,
and in the World's Fair of 1967—their way of celebrating 100 years
of Confederation. Many of them hope that this anniversary will also
celebrate the advent of a larger constitutional position for what in
anticipation they call the *État de Québec*.

Greatness is not without its problems. The pace of urbanization has
.outstripped that of employment. Unemployment is high enough—
generally above 6 per cent—for Canada as a whole, and for the Province of Quebec the latest labor-force survey shows 192,000 unemployed
out of 1,833,000, or more than 10 per cent. Whatever economic causes
may underlie these figures, French Canada looks for the resolution of
the problem in a better place for its members at all levels of the labor
force of the country. It is concerned about both these unemployment
levels, which reflect difficulty in getting a grip on the bottom rungs
of the labor-force ladder, and the even better known fact that the
leaders of industry are English, as they were thirty years ago.

French Canadians see both these facts in terms of their coming
second to industry and so being threatened with a permanent disadvantage; indeed, having left behind the claims to merely formal rights
which made up much of the past history of relations between the two
groups, French Canadians are now seeking substantive equality.
Survivance of language and religion are no longer an issue; they are
taken for granted. The search for a scapegoat described in the first

printing of this book has been abandoned and replaced by a bold attack on the very citadels of English power. Equally out of date is the aspiration to a *victoire des berceaux;* the sharp differential between French and English birth rates of thirty years ago seems as much as anything to have been a phenomenon of the earlier urbanization of the English (see table). Nationalism, everywhere an urban phenome-

BIRTH RATES PER THOUSAND: CANADA,
QUEBEC, AND ONTARIO, 1921–61

	Canada	Quebec	Ontario
1921–25.......	27.4	35.5	23.7
1941–45.......	23.5	28.4	19.9
1960..........	26.9	27.0	26.2

non, tends to clash with religion, at least in the forms that were appropriate to the rural scene, and religion is changing rapidly in consequence. The whole process of change finds its culmination in the educational system, now discovered to be inadequate to produce either the technicians or the leaders that the new situation demands.

The industrial frontier between English and French Canada is still drawn in Cantonville at the same point where it was a quarter-century ago. That is why it seems useful to reissue this study without change from the original. But the interaction on this frontier is affected by a new and much more confident nationalism which pervades the whole of French Canada. That is why the need for research and analysis is ever more pressing than it was twenty five-years ago.

NATHAN KEYFITZ

MONTRÉAL
April 1963

PREFACE

IT HAS been a doctrine of our time that the earth's surface should be divisible into clearly bounded territories, each occupied by a racially and culturally homogeneous people who can celebrate their past, their present, and their hopes in common ceremony and who can act together to administer their domestic affairs and to defend themselves from outside dangers. Few countries conform, in all particulars, to this ideal. This fact, together with the continual expansion of economic regions without too much respect for national boundaries, and along with all the dynamics of human increase and migration, makes the relations between races and peoples more important and complicated than ever. While these relations seem to require more diplomatic activity than in the past, they have become less capable of being settled by agreements between diplomatic agents; for peoples penetrate one another, upsetting internal as well as external adjustments; and the diplomat is powerless to deal with internal problems.

The two great countries of North America notoriously fail, by virtue of internal ethnic and cultural diversity, to conform to the ideal of the nation-state. Both were settled by immigration from many countries. The problem of immigrant populations they have in common, although it is more intense in the United States. The United States has the peculiar problem of adjusting relations between the Negroes and the rest of the population. Canada, in turn, has the special problem of maintaining workable relations between her two chief ethnic elements —the English Canadians and the French Canadians. This is a minority problem, in the strict sense; for two ethnic groups, each living on what it considers its native soil, maintain a common government.

The French Canadians, descended from people who were in Canada before the middle of the eighteenth century, are the more homogeneous and have the richer tradition of strictly Canadian life. The English Canadians came much later and are more diverse in culture. But they are the more numerous and, in certain spheres, the more powerful. It is the French who are, in both number and mentality, the minority.

Relations between the two groups have several times reached something of an equilibrium, only to be disturbed by some new impulse of mutual penetration or by the strain of some crisis, notably war. The French Canadians continually threaten their own inner equilibrium between population and land by a high rate of natural increase. Like some prolific plant that hugs the earth, they spread at the expense of surrounding populations. The English, for their part, sporadically and dramatically plant industries and new commercial enterprises on the grand scale in the very heart of the French-Canadian world. They thus relieve, temporarily and without intending to do so, the pressure of population. Since they also upset the existing social and economic equilibrium of the French Canadians, they get little thanks.

The current changes in French-Canadian life and problems are those of concurrent industrialization and urbanization, both brought about by expansion of the Anglo-American world. The completely rural parish described by Horace Miner in his *St. Denis, a French-Canadian Parish* (Chicago: University of Chicago Press, 1939) may be taken as the prototype of Quebec communities as yet scarcely affected by these changes. Montreal, the metropolis of Quebec and of all Canada, represents the other extreme. This book deals mainly with a community which stands between these extremes, a smaller town recently enlivened and disturbed by the establishment of a number of large new industries, all started and managed by English-speaking people sent there for the purpose. The facts, relationships, and changes discovered in this community are also to be found in many others. Together these smaller industrial cities are the lively front on which people mobilized from the rural parishes meet, for the first time, modern industry and city life, where solid French middle-class townspeople must face an English-speaking managerial class of different mentality and ways of working and where, finally, the traditional institutions of French Canada meet crises occasioned by the presence of those of extreme industrialism and capitalism. The analysis is intended to suggest comparisons with other regions where industrialization and urbanization are complicated—as they generally are—by ethnic differences.

The French Canadians, a self-conscious and sensitive people, have written voluminously of their own past and present problems. The literature consists of poetry, fiction, historical works, critical essays, and stirring polemics. My apology for daring to write on problems with which the French Canadians themselves have dealt with brilliance, insight, and passion is that it has fallen to English-speaking people to do the pedestrian kind of job I have undertaken. Such has been the division of intellectual labor between the French Canadians and their neighbors. And, if they slay me for my temerity and errors, they will do it with rhetorical rapiers, not with statistical bludgeons.

My wife, Helen MacGill Hughes, and I jointly did the field work for the study. We jointly thank the Social Science Research Council for a grant-in-aid. We are grateful also to the citizens of Cantonville and especially to the curé of the mother-parish of the community.

The Social Science Research Committee of McGill University gave encouragement from the beginning. It continued its support after I left McGill University and has now, with generous aid from the Rockefeller Foundation, made publication possible. Leonard Marsh, director of Social Research at McGill University, has patiently borne the brunt of my delays. I have freely exploited the work of William H. Roy, Stuart Jamieson, and other former research fellows of McGill University. To George V. Haythorne I am especially indebted for maps and data which he subsequently published in his valuable study of Canadian agriculture, *Land and Labour*. The Social Science Research Committee of the University of Chicago enabled me to have the intelligent and generous collaboration of Margaret L. McDonald in this and related projects. My thanks to them all; and to those especially loyal friends and colleagues, Carl A. Dawson and Joseph C. Hemmeon, affectionate salutations.

EVERETT C. HUGHES

QUEBEC
February 1943

PREFACE TO PHOENIX EDITION

F FRENCH CANADA is still in transition, it is in part because, now as earlier, *Jean-Baptiste Comes to Town* (to use the title friends and publisher talked me out of). Cantonville has nearly twice the population and labor force it had when my wife and I were there twenty-five years ago; but now, as then, it is a French-Catholic town.

GREATER CANTONVILLE THEN AND NOW*

	Circa 1941	1961
Total population (1941).....	20,503	37,271
Catholic (1941)............	95%	97%
French (1941).............	94% *(ca.)*	94%
Labor force (1938)........	6,733	12,550

* Nathan Keyfitz, Canadian demographer and sociologist, furnished the tabulations from the 1961 census on which this table is based. What I called the "Parish of St. Jerome" and a newer outlying parish have been incorporated into the city. The parish of St. Bernard is now a municipality with a secular name; a growing settlement east of the river has also become a municipality. It is this group of municipalities which I have included in the 1961 population. They cover approximately the territory included in the tables in the book. The labor force figures for 1938 are from Table 15 (p. 47) of the book; that for 1961, from the Canadian census, refers to the Cantonville Major Urban Area which appears to include a slightly larger territory. Since, however, only fifty people engaged in agriculture are included, it is clear that the labor force is mainly that of Greater Cantonville.

There is no reason to believe that the higher management of the leading industries is not as English now as then. I wager that more French have come up in the service end of the industries (accounting, personnel, shipping, clerical work) and that the lower supervisors are predominantly French. The town non-industrial labor force is, I wager, more French than ever although chain stores probably have a larger part of local commerce than before. For such are the trends one finds in cities and economies where industry is run by an outside itinerant managerial and technological elite. The local business and professional people and landholders adapt themselves to the new state of things; the little people of the town and surrounding territory come up by degrees in both the industries and the local businesses and services. The process is the same whether the itinerant innovators are of the same ethnic background and religion as the local people, as in the American South or even in small cities in the North; whether, as in the Rhineland, the innovators are of the same language but different religion (Protestant) from the local people (Catholic), or whether, as in Quebec, the innovators are strangers in religion, language, and national identity and are the ancient political enemy of the proud local people. Ethnic difference may affect the rate of the various changes; it may give focus and heat to whatever conflict smolders or breaks out.

The process itself is to be observed in many parts of the world; in more parts in 1963 than in the late 1930's. For "economic development," as it is now often called, has reached not merely into the less industrial and urban parts of the older industrial regions, such as Quebec, the Canadian North, and the southern states in North America; it has gone at accelerated rate into South America, the outlying parts of the Soviet Union, Asia, the Middle East, and North and Sub-Saharan Africa.

The Quebec case belongs, in its major dimensions, with those of the Walloons and Flemings in Belgium, the Catholic Rhinelanders and the North German Protestants in Germany, and the Afrikaners and the English South Africans (except that the whole situation is altered in South Africa by the presence of the African natives in much larger number than all Europeans). But if one does put Quebec with these cases, it appears archaic. For the Flemings have taken over Belgian politics; and the Catholic Center party born in the Rhine country, is, in effect, in power in Germany, while in South Africa the former minority, the Afrikaners, are firmly in the political saddle. The minority in these case outvotes the erstwhile majority but does not displace them in positions of economic control. The leaders of the minority thus did not have to advocate the breakup of a major industrial economy by political separation, as French-Canadian separatists do, at least by implication. Quebec has no hope of outvoting the rest of Canada; the difference of birth rate is much too slight to shift proportions, especially so since few immigrants to Canada are French.

French Canadians are thus now the senior national minority in the western world; perhaps, instead of being proud of that position, they are wounded to think that minorities—younger, poorer, less educated and cultivated than they—have achieved a national status which they, the French Canadians, have really never sought in large number and with continued determination. Another reason for the present wave of separatism in Quebec may be the cold war. Henri Bourassa, nationalist leader during and after World War I, did not want French Canadians to fight for Britain. In the depression and World War II, the United States became co-villain. Now, in the cold war, Britain is forgotten and French-Canadian votes can apparently be rallied against those who would, in their opinion, make Canada a satellite of the United States. I wish I were in Cantonville to hear the 1963 debate, as I heard the 1937 version when the Union Nationale of the late Maurice Duplessis was campaigning its way to a provincial victory. Cantonville was then and is now interesting in its own right as a place where people live and strive. Cantonville—and the province of Quebec—was then and is now a crucial spot for observing changes of a kind which are occurring in many parts of the world.

Cantonville was to have been the first of a series of industrial towns to be studied; it was to represent the older established French town to which major light industries had come. There were, and are, also towns which were once English and are now French; new one-industry towns (non-ferrous metals, pulp and paper) where nothing was before; older mining towns in the asbestos country; and growing towns and cities with diversified industry. Quebec itself has become a major industrial city as well as remaining a seat of government and of French-Canadian culture. Montreal is larger than ever as a French city and has become more than ever the center of economic, intellectual, and culture change. While I did not do any other Quebec community, many other people have studied and are studying social change in French Canada. Both major French universities, Laval and Montréal, now have large and lively faculties of social science, as does also McGill University. They are studying, in their own ways, with newer techniques, and on a grander scale, essentially the same problems as those I approached in a small way in this book. I have had and still have the pleasure of working with many of them.

I thank Nathan Keyfitz for providing me with the new census data, and especially for writing the piece which I have made bold to use.

EVERETT C. HUGHES

April 1963

TABLE OF CONTENTS

LIST OF ILLUSTRATIONS

LIST OF TABLES

LIST OF TABLES   XX

PART I: THE BACKGROUND

CHAPTER I

THE QUEBEC CONTRAST

THE Quebec of fiction and of the travel posters is a rustically quaint countryside in which the very houses and the layout of fields proclaim a rural culture unlike that of neighboring Ontario, New York, and New England. The stereotype includes also towns and small cities of a certain European cast in which a cathedral and monastery look down from a hill upon quiet rows of stone houses built wall to wall. Such a Quebec exists. After seeing it, the skeptical tourist begins to believe that the *habitant*, the French-Canadian farmer, speaks French not as a pose but simply because it is his native tongue.

The Quebec of the news dispatches of the last decade is quite different. The newspapers and magazines report strikes, demonstrations of passionately nationalistic students and mass meetings of protest against conscription. This Quebec, too, is real. The French-Canadian province of Canada is, indeed, the seat of North America's most stable and archaic rural society. It also contains great modern industries and restless urban masses. Some of the factories, smelters, and mills—modernistic monsters hard of line and huge in their bulk—stand incongruously against a landscape of wooded mountains and foaming rivers. Others, rising above cultivated fields, distract the traveler's eye from graceful church towers that formerly dominated market towns. But the largest share of the factories and more than 600,000 of the French Canadians are in Canada's metropolis, Montreal.

The contrast between the rustic and the urban, the agricultural and the industrial, strikes the eye more sharply in Quebec than in most parts of North America. The physical change from town to country seems abrupt and complete. A town does not cast its shadow as far as the American or English Canadian expects it to. City newspapers and city ways do not penetrate so deeply into the countryside. Yet it would be absurd to suppose that the new industrial communities and the old agricultural parishes of Quebec are merely contrasting tiles in a mosaic. There are organic ties between the two.

1

The urbanization of the French Canadians drawn from the country to the town is complicated by ethnic difference. Quebec's modern industries, those which are changing the face of the province, are not simply old, small industries grown up. The latter were owned and operated, in fair proportion, by French-Canadian entrepreneurs. The new industries are brought by invading agents, armed with capital and techniques from the older English and American centers of finance and industry. These efficient modern managers and technicians are alien to the French-Canadian world in culture—always so in language and temper, generally so in religion. The hands who work in the industries and who make up the bulk of the population of the growing towns are natives of the region—French Canadians bound by sentiment, tradition, and kinship to the surrounding countryside.

Thus the French Canadian, in becoming an industrial worker and a town-dweller, gets a culturally alien employer. He works under a system whose spirit is English-American, rather than French. The precedents for becoming proletarian and for meeting industrial and urban problems in America stem from an essentially Protestant mentality. The French-Canadian city-dweller and industrial worker, even he who speaks no English and has no English-speaking neighbors, feels the impact of alien influences.

These paragraphs oversimplify the situation. For the French Canadians are a people. They number millions and are of many kinds: corporation lawyers, financiers, savants, sophisticates, artists, women of fashion, city slickers, criminals, as well as the rustic farmers of the Lower St. Lawrence Valley, the woodsmen of the north, and the fishermen of the Gaspé Peninsula. In villages, towns, and cities are small merchants, artisans, and the honored priests and professional men. In spite of this variety, the outstanding thing about Quebec of recent years has been the drawing of masses of its rural population into industry.

Quebec is, of course, but one of many places in the world where people of a somewhat rural cast of mind and with a close-knit traditional culture are being drawn into a new way of life by the expansion of industry. Again and again a few people, possessed of technical knowledge and capital, have gone to new regions and there brought about an industrial and social revolution among people accustomed to simpler modes of living. Such colonial expansion is more fateful than mere military conquest, for eventually it changes social structures, the ways of making a living, people's wants, and all those aspects of culture which have to do with creating and attaining ambitions. Since the agents of the industrial revolution are so often strangers, it is not surprising that the process should bring, as a by-product, a sharpening of the consciousness of cultural differences, of minority feeling. For minority feeling is not so much a matter of number as of a felt disadvantage in some hierarchy, accompanied by the sense that strangers and strange institutions are wresting from one's people mastery over their own fates.

The peoples who have undergone such industrial invasions are of many kinds. Some have been completely outside the sway of European culture, with its basic institutions of property and capital, enterprise and wage work. Others are of the European culture but have stabilized their life about the earlier and simpler institutions of the capitalistic system of production and exchange. The French Canadians are of the latter sort. It is the quintessence of capitalism, not its essence, that disturbs their culture. For those of them who have been reared in a rural folk society, the change from essence to quintessence is very great. For others, oriented to a town economy of smaller enterprises and professional pursuits, the change questions a way of life which has given them and their ancestors much satisfaction and an enviable status.

The major part of this study concerns a single industrial town. Its population includes many people who have moved directly from *habitant* farm to work in large industries. But it also has people long accustomed to commercial and professional pursuits and to the more sophisticated aspects of the French-Canadian culture. Its town institutions are intact under the leadership of people of the latter kind. It was because of the presence of these townspeople with their traditional institutions, the middle term in the Quebec contrast between old and new, that this town was chosen. For the accelerated industrial revolution and urbanization of recent decades involve not only individuals who have deserted the rural life, leaving their institutions behind them; its impact falls also upon the people and the institutional structure of the towns and cities.

CHAPTER II

THE RURAL SOCIETY

QUEBEC's distinction among the more rustic and quaint areas of North America lies in the fact that hers is not the rusticity of poverty. The Quebec farmer, or *habitant*, is not a sharecropper wandering with his mules and children from one plantation to another. He may sing old songs and dance old dances, but not on the porch of a dilapidated cabin, as does the southern mountaineer. He is religious and even superstitious, but his is not the disorderly religion of the hill revival, the camp meeting, and the snake-handling fanatic. On a few chronic frontiers in Quebec's more mountainous districts something approaching the poverty and instability of sharecroppers may be found; but it is only an approach, for the steadying hand of the church is even there not without effect.

If the Quebec farmer is not poverty-stricken, he is, nonetheless, rustic. He is not so likely as is his English-speaking rural compatriot of Ontario to own an automobile or a radio, to have a telephone, or to take a city newspaper. The road before his house is not so good. The district school is a poorer structure. The teacher has less training and is worse paid. But this Quebec farmer, although he has fewer of the urban services and conveniences, is more likely to own his own farm.

THE FAMILY

The society of rural Quebec is one of landholding families. It is so described, and with a precision that leaves little to be said, by Léon Gérin, French Canada's pioneer sociologist:

> The French-Canadian countryside presents itself as a simple juxtaposition of families which are very nearly all equal; nearly all engaged in farming; nearly all sufficient unto themselves; but none of which puts any ambition before that of transmitting intact the goods of the family to some one of its children, although favoring—according to the measure of its resources—the establishment of the other children outside the family foyer.[1]

---

[1] *Le Type économique et social des Canadiens* (Montreal, 1937), p. 84 (translation of this passage by Everett C. Hughes). Gérin's is the classic analysis of the French-Canadian rural family in sociological terms. Horace Miner, in *St. Denis, a French-Canadian Parish* (Chicago, 1939), carried the analysis further to include the relation between family and parish. The well-known novel of Louis Hémon, *Maria Chapdelaine*, tells the story of a family in the north-

Gérin puts this into a diagram:

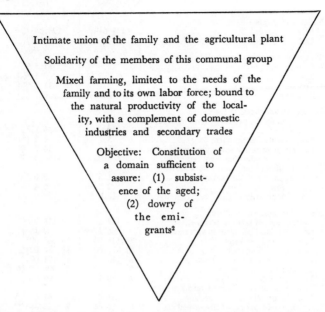

Intimate union of the family and the agricultural plant

Solidarity of the members of this communal group

Mixed farming, limited to the needs of the family and to its own labor force; bound to the natural productivity of the locality, with a complement of domestic industries and secondary trades

Objective: Constitution of a domain sufficient to assure: (1) subsistence of the aged; (2) dowry of the emigrants[2]

Gérin's description represents the ideal rural life of which French-Canadian leaders and poets speak. It is also a reality for a good part of rural Quebec.

The intimate union of the family and its farm plant is represented by proprietorship. In 1931, 93 per cent of all farms in Quebec were operated by their owners, and another 3 per cent by part owners. The familial character of Quebec farming may be shown more sharply by comparing it with Ontario farming. As Table 1 shows, fewer Quebec farms hire labor. The Quebec farm has more adult members of the operator's family at work upon it. Even the ownership of machinery shows the same difference, for, while the Quebec *habitant* is much more likely to own his own threshing machine than is the Ontario farmer, it will be of an old model, small enough to be operated by the family. Power will be furnished by a horse or a small gasoline engine. On the

___

ern colonies of Lake St. Jean. The more recent *Trente arpents*, by Ringuet (Paris, 1939), adds a mordancy not found in previous stories of the *habitant*. His characters go so far as to harbor—for a moment now and then—resentment against the burden which life, the church, and family put upon them.

[2] *Op. cit.*, p. 83.

TABLE 1
FARMING IN QUEBEC AND ONTARIO, 1931

	Quebec	Ontario
Number of farms:		
1921.............................	137,619	198,053 ⎫*
1931.............................	135,957	192,174 ⎭
Tenure of occupied farms, 1931:		
Owner.............................	92.8 %	81.5 % ⎫
Manager...........................	0.3 %	0.4 % ⎬†
Tenant............................	3.7 %	11.2 % ⎪
Part owner........................	3.2 %	6.9 % ⎭
Population and working force:		
Farm population per 1,000 acres of occupied farm land.........................	44.9	35.1 ⎫‡
Farm population per farm...............	5.7	4.2 ⎭
Percentage of farms employing hired labor.	28.2	44.7 §
Wage bill for labor per farm reporting.....	$70.00	$154.00 ‖
Distribution of male farm workers:		
1. Members of the family.............	81.6 %	65.6 % ⎫
2. Permanently hired.................	2.5 %	6.4 % ⎬¶
3. Temporarily hired.................	15.9 %	28.0 % ⎭
Size, value, and expenditure:		
Average size of farm in acres.............	127.3	118.7 **
Improved land per farm in acres..........	66.2	69.1 ††
Value of land per farm...................	$3,135.00	$3,048.00 ⎫
Value of buildings per farm..............	$1,897.00	$2,534.00 ⎬‡‡
Value of implements per farm............	$ 715.00	$ 791.00 ⎭
Value of livestock per farm..............	$ 705.00	$ 900.00 §§
Taxes per fully owned farm..............	$ 50.15	$ 99.01 ‖‖
Percentage of fully owned farms reporting mortgage debt....................	31.8	41.0 ¶¶
Average debt per acre fully owned........	$ 16.64	$ 23.88 ***
Operating expenditures per farm reporting:		
1. Feed.............................	$ 128.00	$ 146.00 ⎫
2. Seed.............................	$ 33.00	$ 41.00 ⎬†††
3. Fertilizer........................	$ 43.00	$ 69.00 ⎭
Machinery and conveniences (percentage of farms reporting):		
Auto...............................	18.9	60.3 ⎫
Binder.............................	30.7	60.9 ⎪
Cream-separator.....................	65.8	66.1 ⎪
Electric motor......................	2.1	3.7 ⎪
Gasoline engine.....................	25.0	20.9 ⎪
Milking machine....................	0.6	2.1 ⎪
Motor truck........................	3.6	7.2 ⎪
Silos...............................	4.3	17.3 ⎬‡‡‡
Threshing machine...................	28.9	4.3 ⎪
Running water in kitchen..............	32.0	10.5 ⎪
Running water in bathroom............	8.2	6.3 ⎪
Telephone..........................	19.5	54.1 ⎪
Radio..............................	6.3	21.5 ⎪
Electric light or gas.................	14.0	16.8 ⎪
Tractor............................	1.7	9.5 ⎭

* *Census of Canada, 1931*, VIII, xxvii, Table I.

† *Ibid.*, p. lii, Table XIX.

‡ *Agriculture and the Farm Population* (McGill University Social Research Bulletin No. 1), pp. 82–83, Table 20.

§ *Ibid.*, pp. 94–95, Table 24.

‖ *Ibid.*, pp. 102–3, Table 26.

¶ *Census of Canada, 1931*, Vol. VIII. Calculated from figures given on p. 208, Table 21 (Quebec); p. 392 (Ontario).

** *Agriculture and the Farm Population*, pp. 8–9, Table 3.

†† *Ibid.*, pp. 6–7, Table 2.

‡‡ *Ibid.*, pp. 110–11, Table 28.

§§ *Ibid.*, pp. 74–75, Table 19.

‖‖ *Ibid.*, pp. 126–27, Table 32.

¶¶ *Census of Canada, 1931*, VIII, lxiii, Table XXIV.

*** *Agriculture and the Farm Population*, pp. 126–27, Table 32.

††† *Ibid.*, pp. 118–19, Table 30.

‡‡‡ *Census of Canada, 1931*, VIII, lxxiv, Table XXIX.

other hand, the Ontario farmer is much more machine-minded, as is shown by the greater frequency of automobiles, trucks, tractors, telephones, and radios. The Quebec farmer regards what machinery he has as part of the estate which keeps his family independent.

In old parishes where the land is good and where there are no urban markets near by, the farms are most nearly sufficient to themselves. The farm-grown sheep furnish wool, which is spun, woven, and made into clothing and blankets. Handsome linen towels and sheets are made from local flax. Such home industries have declined in most parts of the province. They are rare in the neighborhood of the larger cities. They seem also to be lacking where the land is too poor to allow crops that bring no cash or food or when the family is too short of capital to keep people at home doing such work.

But, even where the home industries flourish, the farm is not completely self-sufficient. Some hay and grain are sold, as well as such produce as milk, butter, maple sugar, and firewood. Along the south shore of the St. Lawrence between Montreal and the city of Quebec are several old, very rural counties which are devoted largely to growing timothy hay for the cash market. About the cities dairying and market gardening are making great headway; such cultivation demands capital and much turnover of money. In many of the poorer colonization parishes in the far north and in the hilly counties of the southeast the farms produce so little that the men must work for wages in lumber camps during the long winter season.

With these qualifying remarks it must still be admitted that the Quebec farm, operating at its best, is highly self-sufficient. It produces most of its own food; generally all of its own fuel; in some districts, its own clothing. It breeds its own animals and uses relatively little machine power. And—the crux of the matter—it produces its own labor force by a tremendous rate of natural increase.

Gérin's next point—the determination to pass on the family farm and appurtenances intact to one, and one only, of the children—is the great vulnerable spot of the system. For, if a man has enough children to work his farm without outside help, he has more children than he can provide with land. If, however, the farm were split up among them, none would be provided for. It is a question, not of all or none, but of one only or none. The one having been provided with a farm— or, rather, the farm having been provided with an owner who will devote himself faithfully to it—the family hopes to provide something for the numerous other children who have been rocked in the family cradle and have done children's chores and man's or woman's work in field or house. If this provision is made at all, it must be made in cash. In an earlier day the farmer hoped to acquire a second farm for a son other than the *fils héritier*. Nowadays no such farm is available unless some other family has failed or otherwise been led to leave its family land.

A farm, however prosperous, which provides only for the immediate wants of its family is not self-sufficient. The family is sufficient to the land, but not the land to the family, if by the "family" we mean not only growing children but those children grown to men and women, and, in turn, their children. The system demands the departure of all children but one son, with provision of money or a trade, if possible— but departure, provision or no.[3] The rural society turns, then, about a relation of family to land. The farm must be fertile enough and large enough to feed and clothe the family—ideally, enough so to provide money for education or a start elsewhere for the children who do not inherit land. The family, in turn, must be large enough and possessed of enough skill and solidarity to run the farm and to keep it free of burdensome debt. But such a family, by its very size, endangers the farm in every generation. It becomes a function of the family to scatter its members, leaving but one son behind to inherit and to sire the next generation of farmers.

The psychological accompaniments of this system have not been explored. The child is reared in a homogeneous community, where he shares the respected status of a farm-owning family. But within the bosom of each family all must be ordered toward future diversity of fate for the several children. One will be a farm proprietor and will carry on the family in the native parish. The others, even while at work on the farm, are to be turned into potential priests, nuns, doctors, teachers, businessmen, artisans, colonists, or simply into grist for the mills of industry. The adult proprietors are of one class; their children are destined for dispersion among the various estates of an urban and industrial civilization. The remarkable thing is, not that family solidarity keeps the several individuals at work, without conscious or unconscious sabotage, for the maintenance of an indivisible family property, but rather that they do this in face of the fact that most of the children will have no part or parcel of the farm and will be able to call it "home" only in reminiscence.

Of French-Canadian novelists, only Ringuet, author of *Trente*

[3] Miner (*op. cit.*) gives a very good account of the composition of the family and of its problems at each point in the cycle which is run through from the coming to ownership of the young man to his aging and the coming of the next owner.

arpents, gives any hint that the father who has to so distinguish among
his children bears a heavy burden of guilt which he expresses in propi-
tiatory behavior to noninheriting sons; and that these noninheriting
children themselves feel the burden of renunciation heavily and show
signs of resentment. The writer also had a hint from one priest that the
call to be a nun was perhaps related to the fact that a French-Canadian
farm girl is schooled to a life of hard work for a family in which, as an
adult, she would have no place. That there is a problem comes to the
casual visitor; fathers, and even other members of the family, openly
solicit jobs from him for their potential supernumeraries. The solicita-
tion may occur even when all concerned know that it can come to
nothing. To discover what lies behind these overanxious gestures
would require a more penetrating study than has as yet been made.

THE PARISH

So long as a French Canadian remains on the family farm, he is as
inevitably associated with his native parish as with his family itself.
Rural Quebec is a series of parishes with clear boundaries; all families
within a parish are of it, and known to be so. If, in driving through
the country, one asks where he is, the answer will be the name of a
parish; if he asks who a given family is, he will generally be told the
name of the parish in which it originated.[4] The parish is not like a
midwestern township, merely a place; it is the other key institution of
Quebec rural society. Family and parish, father and curé, work together. The curé, the more sophisticated partner, tells his people what
actions respectively prepare or make them unfit to receive comfort
from the means of grace which he administers. The relevant actions
relate, in no small measure, to the family. The curé brings together
the powerful sanctions of religion, as stated in the august doctrine of the
church, and the crises and problems of everyday life.

While each soul must seek his salvation individually, the church
recognizes the family as the most potent instrument to use in saving
him. The family owns a pew. The tithes are defined as a portion of the
produce of a family property. While it is the individual who receives
the call to the priesthood, it is the family which deprives itself of his
services and pays his way through the long years of training. The curé
urges the family to make sacrifices for the sake of an individual soul
and uses the conscience of the individual to enforce his prescriptions
upon the family.

[4] See Miner, *op. cit.,* p. 63, for a statement of the importance of the parish as a symbol
by which people are identified.

The parish was historically the first institution of local self-government in rural Quebec; it remains the point of active integration of religious and secular matters. The roles of parishioner and of citizen are scarcely distinguishable. The heads of families vote on such matters as the erection of a new church, the floating of a bond issue to pay for it, or the placing of a roadside cross. These things they do not as zealots but as responsible citizens, heads of houses, and owners of land. It is assumed that all are good Catholics. The assumption is so well founded that such differences of wealth and station as exist can be reflected, without any sense of contradiction, in the selection of church wardens and in the allotting of pews.

Civil functions have become more elaborate through the necessity of building roads, maintaining schools, improving methods of farming, etc. There are now rural municipalities, whose main function has been the building and maintenance of roads, and school municipalities, which tax themselves for the building and maintenance of local schools. The imprint of the parish is heavy upon these newer units of local government. In many places they correspond in territory, and hence in membership and leadership.

In the rural districts such social life as exists on any other than the familial basis is a matter of the parish. The rural people are not joiners. The parish provides certain organizations, in which membership is based on age, sex, and marital status. These are natural divisions of the population for the purposes of church ceremony and for the expression of piety.

Many of the features of the parish here described depend upon the class and ethnic homogeneity of the population. The parish consists of families, the great majority of which own farms of comparable size. Between such families jealousy may exist; but there is little room for snobbery, and there is an essential likeness of interest which does not favor the setting-up of associations on class and interest lines. In most parishes of rural Quebec there are few, and in many no, families who are not both French and Catholic. It is thus possible for the community to deal with education, or even the marketing of produce, through a Catholic organization.

This same homogeneity allows the parish to be the backbone institution of the larger society of Quebec. From the rural family, through the agency of the parish priest, come the candidates for the priesthood and for the various religious orders which do much of the nursing and teaching. The parish itself is not specialized, but in the rural family is begun that specialization of personality, of piety and ambition, which —in the schools, colleges, and convents—is developed to the point of providing the auxiliary institutions with their personnel. The great excess of children in each generation puts upon the farmer a heavy burden, both of money and of conscience. He pays for types of education which he himself does not understand but whose value he appreciates at least in terms of piety, prestige, and security.

In the close contact of curé and family there is opportunity for some solution of the family's problem of placing its children and of the church's problem of personnel by the selection of certain children for the call to the religious life. The curé knows which families can afford it. Thus, out of the cradle of the parish, and through the connection of the parish with the overseeing diocese, the children of farmer proprietors are fed into the training institutions, all of which are closely integrated with the church. This provides a circulation of functionaries from parish to parish. And, since most of these functionaries are celibate, they must be recruited anew in each generation from the fecund class of peasant proprietors.

The curé is outside his native parish, but he was bred in another like it. His parishioners may not know his parents, but they are sure to know where he was born. They know some son of their own parish who is performing similar functions in some other parish. The curé is, they know, of their own breed. This circulation of their own people, in the respected and hallowed costumes of the religious orders, gives coherence to the society. The recognized dignity of the cloth saves the peasant-bred priest from too great familiarity. His use of the vernacular, his knowledge of local customs, his general homeliness of demeanor, his hearty presence at family reunions—all save him from being too distant. In spending their good money to send their own children into the religious orders, the *habitants* not only acquire merit but provide for their children and secure for themselves those higher and more specialized services which the parish alone could not manage.

This type of parish life is carried over into the towns and cities as ideal and symbol. Sometimes the clergy overwork it, being themselves too much bound by their own rural experience. But, at any rate, the urban society of French Canada cannot be understood without knowledge of this historic, and still existing, integration of family and parish and of parish with the larger society through colleges, hospitals, monasteries, convents, and seminaries.

CHAPTER III

THE RURAL POPULATION

ONLY a small fraction of all French Canadians in the province of Quebec, and a still smaller one of all people of French-Canadian origin in America, now live the traditional life of the farm.[1] Yet the question of the rural population cannot be ignored, for rural Quebec is still, as in the past, a fruitful mother producing great numbers of people who must, unless the rural system changes radically and quickly, go to live in cities or other parts of the country. The conditions which have driven the French Canadians to town still exist unabated. The question, in essence, is whether there are signs that these conditions may soon change.

Let us assume that the rate of natural increase of the rural population will not soon decline to the vanishing-point. What, then, does the history and present state of the population tell us of the probability that agriculture will expand sufficiently to absorb the natural increase of population without considerable migration to towns or to agricultural regions outside the province? Such expansion might take the form of settling new land or of supporting many more people on land now occupied.

The urban population of Quebec has multiplied several times over since the first dominion census in 1871. The rural population, including villages, has increased by only 29 per cent. As to agriculture itself, the number of persons engaged in it has remained singularly stable; in 1931 there were only 14 per cent more than in 1881. The number of farms decreased slightly (from 137,863 to 135,957) in the same period. The land occupied, improved, and cropped had increased by 37 per cent, 40 per cent, and 47 per cent, respectively. Increase of occupied and farmed land has not been accompanied by a proportional increase in the number of farms and farmers. Since it is generally agreed that the land as yet unoccupied is poorer than that already settled, no great relief may be expected from expansion of the area cultivated.

Only a small part of Quebec has ever been successfully farmed. Even if colonization should attain the proportions hoped for by its

[1] It must be remembered that in 1931 the farm population of 743,598 was only 70 per cent of the total rural population of Quebec. See *Census of Canada, 1931*, I, 161, Table XIII.

more optimistic advocates, the great northern wilderness will long remain several times as large as the occupied parts. At present, nearly all of Quebec's self-supporting farms are found in a belt of lowland following the St. Lawrence River and in the hither parts of the flanking hills. The belt is widest in the south and west, where the province abuts New York and Ontario. Down the river, to the north and east, it becomes narrower, until it is finally pinched to nothing by the Laurentian Mountains on the north and the Appalachian Hills on the south.

The concentration of farming population in the level lowland and the foothills is what one would expect. The additional and crucial point is that the rural population of this belt has been stationary for a long time except for a couple of minor exceptions. Map II shows the growth of rural and village population in the various counties of Quebec from 1871 to 1931. It is the exceptional county in the lowland which has gained rural and village population in that long period; many have actually lost. The exceptions are near Montreal or other growing cities, where many people work in town but live outside.[2] The other counties with significant increases are those with unsettled frontiers. The old, settled counties, unless they change their ways, will not provide places for many additional farmers, even though—as has been shown in a study made by the Dominion Bureau of Statistics—the decline of rural population in the past has been mainly among the nonfarming and part-farming elements. When one notes, in addition, that the increase of rural and village population for the whole province was only 29 per cent from 1871 to 1931, the significance of the frontier itself dwindles.[3]

Within the old settled area there have been changes in farming, and some parts show types of exploitation different from the others. Le Mieux, in the study cited, shows that, even in the counties of de-

[2] *Census of Canada, 1931*, I, 128.

[3] The strictly rural population increased by only 17 per cent. These results were got by comparing the population of the open country and of incorporated villages of less than 1,000 population as of 1931 with the population of the same areas in 1871. The computation tends to exaggerate slightly the growth of rural and village population (*ibid.*, Vol. II, Table 12).

Exhaustive analyses of the processes of growth and decline in rural population are to be found in *ibid.*, I, 107–32, and in a study by A. O. Le Mieux, "Factors in the Growth of the Rural Population in Eastern Canada," *Proceedings of the Canadian Political Science Association*, VI (1934), 196–219. I have discussed the Quebec rural population in "Industry and the Rural System in Quebec," *Canadian Journal of Economics and Political Science*, IV (August, 1938), 341–49.

MAP I

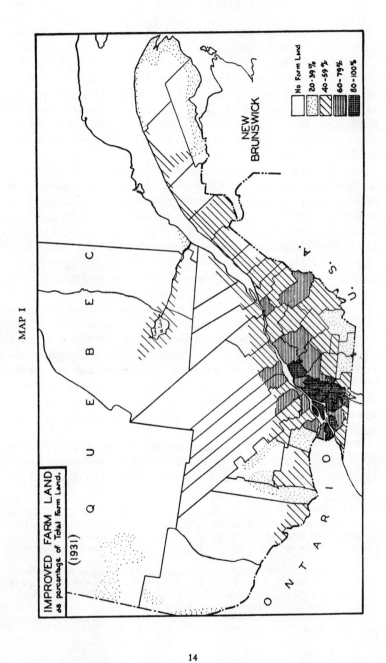

IMPROVED FARM LAND
as percentage of Total Farm Land.
(1931)

No Farm Land
20-39%
40-59%
60-79%
80-100%

QUEBEC

NEW BRUNSWICK

ONTARIO

U.S.A.

14

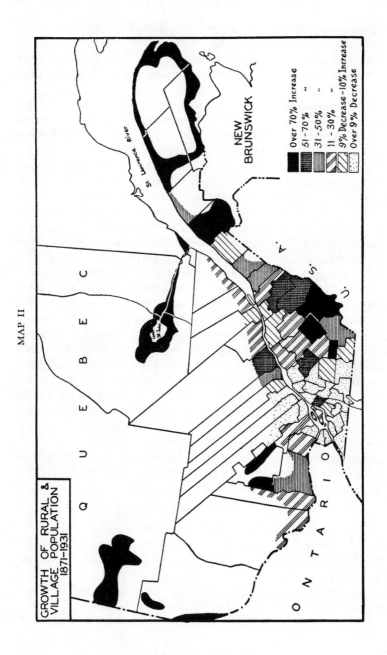

MAP II

GROWTH OF RURAL &
VILLAGE POPULATION
1871-1931

Over 70% Increase
51-70%   "   "
31-50%   "   "
11-30%   "   "
9% Decrease-10% Increase
Over 9% Decrease

QUEBEC

St. Lawrence River

Lake St. Louis

NEW
BRUNSWICK

U. S. A.

ONTARIO

15

clining population, the farms are larger than they once were. About the city of Montreal, however, farms are smaller than average and are more intensively cultivated. The city markets have stimulated truck farming and poultry-raising, although not so much so as around large cities in Ontario.[4]

In a considerable region of the south shore of the Middle St. Lawrence, one of the most completely French and rural parts of Quebec, the farmers have long devoted themselves to production of timothy hay.[5] Other features of the traditional system are modified in keeping with this cash-crop farming. The essential features of family and parish life are the same, but home industries seem to have waned in this district long ago. Elderly women barely remember seeing their mothers or grandmothers at the loom and spinning wheel. In this and in other regions of cash farming, and especially near cities, the support of the aged does not always follow the old pattern, for provision of clothing and of medical care must be made in cash; in the traditional farm family the aged wore homespun and sat in a warm corner until death.[6]

Generally speaking, there is a trend toward production of more and better livestock, toward increased use of fertilizer, and toward a better rotation of crops. But these changes have not been rapid or drastic enough to prevent the exhaustion and even the abandoning of many farms. The French-Canadian farmer, set as he is on conserving family goods, has not included in his thrift careful watch over the fertility of his fields. And, if he wished to do so, much of the soil, even in the older settled parts of Quebec, is but a thin layer over a bed of sand. Whatever a soil expert might say of possibilities of supporting a larger population, it seems safe to say that the French-Canadian farmer will not make drastic improvement in his methods until he is under much greater pressure than he has yet felt. And when he does undertake to intensify agriculture, he will require capital, and hence credit, of a magnitude that would frighten him.

THE FRONTIERS

The remaining counties of Quebec form two frontiers. One, on the north, includes the Laurentian Highlands, the valley of the Saguenay River and of Lake St. John. The other, on the south, starts with the

---

[4] *Agriculture and the Farm Population*, p. 6, Table 2; p. 14, Table 6.

[5] Raoul Blanchard, "Etudes canadiennes, 1ᵉ série, I: La Région du fleuve St. Laurent entre Québec et Montréal," *Revue de géographie alpine*, XXIV (1936), 79 ff.

[6] No statistics are available on these points, but the testimony of residents is quite consistent.

rough Gaspé Peninsula on the northeast and extends west and south along the United States border. On both these frontiers life is rustic and the population is French-Canadian, but agriculture is neither prosperous nor self-supporting. Blanchard estimates that from one-half to three-quarters of all the men of the Gaspé coast go into the woods to work in the lumber camps in winter.[7] There are various seasonal combinations of fishing, farming, and work in the woods; although nearly all the men are listed as farmers in the census, few of them make their livings from farming alone.[8] Farther up the south shore, one finds parishes which conform more closely to the ideal type. But only a few miles back of them are the hilly "colonization lands," where the *habitant* is more of a lumberjack than a farmer and where— in spite of the newness of settlement—clearing of land is already at a standstill and many of the parishes are declining in population.[9]

On the lower north shore, only the coast is settled, except for the Saguenay–Lake St. John district.[10] Even in the latter, the most famous colonization country in Quebec, agriculture depends largely upon industrial towns for markets. The people collect wild blueberries for extra cash. The men work in the lumber camps in winter, and there is even a class of rural day workers who depend upon winter wood-chopping for a living.[11]

Farther west the north-shore farming country has the Laurentian Highlands as its northern boundary. These highlands have been the scene of many attempts at agricultural settlement; but, as Blanchard shows, the turnover of population has been terrific, and farming has made little real headway. Forest industries, water power, and the increasing summer and winter tourist traffic keep the local population alive.[12] In general, the frontier farms are, in a crucial particular, the reverse of the ideal type of farm described by Gérin. Instead of providing the living of the family and the dowry of departing children as they grow up, the farm itself must be kept going by cash which the members of the family earn away from home.

The one really inviting rural frontier has been the hills of the

[7] Raoul Blanchard, *L'Est du Canada français* (Montreal, 1935), I, 90.

[8] *Ibid.*, pp. 75–100.

[9] *Ibid.*, I, 196–228, especially pp. 213, 215, 225, 226.

[10] *Ibid.*, Vol. I, Part III, chap. ii.

[11] *Ibid.*, I, 123 ff., 131, 132, 134.

[12] Blanchard, "Etudes canadiennes, 2ᵉ série, III: Les Laurentides," *Revue de géographie alpine*, Vol. XXVI (1938).

MAP III

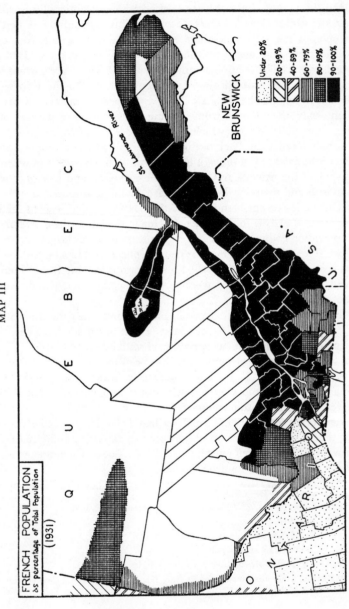

FRENCH POPULATION
as percentage of Total Population
(1931)

Under 20%
20-39%
40-59%
60-79%
80-89%
90-100%

St. Lawrence River

Lake St. John

QUEBEC

ONTARIO

U.S.A.

NEW BRUNSWICK

Eastern Townships, rising from the St. Lawrence plain and continuing southward to New England. The more arable parts of this country were first settled by English-speaking people. By as neat a process of invasion and succession as may be imagined, the prolific, land-loving French have displaced the more progressive and individualistic English. Two prevalent notions concerning this invasion should be corrected. The first is that it is recent and that the Eastern Townships still offer an outlet for excess French population. In contradiction to this, Blanchard shows that the expansion into this district began more than one hundred years ago and that by 1871 the French were in the majority in the townships colonized by the English.[13] Even before they have completely displaced the English farming population, the French must emigrate in large numbers to maintain their equilibrium of family and farm. The second mistaken notion is that the French bought the farms of the Eastern Townships with money brought, by some magic or cabal, from the older French districts. This is a little harder to refute, but certain indications may be found to support my view. Blanchard records that the French came to the lower Eastern Townships as labor when the railroads were built, and then dug in. His suggestion is that they earned in the new district the money which enabled them to stay.[14] In the neighborhood of the industrial town which we have especially studied, the indications are clearer. The English settled the better farms and established local industries. The French came as laborers; they stayed and succeeded the English as owners of the land. It is doubtful whether a large-family farming system can produce enough free capital to establish its children on farms at a distance. It seems more probable that the invaded territory must give a welcome to the invader—some source of ready money to give him a start. The French Canadian brought with him, of course, standards of living and work which enabled him to succeed in competition with the English people of the area. In any case, the excess rural French of the future will not find much place in the Eastern Townships.

In the United States the open frontier receded farther and farther west; when it disappeared, it was several days' railway journey distant from the old settlements of the east. In Quebec, frontier and old settlement remain side by side. It is a frontier that is chronic; much of it has remained in a semisettled state for generations in spite of successive

---

[13] *Idem*, "Etudes canadiennes, 2ᵉ série, II: Les Cantons de l'Est," *Revue de géographie alpine*, XXV (1937), 181, 197.

[14] *Ibid.*, pp. 176–77.

attempts to conquer it. Parts of it are given a chance of more permanent settlement by the establishment of large industries which do not depend upon the supply of timber. Other parts are temporarily enlivened by pulp and paper mills, which stimulate the wood-chopping that gives winter employment and cash to the colonist. But, at no time since the Confederation of Canada in 1867 has the frontier absorbed all, or even a good part, of the excess population from the settled portions of Quebec.

The frontier is, however, a lasting symbol and a perpetual political problem. It stands for the openness of the province. It allows leaders to say that if the French Canadian but retained his original hardiness he could go farther into the hills and into the north woods to pursue his traditional mode of life instead of being lured to the easier but more treacherous life of the city. Colonization serves also as the perennial nostrum for unemployment; for would not any man worth his salt rather go north and carve himself a place in the forest than to rot on relief in city idleness?

In summary, the rural population of Quebec has been maintained at a certain level; it is like water kept behind a dam, with a spillway to run off the excess. But suppose there were no place for the water to run off to. This is the outward contingency to which the system is subject. The frontier has looked like a place for the excess, but for all its size it doesn't seem to hold many people.

The really great runoff has been to towns and cities. New England, which took unlimited quantities of labor in the late nineteenth century and on until the war of 1914–18, is crowded. Its industries are moving out to areas where labor is unspoiled by high standards of living and correspondingly high demands. Quebec, with its growing industries, has been insatiable until lately. But an end may come to the rapid growth of Quebec's own towns and industries—at least, an end may soon be expected to the great demand for labor from the farms[15]—for the city population itself is prolific enough to provide the next generation of city labor if no great expansion of industry occurs.[16]

These things being true, Quebec's rural population may back up and swamp the farms. Indeed, there are signs that it has already

[15] W. B. Hurd and J. B. Cameron, "Population Movements in Canada, 1921–1931; Some Further Considerations," *Canadian Journal of Economics and Political Science*, I (1935), 222–45.

[16] W. B. Hurd, "Population Movements in Canada, 1921–1931, and Their Implications," *Proceedings of the Canadian Political Science Association*, VI (1934), 233.

started to do so. The farmers of Quebec were, on the average, two years older in 1931 than in 1921; and their unpaid adult family helpers were a year older. This change is no bigger than a man's hand, but it has significance. It probably means that young men do not leave home so quickly to seek their fortunes elsewhere. Miner reports that in St.

TABLE 2

MEDIAN AGE OF FARM OPERATORS AND UNPAID FAMILY
FARM WORKERS IN QUEBEC, 1921 AND 1931*

	1921 (Years)	1931 (Years)
Farm operators.................	44.2	46.2
Unpaid family workers..........	19.1	20.1

* G. V. Haythorne, "Agriculture and the Farm Worker in Eastern Canada" (Ph.D. dissertation, Harvard University, 1938), p. 446.

Dénis the curé felt impelled to call upon the young men to get out and find jobs. The depression, the curé said, was over. Perhaps it was merely depression, but it may be that the day of unlimited runoff of Quebec rural population is about over.[17]

[17] Hurd, *op. cit.*, pp. 221–37.

CHAPTER IV

INDUSTRY AND CITIES

AGRICULTURE was the occupation of 471 out of every thousand gainfully employed persons in the province of Quebec in 1871. Although the number in agriculture had increased somewhat by 1931, the proportion was only 225 per thousand of all employed and a somewhat larger proportion (322 per 1,000) of employed French males.[1] This trend continued throughout the period. It probably still continues, for in the decade from 1921 to 1931 the number of French in agriculture in Canada increased by only 5.4

TABLE 3

NUMBER EMPLOYED IN AGRICULTURE PER 1,000 OCCUPIED
PERSONS IN QUEBEC, 1871–1931

1871	470.8*	1911	313.2‖
1881	466.1†	1921	281.4¶
1891	455.1‡	1931	224.8**
1901	382.6§		

* *Census of Canada, 1871*, Vol. V.
† *Ibid., 1881*, II, 279.
‡ *Ibid., 1891*, IV, 450.
§ *Ibid., 1931*, VIII, xxvii.

‖ *Ibid.*
¶ *Ibid.*, VII, p. 12, Table 8.
** *Ibid.*

per cent; the number in other occupations, by 31.2 per cent.[2] Thus, however rural French Canada may be in spirit, the French Canadians are not a predominantly agricultural people. They are, in fact, proportionately only slightly more occupied in farming than are English Canadians.

Even at the earlier date, more than half the employed population was in occupations other than agriculture. Many of them were engaged in industrial occupations.[3] There has always been industry in

---

[1] *Census of Canada, 1931*, Vol. VII, Table 8. The earlier occupational census did not separate French from English.

[2] *Ibid.*, Tables 49 and 69. In Canada as a whole, 34.1 per cent of occupied French males and 31 per cent of occupied British males were in agriculture in 1931 (see below, Table 4, p. 22).

[3] Mr. D. M. McDonald, former social research assistant at McGill University, has compiled figures which show that 12.1 per cent of the province's gainfully employed of 1881 were in manufacturing and that this is but slightly less than the 14.4 per cent so employed in 1935. The qualifications necessary in appraising this apparently slight difference will appear in the text of this chapter.

Quebec, even in the rural parts. Indeed, much of the early prosperity of the farmers came from industries either on the farm or near by. Pot asheries, tanneries, foundries, small smelting furnaces, and sawmills used the wood cleared from the land. Quarries and brickyards abounded. Part of the market for these industries was local, but some of the products went to the outside world. Decline of these industries, through want of local wood, as well as because of growing competition from industry elsewhere, threw the rural population more completely upon farming for its living. In the neighborhood of the town which we have especially studied, most of the small industries dependent upon

TABLE 4

DISTRIBUTION OF FRENCH AND BRITISH MALES IN CANADA GAINFULLY
EMPLOYED IN AGRICULTURE AND NONAGRICULTURAL
OCCUPATIONS FOR 1921 AND 1931*

| | 1921 | | | | 1931 | | | | PER CENT INCREASE 1921–31 | |
| | Number | | Per Cent | | Number | | Per Cent | | | |
	French	British	French	Brit-ish	French	British	French	Brit-ish	French	Brit-ish
Total males gainfully employed, ten years of age and over........	668,834	1,560,615	100.0	100.0	808,777	1,729,758	100.0	100.0	20.9	10.8
Males employed in agriculture..............	262,682	557,772	39.3	35.7	275,738	536,997	34.1	31.0	5.0	−3.7
Males employed in other occupations.........	406,152	1,002,843	60.7	64.3	533,039	1,192,761	65.9	- 69.0	31.2	18.9

* Compiled from *Census of Canada, 1931*, Vol. VII, Tables 49 and 69.

local resources disappeared in the eighties and nineties; with them declined the population of the town as well as that of many neighboring villages and rural parishes.[4]

Some rural industries were integrally related to the farm economy. Even in the days when women spun and wove at home, small mills, dotted about the countryside, carded the wool on a custom basis. With the decline of home spinning, the carding mill has practically disappeared from rural Quebec. Carriage-makers and manufacturers of simple farm machinery were found in the towns. Such establishments had but few workers, and those few were oriented toward rural life. These were the dominant kinds of industry in Quebec in 1871. Inspection of the census of that year shows that the industry was done mainly in small shops in small towns. Furthermore, manufacturing was

[4] Raoul Blanchard, *L'Est du Canada français* (Montreal, 1935); also "Etudes canadiennes, 2ᵉ série," *Revue de géographie alpine*, Vols. XXV ff.

not then clearly marked off, as now, from repair and the other activities incidental to production. Communication, transportation, and construction now occupy large numbers of people. In Table 5 the occupations listed in the most recent Canadian census are put into three groups: the agricultural, the industrial, and the services (including

TABLE 5

FRENCH GAINFULLY OCCUPIED, TEN YEARS OF AGE AND OVER, BY
OCCUPATIONS (GROUPED) AND SEX, QUEBEC, 1931*

OCCUPATIONAL GROUP	TOTAL		MALE		FEMALE	
	Number	Per Cent	Number	Per Cent	Number	Per Cent
Total.............	769,572	100.0	621,979	100.0	147,593	100.0
I. Agriculture†.........	207,854	27.0	203,956	32.8	3,898	2.6
II. Industry‡............	282,634	36.7	245,382	39.4	37,252	25.3
III. Commerce and services§...............	279,084	36.3	172,641	27.8	106,443	72.1

* Compiled from *Census of Canada, 1931*, VII, 430 ff., Table 49.

† Grouping agriculture and fishing, etc. (All but 3,704 males and 7 females are in agriculture.)

‡ Grouping logging, mining, etc., manufacturing, electric light and power, labor, and unskilled and unspecified (last category has but 215 males and 48 females).

§ Grouping transportation and communication, warehousing and storage, trade, finance and insurance service, and clerical.

TABLE 6

DISTRIBUTION OF PERCENTAGES OF MANUFACTURING EMPLOYEES IN ESTAB-
LISHMENTS OF GIVEN SIZES IN QUEBEC, ONTARIO, AND CANADA, 1935*

	NUMBER OF EMPLOYEES IN PLANTS					
	1–50	51–100	101–200	201–500	501+	All Plants
Percentage of Quebec employees..	24.6	10.4	14.5	22.1	28.4	100.0
Percentage of Ontario employees..	26.1	13.0	15.2	20.7	25.0	100.0
Percentage of Canada employees..	27.5	12.6	14.9	20.3	24.7	100.0

* *The Manufacturing Industries of Canada, 1935: Summary Report* (Ottawa: Dominion Bureau of Statistics, 1938).

commerce). Thus grouped, industrial pursuits occupy nearly 40 per cent of Quebec French male workers.

In the narrower field of manufacturing, in Quebec and elsewhere, plants are now much larger. They occupy more hands each and use more capital goods per hand. In Quebec the plants, in terms of hands employed, are slightly larger than in Ontario, the other great industrial province, and in Canada as a whole. The average size of plants in pulp and paper and in the textile manufacturing industries appears in Table 7. These are two of the outstanding industries of Quebec. Of course, there are even today many small industries, but they are over-shadowed by these great new ones, which are financed by outside capital, run by imported managers and technicians, and whose products are sold in a national or even international market.

TABLE 7

NUMBER OF ESTABLISHMENTS AND NUMBER OF EMPLOYEES IN
PULP AND PAPER AND IN TEXTILE INDUSTRIES
IN QUEBEC, 1934*

Industry	Number of Establish-ments	Number of Employees	Average Number of Employees per Establishment
Pulp and paper..................	41	13,157	321
Textiles grouped.................	*88*	*23,735*	*270*
Cotton yarn and cloth..........	16	11,812	738
Silk and artifical silk............	19	6,654	350
Hosiery and knitted goods.......	53	5,269	99

* *The Manufacturing Industries of Canada, 1934* (Ottawa: Dominion Bureau of Statistics), p. 46, Table 12.

DISTRIBUTION OF INDUSTRY

The first impression given by the statistics of the distribution of industry in Quebec is of a great concentration in the Montreal district. Of 188,907 manufacturing employees in the province in 1935, 102,112 worked on Montreal and Jesus islands, which include most of Greater Montreal.[5] The city of Quebec, the next in size and industrial importance, had less than 10,000 so employed. Outside Montreal, Quebec towns are small. Yet there are forty-three of them that each produced more than $1,000,000 worth of manufactured goods in 1935.[6] In each of seventy-six towns outside Greater Montreal more than 100 persons were employed in manufacturing.[7]

[5] *The Manufacturing Industries of Canada, 1935: Summary Report* (Ottawa: Dominion Bureau of Statistics, 1938).

[6] *Ibid.*

[7] Inspection of reports shows no town which has as many as 100 manufacturing employees without at least one plant with 50 or more employees. That is to say, in towns where there is no fairly large plant, the workers in creameries, sash-and-door shops, and other such small local industries do not add up to as many as 100.

The figures given in this section are not all for the same year, because the items reported vary somewhat from year to year.

After what has been presented already, it seems needless to say that the urban population has far outstripped the rural in Quebec. Table 9 shows that, while in the sixty years ending in 1931, the rural and village population had increased by less than one-third, the population of Montreal and Jesus islands had multiplied by seven and a half, and that of other towns and cities by five. Montreal, with its environs, still has more population than all other towns and cities combined; but in the last two intercensal periods the other urban areas have, for the first time, increased more rapidly than Montreal.

Among these other towns are many of a few thousand people with one or perhaps several industries of the modern mass-production type. The advantages which such a town offers to industry are described as follows in a pamphlet issued by the promotion department of a large power company.

Ste. Mathilde is mainly an industrial centre of quite recent growth. Ample power, contented and industrious labour combined with good transportation facilities and the generosity of the city authorities in easing the burden of new industries are rapidly building this city into an important industrial centre.

Ste. Mathilde is also well known as a point to which pilgrims converge every year . . . . to venerate the shrine of Ste. Mathilde.

  Total population: 10,000 (approx.)
  Total number employed: 600 (approx.)
  Number to be drawn from surrounding territory: male, 750; female, 250
  Race: French-Canadian (95 per cent)
  Degree of unionism: No unions
  Annual labour turnover: Practically nil
  Strikes or shut outs in last few years: None in ten years
  Usual hours of work: male, 60 hours; female, 55 hours

The towns vary somewhat, corresponding to the region in which they are found and to the type of industry. The pulp-and-paper town is characteristically near the woods, whence comes its material, and near waterfalls, its source of power. Its workers are men, many of whom have tasted the rough, wandering life of the woods. The mining towns are—mining towns. The centers of smelting of nonferrous metals are typically company towns, located where there is an abundance of cheap power.

The textile town is generally in the older and more settled parts of the province. Labor is drawn from near by. Since textile plants use both male and female labor, the newcomers to such towns come as families and are probably more stable. Also, in such towns the main institutions of French Canada are already in operation, with local

TABLE 8

Towns outside Greater Montreal Having More than 100
Persons Engaged in Manufacturing, 1934*

Number Employed in Manufacturing 1934	Number of Towns	Total Population	Average Population	Total Employees	Average Employees
101– 200.....	17	60,520	3,560	2,536	149
201– 500.....	30	100,772	3,359	8,996	300
501– 1,000.....	13	49,341†	3,795	8,575	660
1,101– 2,000.....	6	41,261	6,877	8,232	1,372
2,001– 3,000.....	5	71,654	14,331	12,657	2,531
3,001– 4,000.....	3	48,990	16,330	11,200	3,733
4,001– 5,000.....	....	....	....	....	....
5,000–10,000.....	2	166,044	83,022	13,791	6,895
Total........	76	538,582	....	65,987	....

* Compiled from *The Manufacturing Industries of the Province of Quebec, 1934*, and from private reports from all but two company towns.
† Population for twelve towns; no population figure available for Brownsburg.

TABLE 9

Comparative Increase in the Rural and Urban
Population of Quebec, 1871–1931*

Population	1871	1881	1891	1901	1911	1921	1931
Rural† and village‡	921,946	1,006,678	1,023,422	1,046,654	1,100,602	1,158,728	1,190,855
Index.........	100	109	111	114	119	126	129
Percentage of increase per decade......	....	9.2	1.7	2.3	5.2	5.3	2.8
Urban§ Montreal and Jesus islands........	132,477	180,684	264,566	348,211	545,115	719,315	993,477
Index	100	136	200	263	411	543	750
Percentage of increase per decade......	....	36.4	46.4	31.6	56.5	31.9	38.1
Urban—outside Montreal and Jesus islands.	137,093	171,665	200,547	254,033	360,059	482,622	689,923
Index..........	100	125	146	185	262	352	503
Percentage of increase per decade......	....	25.2	16.8	26.7	41.7	34.0	42.9

* *Census of Canada, 1931*, Vol. II. Compiled from data in Table 12 (pp. 38–61).
† Rural—unincorporated places in 1931.
‡ Village—incorporated places with less than 1,000 population in 1931.
§ Urban—incorporated places with more than 1,000 population in 1931.

leaders and traditions. Our town is of this type. Industry has disturbed almost every institution, but the fundamental structure of the town is intact. It is the impact of industry on a society such as this that we propose to study.

In the preceding pages we have given a gross and impressionistic picture of the growth of industry and cities in Quebec. The following part of our study will be devoted to what may appear, in comparison, to be minutiae. But these minutiae show, it is hoped, the adjustments which actually take place when industry comes to a small French town. For the purpose we have selected a town, to be called Cantonville, which was in existence before industry came to it—a town located in what was a well-settled farming district but which is now a major center of textile manufacturing.

PART II

CANTONVILLE, AN INDUSTRIAL TOWN

CHAPTER V

THE TOWN AS IT WAS AND AS IT IS

THE OLD AND THE NEW

CANTONVILLE in 1911 was a country trading town. Its population, including that of its rural township, was 2,605. Town and township, closely united by mutual services and family ties, were one Catholic parish. The business and professional men of the town lived off the custom of the farmers roundabout. Twelve small shops, dignified by the census to the status of "industries," employed 128 hands in the production of goods largely from local materials and for local consumption.

By 1937 there had grown about this nucleus a booming community of 19,424[1] persons, of whom approximately 4,600 were employed in industry. Most of the workers were engaged in the manufacture of goods of well-known trade-marks for the Canadian national market. The industries in which they worked were offshoots of British and American concerns; they were in no sense lineal descendants of the small shops of the earlier period. The immediate local cause of growth was the building of two power dams at near-by waterfalls—the same falls which, as barriers to boating, stopped the original settlers at this point on their journey from the St. Lawrence.

The new community included within the territory of the old town and township, two newly incorporated municipalities and several outlying settlements inhabited mainly by industrial hands. The one Catholic parish had been divided into four. The organization and the appearance of the community had changed, but not beyond recognition. The old landmarks remained visible, if somewhat off center, in the midst of the new.

[1] The population of 1911 is that of the dominion census; that of 1937 is from the annual census taken by the catholic parishes. The close correspondence of parochial figures for 1931 with the dominion census of that year make it appear accurate enough for our purposes.

29

Although the names of the town, the township, and the older streets are English, it was into a French community that industry and the new population came. The first settlers were British soldiers mustered out at the end of the War of 1812. They were not numerous enough to

DIAGRAM I

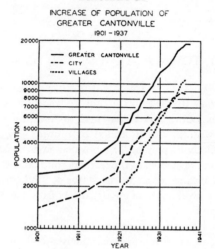

INCREASE OF POPULATION OF
GREATER CANTONVILLE
1901 - 1937

TABLE 10

INDUSTRIAL STATISTICS FOR CANTONVILLE,
1911 AND 1937

	1911*	1937†
Establishments...............	12	26
Capital......................	$173,866	$19,833,345
Employees...................	128	4,558
Salaries and wages...........	$ 37,436	$ 4,499,981
Net value of product.........	$ 73,589	$ 9,036,350

    * *Census of Canada, 1911*, Vol. III, Table XII.
    † *Canada Year Book, 1940*, Table 10.

make more than a small settlement. The French farmers who began to settle about them almost at once were invading not so much an English community as the wilderness itself. By the 1850's a township council had five French and two English members; by 1871 three-quarters of the population was French, and in 1911 more than nine-tenths.

As in many Quebec communities, the English population had had a significance greater than its numbers. The English were, in the earlier days, the leaders in business and the professions. The first lawyers and doctors were English; as time went on they found themselves in competition with French Canadians. By about 1900, English professional men had disappeared from the community.[2] Thirty of the thirty-two business and professional men who met, in 1901, to form an association, were French. They called their body a *chambre de commerce* and recorded the minutes only in French. As a gesture of good will, the office of vice-president was reserved for an English member. In 1939 the death of an aged English resident left vacant the post of registrar of deeds for the county; an almost equally aged, but French, citizen was appointed to succeed him in this lifetime job. Thus was the last English person liquidated from local public office. The elective offices had long since been held only by French; the last English mayor went out of office in 1903. He was, however, elected several decades after the French were in the majority. The truth is that by 1900 or shortly thereafter the few remaining English were not of sufficient importance to be thought of for public office.

When the new dams were built, industry was at a low ebb in the district. But whenever, in the past, there had been industry, English people had had an important hand in it. From time to time in the latter half of the nineteenth century English-speaking entrepreneurs established industries which made the town grow.[3] But the growth was always French rather than English. It has, indeed, been the function of the English in Quebec to create points of activity to which the French population is rallied.

Some of the few relics of old English families in Cantonville today think they remember when the town was mainly English in population; they are really remembering, as people of tradition do, the experiences of their grandparents. By recalling the importance of English persons in the earlier industries they may also be trying to identify themselves with the English managers and owners of the new industries, a breed lately come—as always—from elsewhere. For, although

[2] I have drawn heavily upon the work of a local historian for the facts here presented.

[3] Among the earlier industries were a tannery which used bark, smelting furnaces which used charcoal, sawmills and various other wood-product industries, such as match factories and a bobbin factory. All of them used wood from the forests to the east of the town. The industries declined with the wood supply and with the increasing availability of better wood than grew in the poor soil of this region. Firewood is still an important cash crop for local farmers.

it is true that each succeeding lot of industries in Cantonville has been
started by English initiative, it is not true that succeeding generations
of old local families have done it. Each new industry of importance has
brought in new managers, who, although of the same language and
religion as the earlier English settlers, are as little kin to them as to the
local French families.

The relative position of French and English just prior to the coming
of the new order is reflected in the setting of their churches. St. An-
drew's Anglican Church, a century-old stone chapel, nestled, and still
nestles, beyond an elm-shaded graveyard whose crumbling stones dim-
ly preserve the names of the founders and early settlers—the names
which have disappeared from stores and mailboxes in favor of French
names. The rectory, as if to shelter its tenant from the realities of the
present, is half-hidden behind both church and cemetery. The congregation, a handful of farm families and elderly town *rentiers*, was too
small to support a clergyman alone; their church was a subsidized
diocesan mission. The only other English communal institution, the
Protestant school, had about thirty pupils, who were taught in one
room by a hardy perennial spinster of one of the old families. The
rural cast of the school is attested by a complaint written into the
records that attendance was very poor in the fall harvesting and the
spring planting seasons.

The huge Roman Catholic church, St. Luc's, faced, and still faces,
boldly upon the public park. Its broad steps stand ready to gather the
populace converging upon it from all directions. From the porch of
his near-by presbytery, the curé did, and does, view the comings and
goings of the whole town. On festival occasions, sacred or secular, he
stands, flanked by mayor, aldermen, and other leading citizens, on this
same porch to give his blessing to the parade which will inevitably pass
that way. If the noise of crowds and of the Thursday-night band con-
cert in the park rings too loudly in his ears, he has nothing to complain
of, for, if the presbytery is less quiet than the secluded Anglican rectory, it is because the French Catholic curé, unlike the rector, is the
leading figure in what was, and is, the community's central institution.
In 1911 the Anglican church was a time-weathered monument to the
past; the Catholic parish was a going concern.

The town's Catholic school commission, in close co-operation with
the curé, administered a system of schools in which instruction was
entrusted to the nuns of the local convent. Certain French-Canadian
Catholic fraternal insurance societies flourished under the curé's chap-

laincy and the leadership of prominent laymen. The French community was in full vigor. It was, however, the vigor of a rural town; the organizations affiliated with the parish were simply those required to serve the various age and sex groups without much attention to class and occupation.

If the parish church now is one of the largest and finest in the diocese, it is not because of a revival but simply because the community contains more souls. Other changes, however, are due not only to increase of size but to greater complexity of the community. There are now three new parishes cut from the territory of the old. Each new church faces its own new park and is the center of a new constellation of business and social activities. Each new parish has its own characteristic kind of people; in two of them even the church wardens are factory workers. If the curé of the old parish has six *vicaires* to assist him, that may be because of increased size of the community; but the specialized duties of the six are a product of the more complex social structure. And if the old fraternal insurance societies and the age and sex alignments in the parish are now but lesser organizations among a great number, lay and parochial, which enlist the interest of the population, that, too, reflects the increased occupational and class differentiation.

PEOPLE AND SOCIETY

In this earlier setting a nucleus of French-Canadian business and professional men occupied the leading positions in civic and parish institutions. These men and their families were not aristocratic, for Cantonville is not in the seigneurial country. The family names of the town were shared by *habitants* in near-by parishes and counties, for many of the townspeople, even the leading ones, had come from the farm and had relatives there. If not aristocratic, the leading families nevertheless had that air of dignity and breeding nourished by the Catholic convent and *collège*.

These people, although well known to each other and perhaps because of the fact that they could not escape each other's orbits, were divided into factions. Most of the lawyers were in politics in some way and were rivals for such political advancement as was to be had. One of them was something of a figure even in national politics, as well as being president of the rural bar association of the province. Another line of difference is indicated by the statement that one of the leading men was "close to the curé." This does not mean that any man was anticlerical, but simply that some were closer to the church than others. There arose, in fact, a dispute in the *chambre de commerce* over the matter of compulsory school attendance, which the church unremittingly opposed.[4] Some of the local men wanted compulsory attendance; others spoke militantly for the church's point of view. This line coincided somewhat with the political line, the parish or curé's men generally being Conservative in party affiliation, while the others were Liberals.

Such organizations as there were in the town were led by people of this small business and professional group. A lawyer established the *chambre de commerce*. Another lawyer was founder and moving spirit in the local band. They were school commissioners, town officials, and church wardens. This group, for the most part still intact, has furnished every mayor the town has had even to the present, in spite of the present numerical preponderance of new industrial population. Their position in the town has, however, changed significantly, for the town has changed as a system of positions.

The people of this group lived comfortably either in old houses or in apartments over their businesses. The professional men generally had their offices in their houses; many of them still do. They sent their children away to convents or *collèges*. Some of them traveled, one or two having been to France and to the Chicago World's Fair of 1893.

Their relations with the old English were diplomatic and somewhat friendly. Both Protestant and Catholic graveyards give evidence of some intermarriage, as, for instance, on a large stone in the Protestant cemetery erected to "Mary Harrington, wife of Joseph Marchand." One prominent "French" Catholic citizen had an English Protestant mother and two "English" Protestant sisters. A few Catholics bore English names; there were individuals of whom it is said, "He was more English than French," or the reverse. Occasionally the death of a prominent English Protestant drew a large crowd of French Catholics to the Anglican church in respectful mourning. That, indeed, happened only recently, when an octogenarian of an old English family died.

There is good evidence that most of the older English families knew a good deal of French. Even today one may hear in a downtown office or shop a conversation in which an old resident speaks English and is answered in French, both parties understanding each other perfectly

---

[4] *Chambre de commerce*, Minutes, 1918.

well, "kidding" each other, using first names and without the slightest feeling of being on the defensive.[5]

In the booming industrial town of the present the remnant of the old English clings somewhat to the older French, who know them and respect them for their past, rather than to the new industrial English, who ignore them. It is, on the part of the French, a rather patronizing attitude, for the old English families wield no power and have no future. The attitude is a residue of a forbearing and diplomatic relation between French and English which used to prevail in many Quebec communities. It was the rule in many towns for English and French mayors to alternate in office, for a given proportion of the two groups to sit on public bodies, and for members of the one group to appear at certain ceremonial occasions of the other as a sign of mutual respect. But the effective adjustment of the French of the new order must be to another group of English people, little aware of the gentlemen's agreements of another day.

PHYSICAL GROWTH AND REORIENTATION

In growing, Cantonville has been physically reoriented in a way that affects the relations and interests of people and their institutions. The land of a town is an asset from which the proprietors expect special advantage and profits as the town grows. In Cantonville, as in most Quebec country towns, the land at the center belongs to residents—to business, professional, and even to working men. But the new land brought into use by growth of the town does not gather in a circle about the old town. It forms a fan, whose apex is the old town but whose center of population has been drawn a good half-mile southward from the old business district and lies outside the territory occupied in 1911.

Old Cantonville was huddled below and on the brow of a small rise which runs westward from the falls on the river. Just below the rise

[5] In a local tailor's shop an English customer turned to me and said: "I have been having my suits made by Alphonse for thirty years and he still tries to cheat me every time." The tailor grinned at this good joke of his old friend and customer and passed it off with a remark, in French, to the effect that no tailor could make a cent off a man so big that a whole bolt of cloth was just enough for one suit. During this conversation a Jewish merchant came in to have a ready-made suit altered for a customer. The Jew and the French tailor went after each other in the same chaffing manner, but the Jew stuck to French. One had distinctly the feeling that members of the old English families are given much greater license to "kid" the French and even to criticize them than are the new industrial English or other outsiders.

various roads converge upon the bridge which is the gateway of the region to the eastern part of the province. The town, oriented to the country, centered about the converging roads and highways and straggled out along them to meet the farmer halfway. The old section, known as the Basse Ville, contained the business houses as well as the residences of most of the population, of whatever class and whether French or English.

The industries, except for two quite small ones, have been established to the south on the higher level. The largest plant of all, which employs more hands than all the others together, is the farthest from the Basse Ville on a site which was incorporated into the city only after the industry had decided to put its plant there. The next largest industry is near by. Thus the plants to which by far the majority of the workers make their daily round trip (or two, if they go home to lunch) are at the opposite end of town from the Basse Ville. Houses for the thousands of new people attracted by industry were built everywhere. Some were sandwiched between older houses, crowding the lots to the limit. Apartments were built in open country and in the already closely built Basse Ville. But by far the greater number were built in the direction of the larger industries. On a sandy waste abutting the largest new plant and the road (still generally known by its country name of "Troisième Rang") which forms the western boundary of the town, there has grown up a working-class suburb of more than 6,000 people. From its flimsy, frame, box-shaped cottages and flats streams of workers converge, by way of paths and short cuts, every morning upon the gates of the industrial plants. From a still more rustic suburb people walk along an abandoned railroad track which leads through a jungle of second-growth brush. Altogether, the new building is so distributed that the center of population lies far outside the old town, in the direction of the largest industries. It is not that there are fewer people in the old sections—there are many more than ever before—but that the growth has been even greater to the south and west.

For many of the old proprietors and businessmen of the town the off-center growth has ruined the profit which they expected to enjoy from the expansion of their city. For one thing, many of the new people live so far off that they patronize the miserable little shops scattered haphazardly but too plentifully in the new districts. For another, a new business district is growing up on a broad street two blocks west of the old business section and somewhat to the south. New businesses are seeking the center of population and have practically reached it.

The town's largest theater, many of its newer stores and shops, the new offices of the telephone company, and lately a new city hall have been established in this new and growing business district. A few of the older businesses have established branches there or even moved entirely. But, whether because they were tied down by property in the Basse Ville, because of faith in the older district, or simply because of inertia, most of the old businesses have remained on their original sites, in buildings generally occupied by the family as well. The establishments in the upper town are generally new enterprises, competing with the older merchants. The main banks and many of the old larger stores are still in the Basse Ville, along with new ones and a number of chain stores. The recent establishment of bus lines to the remote sections of the town and suburbs has made it easier for people to come to the old center. The busses, however, serve the new business street as well as the old. This whole series of shifts affects the fates of property and business, the stake of the older population in the town.

The direction of the new growth also shattered many hopes of profit from real estate speculation. The local businessmen looked for their profit from the growth of the town not only in increased patronage of their businesses or professional offices but in the sale of land to new residents and industries. In fact, a few made a great deal of money in this way. Others lost. One very prominent local man went bankrupt from bad guesses. Another is said to have had prospects of a fortune and to have got nothing but debts. All those who looked for development on the east side of the river were disappointed, for industry not only stayed on the west side but even moved farther from the water.

The old residents and proprietors of the Basse Ville got a further disappointment with respect to taxes. They had assumed that the new building would take place mainly within the city limits. But the rural people who moved to the district were not enough impressed with city conveniences to want to pay city tax rates, low as the latter are by ordinary American and Canadian standards. The new jungle suburbs lacked pavements, sewers, and a public water supply. Thither some 9,000 people have moved, leaving unoccupied a great deal of land within the city itself. The city had to provide itself with additional improvements and had to do it without the taxes of about one-half of the occupied buildings of Greater Cantonville. The tax burden did not spread as the old proprietors expected. On the whole, the attitude of those older residents who have not profited much by the expansion of the town is that newcomers have taken the profit the older settlers should have had and that the people of the suburbs are parasites on the taxpayers of the city.

How does all of this—old and new, country town and industrial city—meet the eye?

If the visitor drives in on the main highway he meets first a string town of box-shaped frame houses, cottages of traditional Quebec design, straggling small stores, garages, a couple of blacksmith shops, and a horse-trader's yard cluttered with old vehicles. A railroad switch flanked by a couple of the smaller industries brings this to an end. A turn of the road brings one suddenly into a street of tall elms and maples which shade comfortable houses. This is the Basse Ville at its best, the seat of the families whose names are those of town and county history. If one were to turn to the left, he would find the town golf club occupying the only pretentious estate the community ever had.

Among the older houses are three or four of later vintage where live officials of the first industries to come to town. But even here are some of the modest cottages of thrifty small-town French Canadians. And only a step away are ramshackle tenements whose squalor still reeks more of the barnyard than of the city slum.

This bit of old residential quarter merges into the lower end of the main business street. Across the street from the familiar Woolworth front stands the shaded brick house of the town's most prominent lawyer, who keeps office in his residence. The shops and offices are in all sorts of buildings, from old houses of the traditional type to pretentious brick structures with apartments for the owner and other tenants in the second and third stories. A few of the buildings are obviously new.

Separating the old lower business district from the upper end of town are the Anglican graveyard, a city park, and the main Catholic church, all paralleled half a block farther away by the main line of the railroad. Beyond this formidable system of barriers the old business street soon peters out to nondescript cottages and small shops. One has to go two blocks west to find the broad, newly paved street that has an air of stretching out to something beyond. This is the new business street which leads southward toward the larger factories. Spacious residences, cheap new three-story flats, and new business buildings are found side by side. Only a door or two off this street are new slummy tenements. Lest the impression of the prospering small city be too great, a lone cow comes twice daily down the street on her journey from the pasture beyond the convent to her master's cottage just off Cantonville's most progressive thoroughfare.

In spite of the cow, the new and the urban predominate in this southern spreading part of the town. The industries can be seen. The streets are wide. The apartment dominates over the house, whereas in Basse Ville, the narrow streets, old houses, and the tree-shaded park and church-yards preserve the atmosphere of a Quebec country town. But no part of the town proper is consistently and purely new or old, rich or poor, residential or business, French or English. On the river shore, both north and south of town, are the beginnings of something like suburbs for better-off people, both English and French; these are only beginnings, and there is no room for them to expand. But even these concentrations are not pure, for the cheap new dwelling and the old farmhouse are found among them.

To find something unadulterated one must turn off from the main streets and cross a few blocks of sandy prairie to the workingman's suburb. There all is new, all is cheap and barren, all is French. The most consistent and definitive physical phenomenon of the growth of this town is precisely this satellite of some 6,000 souls, housed in cheap barracks and shanties saved from utter shabbiness only by their newness. The imposing church and presbytery rise from the sand lots in a bare angularity which the few small planted trees have not yet softened.

In sum, the old town stands intact, with its landmarks and its air of small-town comfort. Mingled with it and sprawling about it in nondescript disarray are the new structures. At the extremities of the town, on the river shore, are small patches of the pleasant suburban houses of new people who have city ways and some money to spend. But beyond the industries, spreading over the sandy plain, are the clusters of cubical wooden boxes, urban in form but rural in appointments, which house the masses of industrial workers.

If, in introducing our town, we have played too much on contrast between past and present, it has been to sharpen the reader's eye to the very problems which we propose to discuss: the adjustment of French Canadians to a new kind of life in which their own rather rural past meets industry, the city—in person or through those city influences that spread to smaller centers—and a way of life which, in America at least, is dominated by English-speaking people.

CHAPTER VI

THE PEOPLE OF CANTONVILLE

THE newcomers who have multiplied Cantonville's population several times over are not adventurers from afar; rather are they French-Canadian rural folk who, compelled to move in order to survive, have sought one of the more promising of the near-by stopping-places. Although only a tenth of a sample of 1,346 male heads of families were born in the local town and township, half are natives of three counties.[1] Three-quarters of them were born in a compact block of ten counties. An additional 20 per cent, born in the rest of the province, are from widely scattered places. Natives of Montreal and of the few cities of Cantonville's size or larger are negligible in number. A handful of 71 were born in New England, and only 10 in other Canadian provinces.

The block of ten counties whose people have flocked to the new industrial town include the eastern part of the St. Lawrence River plain, as well as the gentle slope and plateau which rise southward and eastward toward the Appalachian hills. Although the plain continues westward from Cantonville, the town has drawn few people from that direction. That may be due to the counterattraction of Montreal and of many other, smaller cities.

For more than a century the counties on the south shore of the Middle St. Lawrence have produced an excess of population which has moved up and through the foothill counties into the once English Eastern Townships. Cantonville is but the current goal for a migration that is chronic. These river counties are among the most French and rural of the province; certainly they are culturally homogeneous in a degree rare in North America.[2]

The second and third tiers of counties of the block of ten run into the foothills, where rivers are dammed for power. Some industries are to be found there, and the population is slightly more diluted with English. Even so, these counties contain no town of the size or industrial importance of our community. We also know, from personal knowl-

---

[1] Cantonville lies near the center of this group of three counties.

[2] See Table 12.

THE PEOPLE OF CANTONVILLE 41

TABLE 11

BIRTHPLACES OF MALE HEADS OF FAMILIES LIVING
IN CANTONVILLE, 1937*

Recorded Place of Birth	Number	Percentage	Cumulative Percentage
Total recorded..................	1,346	100.0	....
Cantonville and township...........	142	10.6	10.6
Remainder of county and two neighboring counties.....................	545	40.5	51.1
Remainder of region................	305	22.7	73.8
Remainder of Quebec...............	251	18.6	92.4
Remainder of Canada..............	10	0.7	93.1
United States of America............	71	5.3	98.4
Outside of Canada and United States of America........................	22	1.6	100.0
Birthplace not recorded or family without male head...................	2,081	....	....
Total number of family cards†....	3,427	....	....

* This information was compiled from parish records kindly made available by the curés. The clergy take an annual census of all families, both Catholic and Protestant. The birthplace of the male head was recorded for 1,346 (all Catholic) of the 3,427 families listed in 1936–37. Omission of this item ran by streets and blocks, indicating that some census-takers were less punctilious than others. The least complete records were found in an outlying parish whose population is almost completely French and of the working class. A perfect recording would probably show an even larger percentage of people of local origin. There is an underrecording of foreign born; but this does not matter, since the only conclusions drawn have to do with the French-Canadian population.

† The parish census of 1937 showed 3,668 families in the community. We missed some through failure to complete our tabulation for one outlying parish.

TABLE 12

CHARACTERISTICS OF THREE TIERS OF COUNTIES IN THE REGION, 1931

Tiers	Male Heads of Families Born in Counties of Given Tiers	Population*	Percentage Catholic†	Percentage French‡	Percentage Urban (Incorporated Place 1,000 and Over)§	Manufacturing Employees‖
I. River shore.........	372	68,527	99.8	98.5	8.6	720
II. Middle plateau¶.....	494	105,744	96.1	94.5	32.5	5,673
III. Foothill.............	126	70,129	87.8	85.8	38.2	4,333
Total..............	992	244,400	94.7	93.1	27.4	10,726

* Census of Canada, 1931, Vol. II, Table 12.
† Ibid., Table 42.
‡ Ibid., Table 33.
§ Ibid., Table 16.
‖ Dominion Bureau of Statistics, Manufacturing Industries of Canada, 1933, Table 6.
¶ Second tier includes the county in which Cantonville is located.

edge of the English population in our town, that migrants from these counties are nearly all French and Catholic. Cantonville residents who came from this region are now living in a bigger town than ever before. They are living a new life and working at new trades, although they are in the midst of their own kind and kin.

Any person born in the region and now living in Cantonville may, of course, have lived and worked farther afield at some time. The general impression of people in the town, however, is that the migrants have come rather directly from the country and the villages. Our data support that impression. The family records from which we worked allow space for recording the places of birth of all members of the family and for the place of marriage of the parent-couple. Of 969[3] families for whom these records were complete, 710 show no place of birth or marriage outside the ten-county region. Of the 172 wives born outside the region, 109 are natives of the province, 5 of other parts of Canada, and 58 of the New England states, where so many French Canadians have sojourned. The remaining 87 families had records of place of marriage or birth of children outside the region. These facts indicate that most of our people have not lived outside the region and that most of the few who have done so have not left the French-Canadian world.[4] Cantonville is giving them their first experience of life in a large community.

These statements refer to the mass of the population. They are more true of the French than of the English, for the latter were recruited precisely because of previous industrial experience. Even among the French there are many persons of specialized skills learned in other and larger urban centers.

ETHNIC ORIGINS

Ninety-one per cent of the people who lived in Cantonville in 1931 were French. Practically all of the French and another 3 per cent were Catholic.[5] Of the slightly more than 20,000 people recorded in the par-

[3] For this purpose we used the 992 families of which the male head was born in the region. Of these, 969 had complete records for place of birth of husband, wife, and one or more children, as well as place of marriage of the parent-couple.

[4] It is not uncommon to find that a person who speaks no English and is completely provincial has been born in New England during a sojourn of his family in some industrial city there.

[5] Some of the 3 per cent recorded as Catholic but not French were probably French in fact. The French-Canadian census-takers are apparently inclined to count as Irish, Scotch, or English anyone whose name would suggest these origins, although the person be thoroughly French in language, culture, and social affiliations.

ish census of 1940, 95 per cent are Catholic. Inspection of Table 13 shows that the percentage of Catholics has remained practically the same in spite of the multiplication of the population by more than seven in the last thirty years. In the decade from 1921 to 1931, in which most of the industries were established, the proportion of French declined slightly.

TABLE 13

RELIGIOUS AND ETHNIC COMPOSITION OF GREATER CANTONVILLE
1911–40*

	French	Non-French	Totals
1911:			
Catholic...............	2,414	51	2,465 (94.6%)
Non-Catholic...........	....	140	140
Total..............	2,414 (92.7%)	191	2,605
1921:			
Catholic...............	4,103	124	4,227 (95.4%)
Non-Catholic...........	....	206	206
Total..............	4,103 (92.6%)	330	4,433
1931:			
Catholic...............	10,911	405	11,316 (94.1%)
Non-Catholic...........	....	707	707
Total..............	10,911 (90.8%)	1,112	12,023
1940:			
Catholic...............	....	....	19,651 (95.1%)
Non-Catholic...........	....	....	1,021
Total..............	....	....	20,672
Estimated..........	(92–94%)	....	....

* In the *Census of Canada* religions and racial (or ethnic) origins of people appear in separate tables. In making this compilation the row and column totals are taken directly from census figures. In establishing the figures for each cell it is assumed that all French are Catholic. This, no doubt, is slightly in error. From other sources we know that around 1937 there were probably 10 French non-Catholics in the town. A liberal estimate would be 20.

But from 1938 to 1940 the Protestant population has decreased slightly. Since practically all Protestants are not French, this means that some non-French people have actually left the community in these years. In the absence of a considerable increase of non-French Catholics, it also indicates a decrease of total non-French population.[6]

[6] Our knowledge of the community is such that we can say positively that the non-French Catholic population is not increasing in any significant degree.

In short, the establishment of industries and the consequent tremendous growth of the town have not altered significantly the proportion of French and Catholics in the population. This becomes a point of importance when one recalls that the industries which have changed the town were established by English initiative and that each brought an outside non-French manager, together with some technicians and skilled workers. Apparently, no amount of new industry, staffed at the top by English outsiders, will make the population of Cantonville—or of any similar Quebec town—proportionately less French.

Of course, the English (non-French) population of Cantonville has increased in the period under study. It was, in fact, multiplied by six between 1911 and 1931. Whatever may happen to their relative influence, it is not likely that their number will become, either absolutely or proportionately, much greater. The contrary is more likely.

We venture a general statement about the growth of English and French population in Quebec communities. A sudden increase of English population is generally due to some major innovation —a new industry or several of them—in the community's economic life. The English population comes to perform new and specialized functions. It is, in short, a sort of new specialized organ grafted into the local society. The new organ—English population with appropriate capital, machines, and authority—enlivens the town, making it grow and changing its character. But the growth is mainly of French. The changes likewise affect the French primarily, for they get new kinds of jobs and new conditions of living. The English who come to town continue their customary occupations.

Once the new industries are in operation, a settling-down begins. The French learn the skills of the industry and so become occupationally more differentiated. This reduces the need of importing non-French workers and technicians. Meanwhile, by the surer organic processes of breeding and short-distance migration of mass dimensions, the French population will continue to increase. The mechanically induced influx of English population will come to an end. The birth rate of the English being that of the Protestant middle class, and its mobility being high, the English population will then become stationary and perhaps decline slowly. Cantonville is apparently at this phase now.

Thus, the main ethnic element of the community is what it has long been, French-Catholic. The other important element, numerically a small minority, is generally called "English-Protestant." To it are assigned some who are not of English ancestry and even some who are Catholic. The close association of ethnic and religious affiliations in the minds of people makes it logical to present them together. The cross-tabulation in Table 14 shows the variety of tiny religious and

TABLE 14

RELIGIOUS AND ETHNIC COMPOSITION OF THE POPULATION OF
CANTONVILLE, 1931*

	Total (100.0%)	French (90.8%)	British (7.5%)	European (1.4%)	Hebrew	Indian	Asiatic
						(0.3%)	
Total (100.0%).......	12,023	10,911	905	164	21	4	18
Catholic (94.0%)........	11,296	10,911	248	133	....	4	....
British-American Protestant (5.6%)...............	668	....	657	....	....	....	11
European Protestant }	31	....	....	31	....	....	....
Jewish............ }(0.4%)	21	....	....	....	21	....	....
Other sects......... }	7	....	....	....	....	....	7

* *Census of Canada, 1931*, Vol. II.

ethnic groups who do not belong clearly to either of the major groups. If all of these little groups were called "English-Protestant," the latter would still be an insignificant proportion of the total population. How important this small group is, in fact, will appear in the analysis of the occupational structure given in the following chapter.

CHAPTER VII

FRENCH AND ENGLISH IN THE INDUSTRIAL HIERARCHY

OCCUPATIONS AND ETHNIC ORIGINS

In Cantonville's major industries the English hold all positions of great authority and perform all functions requiring advanced technical training. They are in the majority in the middle and minor executive positions, numerous among the clerical workers and skilled mechanics, less so among skilled operating hands, and hard to find among the semiskilled and unskilled help. Altogether, they form but a small minority of all persons employed in industry—so small, in fact, that if they were proportionately distributed among all ranks and specialities they would be scarcely noticeable. It is their concentration in certain ranks that makes them of importance.

The French constitute a large majority of all persons employed in industry. In the ranks of labor they predominate most strongly. They thin out as one goes in from the shop to the office, and eventually disappear as one goes up the authority scale.

Local business and service enterprises are generally owned, and almost all are operated, by French Canadians. Professional and public services lie in their hands. The French are the indigenous population and, as we have shown, constitute an overwhelming majority of the total. Among them are persons of all the ranks ordinarily found in American communities of comparable size. Since the French make up more than 90 per cent of the total population, it follows that more of them are of lower rank than of higher. They are likewise distributed among a great variety of occupations. Those of higher economic standing and of the occupations requiring greater training are, like the laborers, nearly all descendants of farmers or villagers of the region. They are part and parcel of the community.

The English, on the contrary, are an alien minority, consisting of hand-picked individuals brought to town to perform special functions in industry. In business and in the ranks of labor they are rare. A French Canadian has roots in the community. Even without his present job or business he would probably manage some kind of existence there. The English person probably could not remain without his present kind of job or even without the very job he now has.

The detailed account which follows will modify but little this sharp and unqualified contrast. It will, however, show the live points at which friction and change do now or may presently appear.

THE TWO KINDS OF INDUSTRIES

The industries are of two types. The first, owned by local French Canadians, are small shops which produce something for sale to the local population. Sash-and-door factories, combined with general building material yards; a modern creamery; the largest printing shop;

TABLE 15

FRENCH AND NON-FRENCH BY OCCUPATION IN CANTONVILLE, 1938*

GAINFULLY OCCUPIED IN—	FRENCH		NON-FRENCH		TOTAL	
	Number	Per Cent	Number	Per Cent	Number	Per Cent
Major industries	3,983	62.4	287	83.2	4,270	63.4
Utilities	69	1.1	19	5.5	88	1.3
Locally owned industries	66	1.0			66	1.0
Total in industries	4,118	64.5	306	88.7	4,424	65.7
Nonindustrial occupations	2,270	35.5	39	11.3	2,309	34.3
Grand total	6,388	100.0	345	100.0	6,733	100.0

* Tabulated from the town directory, 1938.

and a couple of soft-drink bottling establishments are listed as industries. These are more akin in function and organization to local businesses and service shops—ice and wood yards, blacksmith shops, garages, etc.—than to the major industries. They do not make the town grow but proliferate and grow with it.

Industries of the second type—*nos grandes industries*, as they are called in newspaper editorials and chamber of commerce resolutions—are owned by outside corporations. Local initiative had little or no part in founding them. They have headquarters in Montreal and connections even farther afield. Their local managers are English. The goods they produce are sold in the national and export markets. Such are the industries which changed the community from a small commercial town to one of Quebec's larger industrial centers.

In 1937 eleven industries of the latter type were in operation. Only two of the eleven, employing about seventy people, are managed by

French Canadians. One of these, a foundry and the oldest industry in town, is operated by a hired French manager. The other, while owned by its local operators, is part of the new industrial system. Its product, cardboard boxes, is sold only to the other industries and used to pack their nationally distributed goods. The other plants correspond completely to the pattern of outside corporation ownership, English management, and production for national sale. Table 16 and Map IV present the facts of ethnic origin of managers and place of origin of the mothering companies for these eleven industries.

TABLE 16

CANTONVILLE INDUSTRIES PRODUCING FOR OUTSIDE MARKETS, 1937

Products	Number of Employees*	Origin of Manager	Seat of Mother-Company
Silk goods..........	2,726	Old-country English	England (and U.S.A.)
Cotton goods.......	600	English-Canadian	Montreal (and U.S.A.)
Silk-finishing.......	350	American	U.S.A.
Silk goods..........	300	American	U.S.A.
Silk goods..........	150	Alsatian-American	U.S.A.
Lumber............	100	English-Canadian	Montreal
Novelties...........	60	American	U.S.A.
Rubber goods.......	50	English-Canadian	Montreal
Pencils.............	40	German-American	U.S.A.
Foundry products...	40	French-Canadian	Cantonville
Paper boxes........	30	French-Canadian	Cantonville

* The number of employees is exact for the first industry; the others, given orally by managers, etc., are obviously less exact.

More than half of the industrial hands in the community work in Mill A. The numerical part of the following analysis is based upon exact figures concerning the employees of this factory.[1] The interviews reported are not, however, confined to this industry or even to this town.

Mill A makes artificial silk goods. Although the founding personnel of the Canadian plant came from a mother-plant in England, administrative relations with a United States company are closer.

MANAGERIAL AND TECHNICAL STAFF

The twenty-five men of the general staff of Mill A are all ethnically English except one. That one, the company physician, is a local

[1] The ethnic distribution of the employees of the other industries will be found in Appendix A. Examination will show no significant differences between the distribution in Mill A and that in the other factories. Differences in detail may be accounted for by the fact that small plants cannot afford their own engineers, research technicians, etc. The data were given by management in every case.

MAP IV

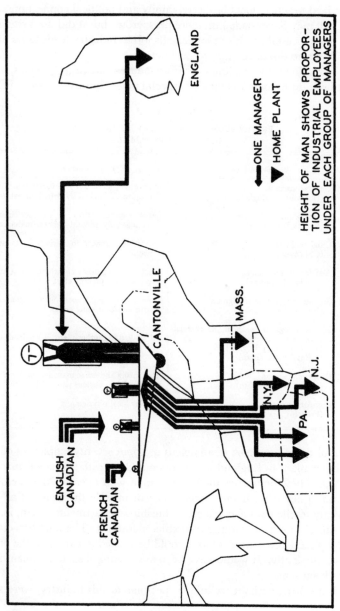

ENGLAND

ENGLISH CANADIAN

FRENCH CANADIAN

CANTONVILLE

MASS.

N.Y.

N.J.

PA.

ONE MANAGER

HOME PLANT

HEIGHT OF MAN SHOWS PROPOR-
TION OF INDUSTRIAL EMPLOYEES
UNDER EACH GROUP OF MANAGERS

ORIGIN OF MANAGERS AND HOME PLANTS

French Canadian who has many other irons in the fire—a thriving medical practice, local property, family and political connections. Industry may have made him more prosperous, but it did not bring him to town or establish his practice. His job in industry leads to no other and has no direct relation to production.

The others, the leading executives and executive-technicians, were all brought to town to take their special places in this industry. Eight-

DIAGRAM II

PREVIOUS CONNECTIONS OF THE MEMBERS OF THE
GENERAL STAFF OF MILL A

Present Positions	Previous Connections
General manager........ (Old-country English)	Managed other concerns in various parts of the Empire, all backed by British investors
Superintendent of labor....... (British West Indian)	Labor superintendent in another industry managed by present general manager
Chief engineer......... (Old-country English)	Executive engineer in various parts of the Empire
Assistant chief engineer........ (English-Canadian)	Electrical engineer elsewhere in Canada. Worked for present chief
Second assistant chief engineer........ (English-Canadian)	Previous personal, school, and work connection with assistant chief engineer
18 major executives, including chemists and textile experts........ (17 old-country English) (1 English-Canadian)	All worked in mother-plant in England
Office manager........ (Old-country English)	Accounting and office management for British concerns in various parts of Empire
Company physician........ (French-Canadian)	Popular local physician

een of them were part of a nucleus of about seventy employees of the mother-plant in England sent to open and operate the new Canadian plant. These emissaries include the man who operates the chemical plant, a key department. Others so sent include the heads of all the strictly textile manufacturing and finishing departments—men, in the main, of practical training in textile operations. The founders of the new plant knew that these men could be trusted to carry out the processes efficiently. It would have been astonishing if such a nucleus had not been sent.

But others, without techniques peculiar to this industry, were sent from abroad. First among them is the old-country English general manager, who has managed several different kinds of industries in widely separated parts of the British Empire. None of these industries produced textiles. Although he is a seasoned and capable manager, the significant link between his varied positions is probably to be found in a common group of English financial backers of these enterprises.[2] This British gentleman—for that he is—is an acceptable guardian of the interests of other British gentlemen—gentlemen, however, who want not only loyalty but a high and profitable degree of efficiency. Once appointed, the manager must gain the confidence of his associates; even before that, in an industry of this size, he must have had the confidence of directors and important investors.

The labor superintendent was likewise brought from abroad without previous textile experience. His functions are the hiring, firing, and transferring of hands; the policing of the plant; and the avoiding and handling of labor conflicts. He stands necessarily in a close confidential relationship with the general manager, whose mouthpiece and agent he must often be. He was chosen by the general manager under whom he had worked in a similar capacity in another part of the world.

The chief engineer also has behind him a career of journeying about the Empire to work at his profession. His chief assistant is, by specialty, an electrical engineer, as one might expect in an electrically driven plant. As a person, he is that young Canadian engineer whom the chief engineer, from previous association with him, judged to be the man to whom he could trust the work most crucial for his own success. The second assistant was brought by the first assistant, who had known him as friend, student, and colleague.

We do not know any previous personal associations of the office manager.[3] He belongs, however, to a breed of man in whom British firms have great confidence—the itinerant Scottish accountant and office manager, hard and loyal at work, genial and friendly among colleagues at play.

[2] A manager in a similar position commented: "Most of the money in our business is British, and it is but natural that a British manager and controlling staff should be appointed. There are deep biases, which I share, behind that."

[3] Had we specifically asked about previous personal and work associations, we would probably have found a great many more than we did. The knowledge which we have appeared in interviews and conversations as something commonly known and presumably of interest to outsiders who were trying to understand the organization. It should be added that in no case was the information given in a spirit which suggested that any man was a "stooge" for another.

Only the company physician stands clearly free of previous relationship with other members of the general staff. He is a prosperous and influential general practitioner. That means that he is French, as are the workers whom he must treat on the company's behalf.[4]

The members of the general staff also stand out in length of service. Twenty of them have been on the pay roll ever since the plant opened ten years ago. Each of the other five has served as long as his job has been in existence. With two or three exceptions, they are on the near side of fifty; several are just turning forty. Stable as to tenure, and with years of service ahead of them, these men are not likely to leave many vacancies in the next ten years. The plant will then have been in operation for twenty years without any appreciable turnover of staff.

These facts should be put into a more general setting, so that they may later be used in discussing the probable future of French Canadians in the higher positions of industry.

We commonly assume that the staffs of industrial organizations are chosen in a mood of impersonal search for the best at the lowest price. It is true that industry demands profitably efficient production and hence wants superior personnel. But in this matter industry is not the haggling trader but the ultimate consumer buying goods in which he has confidence.

The appointment of a major executive or technician is, then, a vote of confidence. Within it are included several component judgments— to wit, that the man knows his technique, that he can and will work satisfactorily in the interest of the appointing authorities, and that he can and will win the confidence and best efforts of his colleagues and subordinates. For some jobs, the appointers may not trust a candidate who cannot be safely and comfortably entertained at dinner; for others, the degree of required social acceptability may be less. In some cases, a personally unpleasant or undesired expert can be thrown in

---

[4] The company physician is not personal physician to the staff, who can and do have most of their medical attention from Montreal English doctors. He is, rather, physician to the labor force, which is French. The range of skill within which a man can be acceptable as a company doctor is very great. This is not a hazardous industry, and the town is big enough to have a few specialists and surgeons available. A great medical center is two hours away. In a hazardous industry so far removed that even the higher staff could not get to a medical center easily, the doctor's qualifications might have to be different. In our case, almost any successful physician would do from the technical side, and the social reputation of the man becomes the crucial point. The man chosen has wide and influential connections and is a good fellow to drink and to play golf and poker with. This combination makes him the right man, seeing that the position of company physician is diplomatic in character.

the faces of colleagues and subordinates; in others, it seems best to cater to the prejudices of the subordinates rather than to those of the appointing superiors. In general, there is probably a strong bias in favor of appointing for higher positions a man of the kind liked and trusted by the appointing group. Ethnic background, religion, and even "the old-school tie" might enter into the case—not in the spirit of looking after one's friends but with the conviction, which might be true, that efficiency is best served so.

For almost any position in industry it may be assumed that there is a certain range between the lower limit of necessary skill and knowledge and the upper limit which can be commanded for the money and social rewards offered. The tendency of modern industry is to push toward the ceiling of efficiency. But within the range of indifference there are generally a number of men available. Within this range judgment is likely to be conservative with respect to personal qualities. This is not the point at which industrial organizations take the long chance.

The road to the higher executive positions is opened to a man by a series of such votes of confidence, each of which gives him access to a new field of experience and to association with the men whose good will is necessary for the next step. At each step on this road the individual himself gathers power to make judgments about others, to accept or reject them as his actual or prospective colleagues, and to make gestures which affect the judgments of others with respect to his equals and his subordinates. In this an industrial organization is like any other human society, with its various circles of close associates, its hierarchy of prestige and authority, and its interplay of social gestures which settle the fate of each individual.

In our community it is evident that French Canadians as a group do not enjoy that full confidence of industrial directors and executives which would admit them easily to the inner and higher circles of the fraternity—and fraternity it is—of men who run industry. This situation prevails throughout the province of Quebec.

It may seem that we have given undue attention to a mere twenty-five men. Let it be remembered that these twenty-five, along with the managers and a few technician-executives in the other industries, occupy the best positions which industry offers in this community. Their high salaries enable them to live in a style which appears conspicuous. They wield great authority directly over the hands in industry and indirectly over other persons, although the local citizens probably overestimate their individual power.

These leading positions, unattainable though they be for all but a few, serve as symbolic goals. They stand for the openness of the road to the top, either for one's self or for others with whose advancement one identifies himself. The French Canadians share with other minorities an acute sensitivity to symbols of this sort. When "un des nôtres" accomplishes something unusual, it is a matter of proud comment, even though the hero be immediately reviled for not using his position to the advantage of his fellows. The French Canadians of our community well know that no major executive of the local industries is "one of our boys" who made good. A newspaper of the region once reported at length and with pride the appointment of a French assistant manager in an industry. Inquiry revealed that he would, at best, be rated as a departmental shop foreman. His appointment was one of a series of actions by which effective management of the plant was removed to company headquarters in another city. Yet that small appointment was news. It was as if someone had announced that the French Canadian could now hope for the higher positions in industry.

THE FOREMEN

Since the French so far outnumber the English in the working force of industry, there must be a point in the hierarchy at which the proportions are reversed. In Mill A, and in many industries in Quebec, the turning-point is near the bottom of the foreman's rank. The staff is exclusively English; the foremen are only predominantly so, for twenty-five out of eighty-two are French.

Since a nucleus of foremen and skilled workmen were brought from England to start the new plant, it is not surprising that English should predominate among the foremen employed in the early years and for some time thereafter. As a matter of fact, this predominance has continued, for, of nine foremen hired in the three years prior to our study, seven are English.[5] The 7.28 years average term of employment of English foremen is almost equaled by an average of 7.00 years for French foremen.

Although our tabulations do not distinguish important from minor and assistant foremen, it is clear that the French are in the lesser positions. Some people responsible for hiring say frankly that they hire

[5] These figures and those in the following sentences refer to years of employment in the mill, not necessarily to years of service at foreman's rank. We do not know the interval between original employment and promotion to foreman. It is obvious, however, that a person employed for only one or two years and already a foreman had most of his training elsewhere.

English foremen and French to assist them. The case is typically put much like this:

> We tried to have French foremen, but it has not worked out. They pay too much attention to family and friends; the British foreman does his job, is friendly with no one, and is just. He doesn't speak French, and that is probably a good thing, too. As it is, he has to work through a French assistant foreman. The foreman might go directly to a man and say: "The next time you do so and so, you will be kicked to hell out of here." As it is, he says to the French assistant foreman: "Tell so and so if he does that again I will kick him to hell out." The assistant goes to the man, and says: "Look here, the boss is pretty sore. You better watch your step." The French assistant foreman acts as a cushion.

TABLE 17

EMPLOYEES OF MILL A IN CANTONVILLE BY NATIONALITY
RANK, AND DEPARTMENT, 1937

RANK	NUMBER			PER CENT		
	English and Other	French*	Total	English and Other	French	Total
Total...........................	389	2,337	2,726	14.3	85.7	100.0
I. Staff, above foremen.............	24	1	25	96.0	4.0	100.0
II. Foremen.......................	57	25	82	69.5	30.5	100.0
III. All others, by departments†........	308	2,311	2,619	11.8	88.2	100.0
1. Main office, etc................	65	97	162	40.1	59.9	100.0
2. Engineering and chemical.......	92	206	298	30.9	69.1	100.0
3. Personnel, final examination, pro-gramming, and shipping........	28	126	154	18.2	81.8	100.0
4. Textile production.............	123	1,882	2,005	6.1	93.9	100.0

* The table of nationalities furnished us by the management showed 2,324 French, 353 English, and 49 "others." Our tabulation, made from the pay roll on the basis of names and personal knowledge, finds 13 more French than does the company's tabulation. Our knowledge of individuals in the upper ranks is so complete that the error is entirely in the lower ranks, where the difference of 13 is of no importance. The error probably comes from our inclination to call any person French whose last name is English but whose first name is French. There are a good many such persons in the community, and it is our judgment that a family which gives a French first name to its child is for all social purposes a French family. If a family calls its son "Narcisse," it isn't an English family.

† The departmental groupings are: (1) general office, general stores, cafeteria, purchasing, factory clerks, and the nurse; (2) as named in the table; (3) as named in the table; and (4) spinning, weaving, textile, knitting, and dyeing departments (the foremen and department heads in this group are mostly Lancashire men).

When the subject of French foremen is raised, the answers come in stereotypes, of which these are the common ones: "The French have to be told what to do and therefore cannot be trusted with jobs requiring initiative and the meeting of crises." "They are good routine workers but are inclined to take things easy if left to themselves." "They are so jealous of one another that they do not yield to the authority of one of their own number." "They have so many relatives and friends that they cannot avoid favoritism."

These clichés become painfully familiar to anyone who talks about this problem in Quebec. The differences between French and English expressed or implied in such statements are sometimes attributed to inherent qualities of the two peoples; in other interviews, to the great disparity in their experience of industry. In either case, it is evident that those who have the power to appoint foremen in Cantonville think that ethnic differences are significant and that the English are superior.

Yet one must remember the twenty-five French foremen in Mill A and the presence of some French foremen in other industries. The very executives who utter derogatory opinions frequently point out exceptions. "Our best dyer-foreman is French." "D'Autel was a mechanic. I made him a foreman, and he is first class. Absolutely fair and loyal." "Hudon is a good, adaptable, reliable man. Old bush Frenchmen[6] are all right."

The foreman is generally a "practical" man who, having come up through the grades of skill, is set over others who do the kind of work he knows. The English undoubtedly had the advantage of skill and experience in Cantonville's textile industries for some time. They may have it still for certain kinds of work. Executives of Mill A say that the new foremen hired from outside in the past few years are mainly men of some mechanical skill required in the maintenance of the plant. A textile mill, and especially a growing one, is not likely to train as many such men as it requires. There is little doubt that mechanical foremen are easier to find in the English than in the French-Canadian world.

In its main textile operations, however, such a plant as Mill A can and does train its own people. The skill and experience required of foremen are got within the mill itself. In these textile departments 94 per cent of the help is French. The great majority of weavers are French Canadians who have, in the space of less than ten years, come from the farm and passed from the lowest to the highest grades of skill. It would be nothing short of remarkable if the 6 per cent of non-French workers should for long retain a distinct advantage in the skill and experience required of foremen.[7] Also, the French will undoubt-

[6] Men who have worked in lumber camps.

[7] It must be said that this 6 per cent of non-French amount to one hundred and twenty-three persons, eighty-six of whom were hired in the five years preceding our study. If they were selected especially with a view to maintaining a supply of English candidates for foremen's jobs and if the selection were well made, no doubt all future foremen could be selected from so small a number. There is no evidence of any such policy, although we had one interview in which an industrial executive said he hired a few English boys each year against the day when he would need foremen.

edly begin to identify their own careers more closely with advancement in industry.

When, therefore, considerable replacement of present foremen becomes necessary in this and other industries, persistence in a policy of appointing English might be taken with less grace than in the past. By that time the current clichés about the French may have lost their force. Already it has become the custom for English industrial leaders to praise the French Canadians for their aptness at learning textile operations and for their loyal and energetic work.[8] These compliments often appear in a context which suggests that the French are more fit for manual than for executive work. Even so, constant vaunting of their superiority, even in the humble capacity of workmen, will scarcely prepare the French Canadians to accept a continued policy of appointing English to "boss" them.

There remain the supposed jealousy of French Canadians for those of their own number who are put in authority and their inclination to favor relatives and friends. Both these alleged traits are in opposition to the emphasis of our secular society upon rational and impersonal selection of persons for jobs. Nothing disturbs an employing executive more than to have employees or outsiders question his appointments; in Quebec, English executives suffer a real *malaise* in the face of the familial claims and jealousies of the French Canadians. It was more in sorrow than in anger that the manager of a small industry spoke thus on this subject:

They are very jealous of one another. If we hire two from the same family, they want to know why we do so when some other large family needs support. The priest even asks about such things. If a man gets $30 a week, he will tell his friends he is getting $50, just to boast and be a big fellow. The others want to know why he is so favored.

French-Canadian society is strongly familial, as well as being a minority. On both counts one would expect personal claims to positions to be pushed strongly. Every family acts as a lobby for its members. The French Canadian in public life feels this pressure to provide for friends, relatives, and French Canadians. Jealousy of those who

[8] Such statements are often made when explaining the movement of industries to this province. This amounts to saying: "We moved here not to get cheap labor but to get good labor." The alleged superiority of French girls is sometimes laid to the prevalence of home spinning and weaving in the rural parts of the province. At other times, however, another theme is introduced, as in the following statements: "These French-Canadian girls are so absorbed in their work that they hardly notice anyone passing by. The English girls will do so much work and no more." This suggests that the French girls are quick because they are unspoiled; that is, because they have not yet developed those conscious or unconscious restrictions of production found among workers in older industrial centers.

get advancement is a natural component of such a situation. Our impression is that English employers and executives have a real fear that French put into authority would yield to these claims and jealousies to the disadvantage of efficient production, or that, not yielding, they could not maintain discipline and morale.

On the other side, one must recall that great numbers of French Canadians have always, and do now, work for employers and under superiors of their own ethnic group. French-Canadian businessmen manage successfully in the midst of these familial claims. In the newer industries managed by English one finds some executives who say that jealousy of a French Canadian promoted to authority appears mainly at the moment of his promotion and dies out as soon as he is established in his position.

It may be that the expressions of jealousy and the pushing of claims rise to a new height when the French Canadians first enter a new system of relationships (such as those of large industries) in which the equilibrium between their traditional claims and their relevant abilities has not yet been established. They may also take some advantage of the English outsider, who does not know the devices by which a French Canadian would keep such claims in check. These are merely possibilities, based on observation and what is known of other peoples. Another such possibility is that longer experience with large industry will make French-Canadian society distinctly less familial and personal.

RANK AND FILE

Employees of Mill A below the rank of foreman vary greatly in skill and responsibility. Our data, however, classify them only according to the departments in which they work. Table 17 shows that the ratio of French to English workers increases as one goes from the office outward through the engineering, chemical, and personnel departments to the textile manufacturing departments. This is a line of increasing distance from management and technical work.

The main office staff of an industry, quite apart from rank, is characteristically oriented toward management. The bookkeeper, the payroll clerk, the private secretary, and the stenographer, though their authority and pay be small, occupy positions of some confidence. The office help of Mill A take lunch and afternoon tea in a staff refreshment room, not in the general workers' room. This very common arrangement is one of orientation and of "social," rather than authority

and salary, ranking. In the office of Mill A there work (in not particularly important clerical jobs) a number of the daughters of Cantonville's better French families—girls who could not possibly work out in the factory for twice the money. In the office they can, while earning necessary money, meet on agreeable terms young men who have good prospects of success in the new industrial order. The English managerial families have these young women in their houses on occasion.[9] Although these girls have no exceptional skill and little hope of advancement, they can and do accept these management-oriented jobs.

If, from the general category of office help, we exclude the semi-clerical factory clerks, the purchasing, storehouse, and cafeteria employees, the remaining strictly office force of seventy-nine people is more English than French. The turn from a majority of English to a majority of French comes precisely at this point. The office force proper is 62 per cent English; the allied departments, named above, are 75 per cent French.

The engineering and chemical departments include many technicians, but also the working forces which maintain equipment and operate the chemical plant. From what we know of the plant, it is certain that the English occupy the jobs requiring greater technical and mechanical training. It follows that these skilled people account for the relatively high proportion of English in these departments.

The labor department requires help, not of exceptional skill, but of undoubted loyalty to management. For these are the people who check employees in and out, watch the plant, and do the policing which becomes especially important in time of unrest and strikes. It is essential, for diplomatic reasons, that most of this staff be French. Yet the chief of the plant police is an English Canadian of long experience in policing and private detective work.[10] The selection of employees in this department seems a sort of calculus problem, with loyalty and diplomacy as the variables.

These management-oriented employees enjoy some measure of prestige and security without much promise of advancement. Like the

[9] Daughters of professional and business families of high social standing in Quebec often keep books, type, etc., for their fathers. This is justified by saying how indispensable the daughter is to her father or, if she works elsewhere, to her employer, who is a family friend. This raises the work above mere clerical work for a living. The necessary techniques—business English, typing, shorthand—are taught in convent boarding-schools, which girls of such families attend.

[10] In Montreal industries of English management we found it common to have English watchmen and policemen of the "Old-Dog-Tray" stamp.

minor bureaucrats of government, they are close to authority without actively sharing it. Theirs are jobs a little aside from the main highways which lead from the humble places to the high places. The presence of French Canadians among this bureaucracy of industry indicates some confidence of the management in the local people and a certain interweaving of factory organization with the local society. It does not presage the rise of the French Canadians to positions of importance in management or the productive operations.

Of the genuine rank and file of 2,005 people who do the spinning, weaving, knitting, finishing, and dyeing, 94 per cent are French. In some local industries they are all French. Mill A brought a few operating hands from England to teach the new local help. They were supplemented by French Canadians from New England who knew both the skills and the prevailing French language.[11] This phase has now passed. The basic labor force of all industries is French Canadian and native to the region.

Meanwhile other textile industries have been established in the province. Working at these operations is no longer something new. The region contains plenty of people who are more or less skilled in textile operations, and it can supply many more. Each industry, furthermore, is normally its own training school in its basic skills. French Canadians have come into their own in these, the main, operations of industry.

The industries which came into Cantonville brought with them, in addition to capital goods, certain people to perform special functions. Local people, in the beginning, occupied only those industrial positions for which little training was necessary—those for which their own cultural experience prepared them.

French-Canadian culture obviously includes the general institutional forms and the basic skills of Western civilization. The people expect to get their living by working for wages, by operating farms or business enterprises, or by practicing the various familiar professions.

[11] We got some indications in interviews that the management in some mills is glad to get rid of the New England French as soon as possible. The old-country English, whatever their sentiments about hours, wages, unions, etc., apparently do not spread discontent among the new French help. That may be because of the little communication, as well as because most of the imported old-country English help hope for promotion. The New England French, looked upon as more sophisticated ethnic fellows by local Canadian French, are more likely to spread discontent by making invidious comparisons between Quebec and New England working conditions. The New England French share with their local brethren exclusion from the fairly solid English group and hence have no great reason for identification with the dominant managerial group.

A system of schools, from infant class to the university and professional school, offers education and occupational training.

As is common in Western countries, the children of middle- and upper-class families generally get more formal schooling than those of the lower classes; town children more than rural. One of the means of getting ahead in the world is to get an education. The higher schools of French Canada train people for the kinds of careers understood and prized in their society. One finds law, medicine, dentistry, and lately commercial studies in the schools and universities. Not much has been offered in engineering and applied science until the last decade. Thus the French Canadians of highest training are not prepared for careers in industry. The masses of the people, while they have no training for industry, also have no well-formed ambitions or training which they have to give up to enter industry. The untrained lower classes are, in short, more adaptable than the educated upper classes. The latter are actually specialized away from industry; they could not turn to industry without loss of the gains which they have already made in their own world. Upper-class French Canadians thus find themselves in a dilemma shared by the upper ranks of any society which undergoes an industrial revolution introduced by outsiders.

Thus it is in the upper ranks of industry that one finds the English outsiders. People of local origin and French culture are in the lower ranks. The latter are, furthermore, from the lower ranks of the local society. The people of the higher ranks of the French-Canadian society find little place in the industrial hierarchy.

Once established, the industries become a social setting within which French and English interact. As humans must do, they interact by means of gestures. A person's action is taken not merely as a thing in itself but as an indication of what he thinks, of what he might do another time, of what others like him may or may not do. The responses which one gets may reinforce or discourage him in a whole line of action which is dear to him. Much of this exchange within an industrial organization will play upon the theme of the chances of advancement.

The English industrial managers, technicians, and foremen undoubtedly make some gestures which would encourage their French subordinates to aspire to higher positions. The following is an example:

The French lack the spirit of adventure. On technical work they are all right, so long as given but one thing to do at a time, such as taking readings. They have no initiative. I have a French draftsman with real ability; he ought to leave here and get broader experience than we can give him. He could make more money in commercial art. I suggested this to him and promised to take him back in case he couldn't get on elsewhere. He talked it over with his relatives and decided he had better stay with his job here. He is afraid to leave.

The response of the draftsman was in keeping with the role of the family in French-Canadian culture. His family had got him trained for a certain kind of job which gave promise of a certain level of income and prestige. The suggestion of his employer was taken as evidence—as the story was interpreted to us—that the young man was secure in his job. That being so, the family objective had been reached. The young man owed it to the family to stay where he was safe, and not to risk their investment in him by undertaking a hazardous adventure among strangers.

The employer, in putting one of his young men in a way to get ahead, was following a folkway of our "individualistic" industrial civilization. The executive loves to recognize merit and have his "boys" make good. But the play involves a challenge. To fulfil his sponsor's expectation and to win the confidence necessary to a second gesture of advancement, the young man must accept the challenge, run his chance, and make good. This the French-Canadian draftsman did not do. In telling the story the English employer expressed a commonly held opinion that French Canadians are satisfied with security and are therefore ineligible for the struggle to the top.

This opinion is probably based upon talk as much as upon experience, for the local air is full of such talk. Whether many executives have had equivalent experiences does not matter. The attitude is real. The French know it quite as well as do the English. The knowledge may well prevent them from making determined efforts for advancement. The attitude of each toward the other may thus inhibit the initial steps by which the situation might be changed.

Another exchange of gestures is suggested by the frequent stories of family pressure among the French Canadians. Whatever the reality, it is a doctrine of modern industry that a superior shall choose and promote his helpers without regard to family or other personal claims. If an individual for himself, or another on his behalf, poses such claims, the superior resists inwardly or openly. The resentment will be greater if the claimant is outside the superior's own social circle. To be sure, one Cantonville manager says he chooses much of his help on the basis of family recommendations. He likes certain families and avoids others. All of the thirty-odd Hudons in the plant are made to feel mutually responsible for their good name. But the Hudons are not there because of a claim upon the industry; on the contrary, the management deliberately chooses to put a certain claim upon them. Furthermore, these people are not destined for positions of authority, in which their kinship would make them suspect both to management and their fellow French Canadians. In general, the English people in industry believe that the French are constantly looking out for their relatives and friends; such a belief might well inhibit gestures leading to promotion.

Thus far we have dealt with what happens in the industrial organization. The occupational orientation of the individual begins much earlier and in the bosom of the family. Nothing so marks a culture as the ambitions fostered by the middle and upper classes. In French Canada boys of these classes are directed toward the liberal professions —law and medicine—with the lesser professions and business as alternatives. In our community no professional man has prepared or is preparing more than one son for his own profession. The others are generally put into business or become administrators of their father's affairs. Careful inquiry turned up no son of a prominent family who is taking or plans to take a university course in engineering! Two boys of such families are receiving a sort of apprenticeship in industries in other communities.

Such young men, of less training than their own fathers, are objects of special family solicitude. In some cases the family has sought positions in industry for them. All that is open to them is minor clerical work without hope of advancement. Family pride would not permit them to work in overalls, as do their ethnic fellows of humbler origin and as several of the English executives and engineers have done earlier in their careers. Indeed, managers often mentioned pride as a failing of the French-Canadian boy with a little schooling, even though he is of humble family; he, and the family which gave him the schooling, are inclined to question whether a job is worthy. Overalls brand a job as not worthy, even though it might offer more chance of advancement than clerical work.

If the French-Canadian boy of "good family" takes the minor clerical job that the industry is willing to give him for his name's sake, he knows full well that he will play second fiddle to outsiders in the very town where his father has been *maître d'orchestre*. The alleged result is a lack of that enthusiastic and competent work which might bring confidence and promotion. The boy's sister may take similar work without loss of face. She is not expected to get promotions. The man is, and no rationalization can save his face. The young man in this position can have from his English contemporaries a social equality on the golf links or at dances if his father will pay for it and if he (the young man) is willing to be seen in company that know his plight. Just such a young man, whose father had got him a job in industry and who took out his frustrations in drink and fast driving, said to one of us: "If I get drunk enough, I can kid myself that I am really a man." His plight is that of a class of young men, helped and almost forced, with too little training and too much pride, into positions of no future in industry. Industrial managers treat them with indulgent tolerance but do not regard them as candidates for positions of importance.

The English person in industry is several times more likely than the French to be an executive, an important technician or engineer, a foreman, or an office worker. The selection lying behind this took place mainly before the English person came to town. In the place he came from his ethnic affiliation was undoubtedly shared by a great number of people who did not get ahead as he did. The manager of one local industry mentioned this to modify his own tendency to explain the position of the French in terms of supposed ethnic qualities. Once in Cantonville, the ethnic factor is so important and apparent that almost everyone accounts for things in terms of it. It is in the air. Conventional phrases express "what everyone knows" about the French. French Canadians know these opinions and sometimes admit that there may be something in some of them. The knowledge, on both sides, that such opinions are held results in a reserve in the conversation of English with French, a reserve which takes the form of talking only social trivialities or of turning aside from touchy subjects by pronouncing profound truisms beyond discussion. Free discussion between the groups is rare. Such an atmosphere is favorable to the elimination of neither actual nor imputed shortcomings of French Canadians in industry.

CHAPTER VIII

FRENCH AND ENGLISH IN NONINDUSTRIAL
OCCUPATIONS

THE people engaged in nonindustrial occupations provide goods and services for local consumption. The employees of industry produce for a large, generally a national, market. The local units which dispense goods and services are, again in contrast to the industries, small, numerous, and often operated by independent entrepreneurs. In many lines the individual may set up shop on his own account without waiting to be hired, although, of course, some of the local dispensers of goods or services are agents for others and some are, like the managers of industry, employees of corporations whose headquarters are elsewhere. Finally, since the business and service units are small, the power to choose, hire, and command employees is distributed among a far greater number of people than in industry.

Freedom to set up shop on one's own account, the wide diffusion of hiring power, and the right of customers to buy goods and services from whom they will may be presumed to make the ethnic selection of the personnel of business and service units much more sensitive to the daily small choices of local people than is that of industry. This chapter is addressed to the actual distribution of French, English, and others among the nonindustrial occupations, to their respective places in such authority hierarchy as exists in business and service units, and to a discussion of available evidence on the way in which the customers of the two main ethnic groups exercise their sovereign choices.

Considerably more than nine out of ten of the potential takers of goods and services are French.[1] Again, the French are of all income groups and of many degrees of sophistication—from the *habitant* now working in industry to well-to-do people of urban tastes. The English are few; although not rich, they are concentrated in the higher positions in industry. Their tastes are those of American and Canadian town and city people of their class, and they are more subject than the French to those pressures which lead to conspicuous consumption. From the French, therefore, comes the great volume of demand; from

---

[1] The rural hinterland is almost completely French.

the English comes a certain enlivening demand for the more urban goods and services.[2]

The French who follow nonindustrial pursuits are numerous; their occupations are varied; and they occur in all ranks, from laborers and servants to large entrepreneurs, managers, and professionals. The mere handful of English follow but a few occupations. The French customer can have almost any want satisfied by an ethnic fellow; the English customer, only a few by his ethnic fellows.

A given kind of goods or services may be offered and wanted, or either, rather indifferently by people of both ethnic groups. It may be offered and wanted, or either, by one or the other group only. Goods or services also vary in the extent to which they are separable from the person who dispenses them. To the many possible combinations and permutations of these factors, each in their possible degrees of variation, it may be assumed that there are corresponding kinds and degrees of competition between the two groups. It is clear that members of each group want for their children education of an ethnically peculiar kind and want it only from their ethnic fellows. At this extreme, competition between the ethnic groups does not exist. At the other extreme are goods admittedly affected little by the hands of the dispenser and wanted rather indifferently by people of both ethnic groups. This is the case of greatest potential competition. These ideas should be kept in mind while reading the following pages.

Tables 18 and 19 show the numbers of French and non-French in various classes of nonindustrial occupations. The non-French are so few that they may be discussed almost one by one.

The five English schoolteachers and the two Protestant ministers do not compete with the nuns, lay brothers, and priests who perform functionally similar services for French Catholics. The only English physician has, by his own account, little French practice; his thirteen French colleagues have and expect little English practice.[3] These professionals administer to the needs and mysteries of soul and body which people are loath to entrust to ethnic strangers.

[2] Interview evidence indicates that the English created effective demand for fresh fruits and vegetables in winter, for fancier groceries, for outside magazines and newspapers. It is impossible to gauge this influence. In favor of it is the fact that only three or four of the numerous groceries carry such goods, and that these are especially patronized and praised by the English. Even these stores, however, could not live without a large body of French customers as well.

[3] See footnote to Table 19 for details concerning non-French in professional and quasi-professional services.

At the other end of the prestige scale, but still in the realm of personal service, we find that no non-French are employed as servants.[4]

TABLE 18

DISTRIBUTION OF FRENCH IN NONINDUSTRIAL OCCUPATIONS
IN CANTONVILLE, 1938*

OCCUPATION	MALE		FEMALE		TOTAL	
	Number	Per Cent	Number	Per Cent	Number	Per Cent
I. Professional and quasi-professional..	74	4.3	27	5.0	101	4.4
II. Proprietors and managers of business concerns.........................	222	12.8	16	3.0	238	10.5
III. Agents and clerks................	331	19.1	132	24.6	463	20.4
IV. Proprietors and persons engaged in service shops and trades†........	393	22.7	52	9.7	445	19.6
V. Servants........................	....	....	295	54.9	295	13.0
VI. *Rentiers* and public functionaries..	96	5.5	15	2.8	111	4.9
VII. Laborers‡.....................	617	35.6	....	....	617	27.2
Total......................	1,733	100.0	537	100.0	2,270§	100.0

* From a tabulation of information given in the city directory, 1938.
† It was impossible to determine in the case of 275 of the 393 males engaged in services or trades whether they owned their own shops or not. The majority of these probably belonged to the category of those working for someone else, such as mechanic, plumber, etc.
‡ It is likely that many of these are employed in industries.
§ This total does not include the 13 Catholic clergy listed in the directory. There are other clergy and nuns who were left out. These people perform services such as teaching, nursing, etc., and would be listed as professionals or quasi-professionals.

TABLE 19

DISTRIBUTION OF NON-FRENCH IN NONINDUSTRIAL OCCUPATIONS
IN CANTONVILLE, 1938

Occupation	Male	Female	Total
I. Professional and quasi-professional*...	6	3	9
II. Proprietors and managers of business concerns..........................	13	....	13
III. Agents and clerks.................	8	2	10
IV. Proprietors and persons engaged in service shops and trades.............	7	....	7
V. Servants............................	....	....	....
VI. *Rentiers* and public functionaries.....	2	....	2
VII. Laborers..........................	....	....	....
Total........................	36	5	41

* One physician; 5 schoolteachers; 1 Jewish music teacher, converted to Catholicism and married to a French woman; 2 insurance agents who do not maintain offices. Two Protestant ministers were not included.

Many French families, some of quite modest income, and a large proportion of the English families hire domestic servants. The usual maid

[4] The directory canvassers evidently missed a middle-aged maid brought out from England by a managerial family. In some months of daily exposure to talk about maids we heard of no other such case.

is a country girl from near by.[5] Some are paid as little as $3.00 a week.
The English housewives complain of their lack of experience and apol-
ogize sometimes for the low wages, but we heard of no one who had
made an effort to get from elsewhere experienced—and higher-priced
—help. In effect, the abundance of cheap domestic help enables the
English families to raise their standard of living. To the maid, work in
an English house is a way of living in town and learning the little bit of
English thought desirable for a job in the industries.

TABLE 20

NATIONALITY OF OWNER OR MANAGER OF BUSINESS AND
SERVICE UNITS IN CANTONVILLE, 1938

	French	English	Jewish and Other	Total
I. Utilities and banks..............	8	3	......	11
II. Businesses:				
1. Wholesalers and distributors.....	47	2	1	50
2. Retail........................	142	2	14	158
3. Hotels and recreation...........	37	1	2	40
Total business...............	226	5	17	248
III. Services:				
1. Professional...................	33	1	......	34
2. Quasi-professional.............	33	......	2	35
3. Service shops.................	116	1	1	118
4. Trades.......................	29	......	......	29
5. Agents.......................	12	......	......	12
Total services................	223	2	3	228
Grand total..............	457	10	20	487

Laborers and more skilled men privately hired to do repairs, gardening, and cleaning are all French. We need not discuss the one English *rentier* and the one English public official, both relics of pioneer
English families; the latter is already dead and succeeded by a French
Canadian.

The remaining non-French in nonindustrial occupations all have
some place in the commercial offering of goods and services to the local
populace. To make their place in the competitive system clear, we
have compared them with the French in two ways which seemed
especially pertinent.

[5] The French family with which we lived, a retired farming couple with grown daughters
engaged in small business, kept a "hired girl." She ate in the kitchen with the family.

Table 21 divides the French, English, and other heads of business and service units into independent entrepreneurs and hired managers.[6] Half of the ten English are hired managers, while the twenty "Others" (Jewish, Greek, and Chinese) and the four hundred and fifty-seven French are predominantly independent entrepreneurs.

Table 22 classifies the same people according to whether their units are locally independent, partially so, or definitely part of an outside organization.[7]

It seems fair to assume that the local entrepreneur is most completely at the mercy of local consumers; the dispenser of goods and services

TABLE 21

HEADS OF BUSINESS AND SERVICE UNITS IN CANTONVILLE
CLASSIFIED AS ENTERPRENEURS AND HIRED
MANAGERS, 1938

	Entrepreneurs	Hired Managers	Total
French.............	434	23	457
English............	5	5	10
Others.............	17	3	20
Total..........	456	31	487

for which special agency is required, less so; the hired manager of an outside concern, least so. Of the latter, the furthest removed from local customer control is the hired manager of a utility which has a monopoly over some service.

Only three English persons operate without any sort of special agency; two additional ones own garages and have agencies for automobiles; the other five are managers of outside concerns—to wit, two banks, one electrical power company, an electrical goods store owned by the power company, and a hotel partially owned by the power com-

[6] These tables are based on material gathered by a house-to-house canvass. We walked every inch of street and lane in the town and outlying districts, noting, among other things, the businesses and services offered in each building or lot. When there was the least reason to believe that a business or service was not French, we made inquiry. We missed services which had no kind of sign or other indication that the premises were not strictly residential. This probably accounts for a few discrepancies between these data and those of the town directory. The unit in the table is a business, a shop with a sign up, etc., offering for sale goods or services.

[7] Into the mixed category are put such things as automobile agencies, certain insurance agencies, etc. The automobile agent is an entrepreneur who generally owns a garage, but the manufacturer can give or take away his right to sell the particular brand of car. To this extent the agent, although an entrepreneur, is subject to outside control.

pany. Medicine, hairdressing, automobiles and automobile acces-
sories, electrical power and services related thereto—these are the
things which English people offer for sale.

The physician brings to town training in an English-Canadian medical school of great prestige. He also brings his English-Protestant person. Given the English attitude toward French-Canadian physicians,

TABLE 22

BUSINESS AND SERVICE UNITS IN CANTONVILLE CLASSIFIED BY
ETHNIC AFFILIATION OF PERSON IN CONTROL AND
BY TYPE OF CONTROL, 1938

ETHNIC AFFILIATION	TYPE OF CONTROL			TOTAL
	Local	Mixed	Outside	
French............	394	48	15	457
English............	3 Auto parts Physician Beauty parlor	2 Auto sales (2)	5 Banks (2) Power company Electrical goods Hotel	10

Others............	17
	Jews
	  11 clothing stores
	  1 jeweler
	  1 trader (hides, etc.)
	  1 music teacher
	
	Greek
	  1 restaurant
	
	Chinese
	  1 laundry
	  1 restaurant
	
	Negro
	  1 music teacher
		0	3
			Jewish
			  3 novelty stores
				20

Total.........	414	50	23	487

he has a special advantage with his own people. The two hairdressers,
formerly clothes models in the United States, counted on the prestige
of the United States in matters of fashion to get them a clientele among
the English of the town. Their success was short-lived, for their shop
has since disappeared. The French, after all, have a certain reputation
in the matter of beauty care. The other English entrepreneurs offer
automobiles and services related to them. These goods come from the
English-speaking world. In things mechanical the English generally

have prestige in French Canada—certainly among the English themselves and to some extent among the French. The English of the town are a select group of customers for automobiles and related services. Even so, the only two solid entrepreneurs among this whole group— the owners of the two garages and automobile sales agencies—are locally bred, bilingual members of pioneer families; they did not come to town to do business but are members of local society who went into business among friends and neighbors.

The outside managers represent organizations of public-utility character and closely related to the financial and industrial superstructure of the region. Customer control may be assumed to be limited. The banks compete for the custom of the local populace, but there is every reason to believe that the more important custom of the industries depends little upon the character of the local manager.[8] At any rate, the two English bank managers are in charge of the local houses, one of which handles the accounts of the power company and the largest industry, and the other of which handles some lesser industrial accounts. The other managers, as well as all other help, are French. Even the two English bank managers are Quebec bred and bilingual.

The power company, whose manager and twelve other employees are English, is more than a dispenser of service to the populace. It manufactures power at two large hydroelectric plants in the community. It was the available power that brought the industries. The power company financed the building of the best hotel, with the aid of some subscriptions from local businessmen, to make the town attractive to industry. The manager of the power company is primarily a technical expert and a strategist in the financial and industrial development of the region.

The electrical-goods store with an English manager belongs to the power company, as does also, in effect, the hotel with an English manager. A French-Canadian political speaker expressed a common opinion when he pointed at this hotel and shouted: "Is that hotel for you? No! They even charge more for their beer so you won't go in there with your dirty shirt. It's for the English big shots [*gros bonnets*] to stay in when they come to collect dividends from your labor."

This analysis shows that no English person conducts an enterprise or offers a service in this community without either some special ad-

---

[8] The banks are all branches of regional or dominion-wide banks, as is true throughout Canada. The great dominion-wide banking companies are each affiliated with groups of industries.

vantage with the English population or some support from an outside appointing authority, or both. Even within these limits, those English who meet customers in competition with French are generally Quebec born and bilingual, as are the car and accessory agents and the managers of the banks and of the electrical-goods shop; for there are completely French houses offering these things. The English hairdressers are already gone. The hotel manager, who speaks no French, is in charge of a hotel of such quality that it is assured of all the first-class trade and doesn't have to make ends meet anyway.[9]

The relative absence of English independent entrepreneurs and givers of service is not necessarily due to French preference to do business with their own, for the few Jews, the Greek brothers, and a clan of Chinese do independent business, with caricature faithfulness to the lines of trade with which they are popularly identified. Certainly these people, alien to both English and French, have no fund of ethnic good will to fall back upon. Yet they come and survive, not, to be sure, by giving personal service, but by selling impersonal goods. They are traders. As such, some of them survive even in the back parts of the community where no one speaks English or is tainted by urban tastes. The Jew survives here, as elsewhere, not by good will or a claim upon friends but by adapting his language, standard of living, and methods of doing business to his surroundings. This the English of our community do not do.

THE AUTHORITY STRUCTURE

Not all English are at the top of the units in which they work. Several work under the authority of other English people. So far as we could discover, however, in only two cases do English work under French. The French owner of the largest garage and automobile agency hires as his sales manager a local, bilingual English Canadian with many kin among both ethnic groups. His forbears have been merchants in the county for nearly a century. In addition to this advantage, he gains from the outspoken preference of the English (who are good customers for his middle- and higher-priced cars) for dealing with their own kind in matters of mechanics.[10]

[9] Since our field work was done, both English bank managers have been succeeded by French Canadians. The English hairdressers have gone. No new English entrepreneurs have appeared.

[10] The Ford and Dodge agencies are completely French. Three makes of cars may be bought from the English. We have no data to show that the English select their cars on the basis of the nationality of the agent. It is, indeed, very unlikely that they do so. But they

In the Woolworth store an English assistant works under a French manager.[11] Since chain-store employees of this grade are moved about from town to town by a central office, this young man was not hired by his French immediate superior. He belongs to an almost unnoticed Quebec-born, bilingual English civil service of business, found in the banks, the utilities, and the chain stores. Neither of these cases is quite a simon-pure case of employment of English by French or of subordination of English to French. Generally speaking, English do not work under French authority.

While some French work under English authority in the nonindustrial occupations, the great majority do not. Of the 487 business and service units, 394 are the local, independent enterprises of French Canadians. They and their employees are not under any discernible English authority. But most of the fifteen French managers of branch businesses, while they are subject to no resident English authority, work for organizations which are admittedly English at the top. The position of the forty-eight French heads of "marginal" units varies. The local French agent for Singer sewing machines has an exclusive agency granted by outside, ultimately English, authority. Yet he is, in effect, a local entrepreneur; he sells his machines to the English minority, but more energetically and resourcefully to the French newcomers from the country. Likewise, the French agents of nationally known insurance companies and breweries, although subject to outside appointment, carry on their local work with relative freedom. Yet the people of the community are aware, even without the constant reminders of nationalistic leaders, that, if the authority hierarchies of these concerns were followed upward and toward central headquarters, the French would first thin out and later disappear. The local and visible authority may be French, but the absent higher authority is English.

---

talk freely of their distrust of French mechanics. The largest garage, French-owned but with the English sales manager, has a high reputation among the English, although the foreman and all the help in the garage are French. Such contradictions are common. We do not conclude that a French salesman would not sell as many cars of this make; we only suggest that the owner was very shrewd to have selected as sales manager a man who would combine in his person qualities which would get the good will of both industrial and town, English and French, population.

[11] From its founding until recently this store was managed by an English person with French assistants; this has now been reversed. The young English assistant says that his function is to be around to straighten out difficulties between English customers and French salesgirls. Evidently the administration attempts to suit its personnel to the ethnic character of the local clientele.

These facts also bear upon the question of competition between French and English. The local independent merchant is in competition with the chain stores. The personally present competitor, the manager of the chain store, is generally French. But, though he meets no English competitor in the flesh, the French-Canadian retailer feels the competition of stores and agencies which he knows are controlled by English people. In the local community French Canadians solidly hold their place, in both number and importance, wherever customers are to be dealt with; in the new remote control which nowadays so profoundly alters the position of the local entrepreneur the French have little part.

Since the English are, on the average, of more urban origin and have higher incomes than the French, it is but natural that they should want more of the urban goods and specialized professional services per capita. Even the English farmer of Ontario demands more of such things than the Quebec farmer.[12]

It might, therefore, be supposed that these more urban things would be brought to our town by English businessmen and professionals. Such is not the case. Automobiles, plumbing, and the other mechanical conveniences are sold, serviced, and installed by French people. Fashionable clothing, magazines, and motion pictures are all brought and dispensed by French alone.

The only English professional man is the physician, who is, in spite of some specialized training, a general practitioner. Several of his thirteen French colleagues are partial or complete specialists. They include a qualified fellow of the American College of Surgeons; a man who has had special training in pediatrics and public health; and an eye, ear, nose, and throat specialist. Some of them have had the specialized part of their training outside Quebec; to this extent their specialized services come from the English world. The local English people, however, go to Montreal for specialized medical services from English hands.[13] A few English people have had glasses fitted by the French eye specialist; at least two wives of middle-rank industrial executives have had babies under the care of a local surgeon. Such cases appear to be rare.

---

[12] See chap xvi; also chap. ii, Table 1.

[13] That the English in Quebec generally want more specialized medical treatment is indicated by our finding that a much higher proportion of English than of French physicians in Montreal are specialists. The English of our town frequently "go in to Montreal" to see doctors, dentists, etc. They even phone a popular pediatrician long-distance for advice; the doctor has a fixed charge for this service.

Dentistry, an American art, is practiced only by French. The one English maid in town was sent by her employer to a French dentist to have a tooth pulled. How frequently the lesser English go to French dentists we do not know. Certainly the bulk of the English go to Montreal for such service. Finally, the lawyers and notaries are all French. The notary, whose services concern estates, marriage contracts, deeds, wills, small investments, and the like, is in the French tradition. The English, who have relatively few local property interests, know little of him. He lives off the affairs of property-owning farmers and townspeople, the *rentier*, and the small businessman. The advocate lives off those matters which come to court or might do so. Again, the English people have few affairs of this kind. The corporations retain lawyers in their headquarters city, although a local lawyer may take charge of local litigation for them. One local lawyer represented a utility company in a damage suit and was finally sent to England to take the case before the Privy Council. But, in the main, the local lawyer lives off the problems of the French local people. The English, like salaried middle-class people elsewhere, have little need of him. It is probably more urban for a family not to have a lawyer than to have one.

To the French professional man, the local English, as individual clients, mean little. The industrial corporations, to one or perhaps two of the lawyers, may mean a little more. But again, the remote competitor is there; the English corporation lawyer of Montreal does the big work. Certainly no local lawyer has grown fat during the period of growth of our town. Some get part of their living by minor municipal clerkships, for which they compete with nonprofessionals.[14] The notary is a rural and town functionary; the growth of large business does him little good. In fact, city life seems to reduce the family's need of him.[15] Certainly, local English people have little work for notaries to do. It is the city way of life, rather than any particular urban institution, that undermines the notary's position. The physicians and dentists, likewise, get little from the English. But there is every evidence that the demand for professional medical services is increasing in Quebec; the local French physicians are probably profiting by the movement of their own people from country to city, if not directly from the English residents.

[14] Even the more prominent lawyers and notaries, without exception, hold some such office—e.g., clerk to the school board, town clerk, township school clerk, etc.

[15] While we have no statistics on this point, a local notary testified that the propertyless city family does not make a marriage contract, draw up family settlements, etc., as do farmers. These instruments are the notary's work.

But, while the English offer the local professional men little patronage, they likewise offer them practically no direct competition. Of the thirty-three professionals—physicians, dentists, lawyers, notaries—only one is English. The young English professional man, of any line, would be foolish indeed to try to establish a practice in the local maze of family and clique relationships. He would be not only an ethnic stranger but also an outsider, in the sense of having no claims upon anyone. The professions are especially dear to French Canadians. Their educational system is oriented to them. The cherished ambition of the French-Canadian family is to put a son into one of them, if not into the priesthood. Training for the lay professions cannot be had without several years' residence in one of the province's two largest cities, Montreal and Quebec. But the men thus trained remain in the province, where their language, religion, and personal associations are an advantage; outside, these would be handicaps. Furnishing, as they do, one of the favorite and surest ways of upward mobility, it is but natural that the French Canadians should be especially jealous of professions. Such is the case. In spite of the lack of English professional competition in our community, some of the lawyers are among the most bitter and outspoken agitators against English—and Jewish—invasion of the French-Canadian domain. Yet, and this is a crucial point, all new and especialized professional services which have been brought to the community have been brought by French and by French alone.

The French who bring such new and specialized services and goods are in competition with their own ethnic fellows who offer less sophisticated services and goods. They may even be engaged in a struggle with their potential clients' rural conceptions and tastes.

The local physicians are in competition with the traditional bonesetter (*remancheur*) and with a woman who, some miles in the country, cures cancer and all manner of diseases by a combination of magical rites and herb medicines.[16] The specialized physicians are in a silent struggle against preference for the rural, unspecialized doctor.[17] Dentists

[16] During our stay one of us sprained an ankle while returning from a meeting at night. We went into a small shop to call a taxi to take us to the doctor. The taxi-driver spent some time and energy trying to get us to go to a bonesetter who, he said, was as good or better than the doctors at that kind of thing and much cheaper. Anxiety was stronger than scientific curiosity at the moment; so we went to the English doctor. He, in turn, took us to the hospital for an X-ray, which was made by a French nun.

[17] There was general testimony as to the great popularity in town of two physicians who lived in small villages some miles away. The rural family with whom we lived were quite

especially complain of the distrust which rural people have of them, and of reluctance to have any work done other than extraction and the fitting of dentures. If the dentist suggests repairs instead of extraction, he is accused of merely trying to get more money, since the tooth will eventually have to be pulled anyway.[18]

The situation is much the same in the sale of goods or in giving non-professional services. The young lady who offers smart gowns for sale has to compete with dozens of local dressmakers. The theater-owners who bring Hollywood to town complain of the parsimonious opposition of country-bred parents who think their children should spend their time without spending money. The French dealer in furnaces and electric cooking stoves finds himself in competition with a strong bias in favor of wood-burning stoves, helped along by numerous dealers in firewood. Even horse-traders—three of them—survive in this community. The business and professional people of the town are aware of, and anxious to talk about, the struggle between rural and urban tastes in the community. These who introduce the new are, however, like those who offer the older and more rural things, French Canadians.

Also pertinent to understanding of competition in business is the fact that Cantonville is a small town, quickly grown large. Before the town grew and while it was growing, the leading business and professional men tried to attract industry by advertising the town and by giving tax concessions. They frankly expressed their hope that they would profit from expansion of the town. What has been the result? Many of the older men remark that, while customers and clients are more numerous, so are competitors.

In the professions the number of practitioners has not increased in so great a ratio as the population. It does not follow that they are all doing well or that the older men have profited greatly by the growth of the town. We have already mentioned the preference of some of the population for health services of rural type. At least one country doc-

---

sure that their own old rural doctor was better than the specialized town doctors. They told tales of his immediate correct diagnosis (for $2.00) of ailments on which large sums of money had been vainly spent with city doctors.

[18] We have observed a number of cases which substantiate this. For instance, a French woman in Montreal was struck by an automobile and knocked off her feet. A tooth was knocked loose. She almost gleefully took the occasion to get all her teeth pulled and false teeth fitted—at insurance company expense, although the company's representative was willing to have her get repairs to her teeth. The latter would, in fact, have been more expensive.

tor, resident in a village some miles away, has a practice in town; a number of people of rural origin made it clear that they liked him just because he was rural. Some of the new physicians are specialists, and so may put the older men at a disadvantage. Two physicians, new to the town, have established private hospitals. At least one of the older physicians is said to be doing very badly. Two of them, already popular, have undoubtedly profited by becoming company doctors.

We did not find out exactly how many businesses of various kinds existed at earlier periods, but rough comparison of present facts with what older people remembered of the earlier day indicates that the increase in the number of businesses has been very great. Formerly,

TABLE 23

PROFESSIONALS IN CANTONVILLE, 1921 AND 1937

Period	Lawyers	Doctors	Dentists	Notaries
Before industry (1921)......	2	4	2	3
After industry (1937).......	7	14	7	5

for instance, there were two hardware stores, run by old families. Now there are nine, two of which are branches of outside firms and are much larger than either of the two older stores. The owner of the oldest hardware store complained that, while the building of new houses had for a time given a great boost to the hardware trade, the industries had not patronized the local stores. It is evident in several other lines that the old respected firm is no longer the first in size or importance. Whatever the quantitative facts, many of the older business people express disappointment with the effects of the growth of the town and especially resent the coming of new businesses.

The older businessmen are especially concerned about the burgeoning of miserable little enterprises of all kinds. The ideal of the French Canadian is to have a modest business, financed from savings. Pressed by the size of their families and by the limited opportunities, small people have swarmed to town. A flour-miller, whose lungs were affected, started a tiny store with a stock of groceries, cigarettes, stockings, and whatnot. Hardware appears on the same counter as soft drinks; dry goods with groceries. These are not the old general stores, of which there are several patronized by the farmers, but pathetic makeshifts in every kind of house or shack. Remnants from the silk mills, sold to employees with the stipulation that they shall not be resold, are offered in "coupon" shops. Your landlady will, when you aren't looking, send your clothes not to the laundry you specify but to some friend who does a little washing; if she hears you call a taxi, a friend who uses his old car as a taxi in off hours will appear at the door before the taxi you called. She will try to persuade you to buy your cigarettes from a retired farmer from her native parish who now has a few groceries for sale in the front room of his house. Any enterprise will do, so long as it requires little experience or capital. The French Canadian, like the Jew, loves an independent enterprise; unlike the Jew, who importunes the passing stranger, he remains among kin and friends, upon whom he can press a personal claim for patronage.

It is of these small businesses that the chief wholesaler of the town speaks thus:

Most of the small grocers were farmers. They think they can run a business without knowing how. I say to them when they come here to start: "Have you had any experience?" They say: "No." I tell them to stay out of the business. But they want to go ahead anyway; so I say: "We have goods to sell, but you will have to pay cash. I can't give credit to people who don't know anything about the business." Many of them, of course, lose their $2,000 or $3,000 savings or proceeds from selling their farms. If a farmer has a son he has put through a commercial course, or even part way through, he thinks this son knows all about business, although he has never had any experience. So he takes his money, comes to town, buys a house, and starts a business for the son. It takes a couple of years to lose all the money, and then it is all over.

People think that, because the town is growing, there is lots of room for new businesses. I think the number of businesses has increased out of proportion to the population. There are lots of failures; I don't know how many. They are mostly the small places.

Many of these so-called "restaurants" are just places selling soft drinks (generally bought for cash). They carry a few groceries as a side line, but they are not well handled. There is not much in it for us. The grocery stores are, in general, better than formerly. We have had to push them in the matter of display, cleanliness, etc., to meet the chain-store competition.

While the wholesaler can speak indulgently of the shoestring businesses, the proprietors of the established retail businesses accuse them of unfair competition. The small people are rebuked for lack of cooperation in limiting the hours of business and in other measures to regulate competition; for opposing steps to improve the town as a trading center; and for shirking civic responsibility. But the major complaint is that they don't have to make a living from their businesses, since members of the family work in industry and so steal custom which rightfully belongs to the merchants who bear the full burden of overhead. The latter consider themselves the bulwark of the French-Canadian middle class, as, indeed, they are. The rift between them and the keepers of marginal businesses is apparent in the alignment of people on various political issues. The more prosperous merchants, united in a chamber of commerce, find their measures for civic improvement stalemated by the opposition of the shoestring shopkeepers.

This situation, common in Quebec towns, is a by-product of the pressure of population in the country and of the growth of the town. The battle, with uncertain front, is fought between French and French; the English are scarcely aware of it. It constitutes an additional threat to a basic and respected class of French-Canadian society, the solid, small-town businessmen who expect, along with professional men, to share the honors and bear the burdens of parish and civic leadership. This group feels *malaise* at the crowding-up of undue numbers of competitors from below as well as at the invasion of their domain by chain businesses.

A few French people have tuned their businesses and services to the urban demands of the English population. A grocer in the end of town where the executives of the biggest industry live has put in the best of groceries and meats and gives credit to this select group. Some of the hairdressers have managed to get select English trade. One French garageman has got the confidence of the English; one insurance broker is called "reliable" by the English; and so on. In speaking of their favorite French dealer—grocer, hairdresser, service-station keeper, druggist, etc., the English person will generally mention that he is an exception—different, that is, from other French people. He is honest, clean, a good mechanic, reliable, competent; she is of a nice family and shows taste in the dresses in her shop; and so on. The fair statement of the case is that as the town has grown, the best store or shop in town in a given line is a better, or at least a smarter and more urban, one than the best when the town was smaller. In general, the English managerial class seek the best and smartest. The corresponding classes of French people do likewise but are a minority among all French. The majority of French are rural and of the working class. From our observations they are the only people seen in the small, marginal shops. But even these poorer people, the younger ones especially, dress smartly and have their hair well coiffed. For clothing, at least, they obviously go to the bigger stores.

There is then a competition among the local French businesses. There are several classes of trade, along the usual income and class lines. The English appear in the upper classes and among the more demanding and sophisticated customers. They also shop in the Montreal stores a great deal. These things would be true in any town with a similar history and similarly located. The ethnic factor, real as it is, probably is emphasized beyond its actual economic value. Emphasized, it certainly is by the English people, as the following account will show:

An English woman, new to the town, attended a tea in an English house. She inquired about a good hairdresser. These remarks poured out:

"Try Mlle Y——. She lives in a lovely old house on the Boulevard. Her father has lost a lot of money in land. They are not poor, but not as well off as formerly. You make an appointment with her, and she does you in a lovely sunporch overlooking the river. She takes her time, talking to you all the time. "

"French girls talk all the time, just like magpies, when they do your hair."

"We English ought to patronize each other's businesses. You know the French want us to buy with them, but actually they owe everything to us. All the factories, which make them their jobs, are brought here by the English. The English businesses deserve to be helped.

"I had been getting my hair done by Rosalie (French). But then I thought I ought to go to an English one; so I went to Miss W. But I don't like her cuts; so I have gone back to Rosalie. There was another English hairdresser here, but she made me tired; she made it plain that we hicks ought to be grateful to her for coming here to show us how we ought to look."

It turned out that all present actually go to French hairdressers.

Another example:

The English hairdresser, while at her work, said to her English customer: "The factory girls come in from the country where they never went to beauty parlors. They don't bother at all, but then sometime another girl says, 'Why don't you get a permanent?' So off they go to some cheap place and get one. They won't go to a beauty parlor again till they get the next permanent. They might not wash their hair for a year. The provincial inspector always says when he comes in here, 'Your place is so clean.' They aren't used to a place like ours. You see some awful places. A little room of a house where a big family lives will be used as a beauty salon. They say some of these places keep a sponge soaked in wave-set and just spread it on the hair of anybody that comes in. You get the cooties passed around that way. We don't want that kind of trade. We do just the high-class work. We have had some business from the better-class French. Mme B., the doctor's wife, and the S. family (a lawyer's family), they are just as nice people as you could hope to meet."

These interviews, and others like them, indicate that the English do trade with the French, even when they might find English people to buy goods or services from. But they also indicate that the English think and talk about the subject, sometimes in a rationalizing way, sometimes in an ill-informed way. So far as we could discover, there is no corresponding talk about the English as business people or customers, although there are open movements to encourage the French to buy from their own people. Certainly no French person would explain to a neighbor that, although her hairdresser was English, she was clean and of upper-class family; or that her grocer, in spite of being English, carried a good line of fresh vegetables and kept his meat on ice; or that his automobile mechanic, although English, was competent. The French do not have this particular set of prejudices against the English, nor do they have much opportunity to trade with the English, for there are few English persons in the community to sell them goods or services. Since the time of our observations, the number has decreased. It is very improbable that it will again increase.

Language probably plays a more important role in competition in the nonindustrial than in the industrial world. The executive and technical language of industry in our community is English. Since, in addition, the persons in authority are English, it is but natural that English should percolate downward among the French workers. The pressure is on the subordinate, whose mother-tongue is French, rather than upon the superior, whose language is English.

The salesman dealing with a customer or the professional talking to a client has to pay more attention to the choice of language. The English people of our town can all buy a package of trade-marked cigarettes from a salesman who speaks no English, but few of them could describe a pain or understand instructions about firing the furnace in French. All of the French professional men speak some English; some of them speak it fluently. The bigger, more specialized, and more centrally located businesses all have salespeople who can speak English sufficient to the purpose. In the smaller and outlying shops many of the proprietors can speak only a few words of English. They have little need to do so. Their shops and goods are not such as would attract people of the economic class of the English of our community.[19]

[19] We made no systematic study of the fluency in English of people in the various shops, but in the course of our observations we got into places of business of all kinds and in all sections of the community. Even in the downtown district there are quite a number of places in which no effective use of English can be made; in the sections which are distinctly workers' settlements, the proprietors assume that any customer will speak French, although they almost invariably made some remark which indicated that they knew we were English-speaking. Some attempted a few words of English, but they seldom could keep it up in any conversational way.

Any kind of goods or services that can be got in the community can be had by talking either language. With one or two unimportant exceptions, French is spoken in all stores, service shops, and professional offices which are open to all who wish to come to buy goods or ask for service. English, on the other hand, is not found in all shops or places where services are given. With very few exceptions the people who sell goods and services in English are bilingual. Of these bilingual persons, all but a few are French. The few English bilingual salesmen, merchants, and managers of businesses are natives of Quebec. We found no Jewish merchant who had not learned to make himself understood in French. In this adjustment it is evident that the vendor of goods and services has adapted his language to his customers. The result is an evident advantage for the bilingual person in a position where a public which can "take it or leave it" must be dealt with. For whatever reasons, bilingualism is not frequent among the English. There are certain conventional reasons given.[20] In fact, the English do not have to learn French to keep their positions in industry. The housewife does not have to learn French to keep her housemaid. If they were to speak French in these relationships—except in a joking or patronizing spirit, as is occasionally done—they would be in some measure reversing roles. For they would then be making the greater effort, which generally falls to the subordinate; and they would speak French badly, whereas the subordinate generally speaks English pretty well. The combination of lack of necessity and reluctance to put themselves into the subordinate position as regards language probably accounts for the failure of the English population generally to become fluent in French. In addition, except for formal relationships, the English population in general has little contact with French people.

For many of the French, in short, English is a necessity, either in dealing with their superiors at work or with customers and clients. The English in industry are so placed that they need not speak French to please or satisfy anyone. In business the few who meet customers are bilingual; but they are and will remain few.

[20] In public or in conversation with French people, English people express regret that they can't speak French. In private they more commonly excuse themselves by saying that the local French is unintelligible to a person who has been taught only "Parisian French." Or they may frankly say that this is an English country, and it is up to the French to learn English.

CHAPTER IX

COMMUNAL INSTITUTIONS: GOVERNMENT

B Y ANALYZING the communal institutions we should be able to gauge the extent of co-operation between the two ethnic groups where the exigencies of getting a living do not require it. Such analysis should, however, be seen against the background of Quebec at large.

Differences of language and religion between the French and English are the most obvious reasons why some of the communal institutions of either group are not acceptable to the other. Important as these factors are, they are but expressions of the existence of two consciously separate groups, each of which has many usages and sentiments not shared by the other.

There is but one system of economic institutions, although in some businesses and occupations and in some positions within a given business organization one group or the other predominates. Some business houses advertise that they are French, with an eye to attracting customers who might prefer to buy from their own. Some of the voluntary associations of businessmen are predominantly, some avowedly, of one ethnic group. But the system is one.

Government, in all of its branches, is but a single system. All residents are subject to the same law, and all citizens vote at the same elections. Only at one small point can the law be said to establish a distinction of status between French and English. An accused has the right to have six members of the jury who speak his mother-tongue, if it be French or English.[1] This allows some play to such difference of

---

[1] This provision, in effect, prevents the accused from being judged by members of the opposite ethnic group. In a recent case (*Montreal Star*, February 26, 1938) some French Witnesses of Jehovah, accused of seditious conspiracy, asked and were denied the privilege of being tried before an English jury. The court decided that, while the accused may ask for six jurymen of his own mother-tongue, he has no right to ask for jurymen of the other language. The offense in this case consisted of distributing pamphlets which said that clergy and civil authorities are tools of Satan. A pre-war English (*de facto*, Protestant) jury would probably not have convicted. A French (*de facto*, Catholic) jury might be expected to take such charges seriously and, in addition, to regard French-Canadian Witnesses of Jehovah as religious and ethnic traitors. The law allows the members of each group to be tried by their own but does not permit them to escape their own.

mores as might affect judgments of guilt within the framework of the one legal system. Apart from this, the ethnic line appears in the mobilization of people for voting and political pressure and in certain conventions, such as the alternating of English and French mayors in some towns. There has never been a major political party composed of one ethnic group only or openly committed to the aims of one group only.

The great separate institutions are the schools and churches. Around them gather charitable organizations, also separate for the ethnic groups. The churches well illustrate the nature of the institutional division. The Protestant churches are the usual ones of English-speaking countries, from the Anglican to the Salvation Army and the Bible halls. French Protestants are few and soon become English. English Catholics, however, remain English.

The Catholic church was established in Quebec by French people, and French it remains. The bishops of all dioceses are French. The province is divided into territorial parishes. It was eventually found advisable, in some cities, to create special parishes for the English-speaking Catholics. They cover territory also included in the original system of parishes, but the boundaries do not coincide. The pastor of the oldest and leading English-speaking parish in Montreal is, formally, only a parish priest; informally, he is a kind of prelate among the English Catholics. Thus the Catholic church yields to the strength of ethnic sentiments.

The law relating to schools recognizes differences of religion rather than of language. Protestants and Catholics may, under certain conditions, set up separate school systems in the same community, each supported by the taxes from real estate owned by people of the appropriate religion.[2] In fact, the Protestant schools are English, and the majority of Catholic schools are French. This is not because the law says so but because of the ethnic facts. The law provides for two official languages in the province—French and English—but it does not say that French shall be the language of Catholic schools; and English, of Protestant schools. Nor does it say how it shall be determined which language shall prevail in a given school.

A Catholic school board is generally all French. The Montreal

---

[2] School taxes paid by corporations are paid into a fund which is divided between the two school boards according to the number of school children of each religion. Jews in Montreal pay the tax into a fund from which tuition is paid to the appropriate school board for each Jewish child in school.

Catholic School Commission has two English persons—really Irish—among its eleven members. The special schools for English Catholics have the grading system of the Protestant schools—a system quite different from that of the French schools. In getting higher education the English Catholic must choose between ethnic affiliation and religion; he generally chooses to study with his Protestant ethnic fellows at McGill University, and after graduation he joins them in professional associations.

A similar division occurs in charitable matters. The French, English Protestants, English Catholics, and the Jews each have their own system of charitable organizations in Montreal. The ethnic difference has injected itself into the institutional structure, separating English—Protestant and Catholic alike—from the French in the more sentimental concerns of life.

The things said of the province at large apply in general to our community. We have already shown the place of each ethnic group in the business and industrial world.

It is well, at this point, to recall the relative numbers of the two ethnic groups and of the adherents of the major religions. For the part played by each group in the common institutions, as well as the kind of separate institutions each can and does maintain, depends, in part, upon proportions and upon numbers. The present distribution approximates what is shown in Table 24. The French Catholics form the overwhelming majority. The English-Protestant group, even with the addition of the marginal groups, is of village size.

GOVERNMENT AND POLITICS

It was shown earlier that the indigenous English population has disappeared from political offices. The new industrial English population shows no sign of attempting to compete for them. All candidates in local, provincial, and dominion elections for years past have been French.

So far as local politics are concerned, the English confine themselves mainly to adverse criticism, expressed in ethnocentric terms. The usual charges are inefficiency, graft, and unfairness to the English and the industries. These charges are directed at the local French without much discrimination between persons. The English are relatively unaware of the pitched battles between various local French citizens and factions over city appointments, expenditures, and alleged irregularities. Quite often they speak of bitter political enemies as being friends and associates. The few "old English" know more about such matters but are equally outside the combat. Their attitude is typically expressed thus:

My husband was born here, and he speaks French as well as he does English. I think he is the only non-French person who takes an interest in politics here. He is the only person ever thought of to represent the English in public office. But he never gets there; they won't have him. Why?—because he understands what they say when they speak French. He breaks right into their arguments, and they won't have any of that.

In campaigns the candidates speak a little in English to get the votes. But they never have a prominent English person on the platform to help campaign or look impressive. I never saw an English person on the platform; just French.

TABLE 24

RELIGIOUS AND ETHNIC COMPOSITION OF THE POPULATION
OF CANTONVILLE, 1940

	French	English	European	Total
Catholics...............	19,151	350*	150	19,651
Protestants.............	0	921	50	971
Jews...................	0	0	50	50
Total..............	19,151	1,271	250	20,672

* The English-Catholic figure is probably too high, for reasons noted in chap. vi. The European-Catholic group is probably also a little high; this group, at any rate, is inclined to mix with the French. The slight corrections would not alter the general proportions significantly.

This statement expresses antagonism not only toward the French, for rejecting the English in politics, but against the new English as well, for their lack of interest in politics.

The chief local issue talked of by the new English is taxation of the industries. The managerial group think that their companies do enough for the community by simply being there to employ people. The major industries all have or have had partial or complete exemption from municipal taxes for a period of years after their founding. In municipal elections the English people invariably rated the candidates according to the current impression as to whether they were "nationalistic," i.e., whether they were likely to try to raise the assessed evaluations of industrial property, or would take labor's side in any dispute. In one election the wires apparently got crossed; some English people thought a certain M. Haute was to be nominated as a candidate favorable to industry and to the leading Conservative French-Canadian faction. In the French end of town it was said that M. Haute's close relative, a very wealthy French Canadian, had told M. Haute not to run because everyone would say that he was a candidate favorable to the companies. He did not run. A local merchant somewhat connected with certain nationalistic movements did run and was beaten. The winner was a former Liberal member of the provincial legislature, who was distinctly middle-of-the-road on nationalistic and industrial issues. He was, however, called a "rabid nationalist" by the English. He was mayor for some four years without showing himself particularly hard on the industries. He still has the reputation of being against industry, and therefore anti-English, mainly because of his refusal to call in the provincial police during a strike.

Among the French, local politics is a great and serious affair. As members of families and factions, they take part, heart and soul, in the local conflicts over honors, contracts, offices, and jobs. The local proprietors are much concerned about improvements and taxes. Through this maze runs the theme of taxation of the industries. Some look upon the question with the eye of the tax-burdened small proprietor who sees the big owners, the industries, going scot-free or nearly so. Some look at the question as workers who see the "foreign" companies making profits off their labor. Some of the more prosperous businessmen, on the other hand, tell their people not to bite the hand that feeds them. The French are also divided over the issue of optimistic but costly expansion of public works in the hope of increased growth of the town, as against the more conservative small taxpayers' desire to keep taxes down.

In provincial politics the county has generally been Liberal. In the summer of 1936 it upset tradition by voting for a Conservative candidate, who ran for the newly formed Union nationale party. This election shows, in caricatured extreme, the role of the French and English in local politics.

The Union nationale combined a good deal of old-line Conservative personnel with some distinctly nationalistic leaders and an equivocal name. In our town the Union candidate was of the leading Conservative faction, which included several prominent and well-to-do business and professional men. The opposing Liberal candidate, then a member of the legislature, also had local factional connections. The socially ranking French-Canadian families, although not now the most wealthy, were and are Liberals. There was no change in the party affiliations of these factions or of the Liberal farmers. The real battle, for the votes of the new French industrial population, was carried on with great vigor and bitterness.

The election, in fact, took on the character of a nationalist crusade among certain elements of the population. A number of young men organized a Jeunesse nationale in support of the Union. Their propaganda accused the Liberal party not only of venal corruption but of having sold the province out to English corporations. On the street corners and in the taverns the younger industrial workers and unemployed attacked the Liberal party, the millowners, and their own French elders. The Liberals, they said, were taking too much money for themselves, their relatives, and their friends. The millowners, they insisted, disregarded French Canadians and hired outsiders to the disadvantage of local residents. To the young men the Union was not a party but a movement to guarantee French-Canadian workers and small people generally a fair deal from the foreign-owned industries. Again and again they protested that they were voting not Conservative but Nationale and that Duplessis, the Nationale leader, although he had been a Conservative, was now free of Tory connections.

Again and again it was said that the old people were too "partisan"; they stuck to the party of their rural fathers and expected their children to do likewise, not realizing that the Liberal party was doing nothing to free the town French workers from the yoke of the English industries. This mélange of feelings is expressed in the following talk, addressed to a tableful of men in a tavern. The speaker, a hairy man of about thirty-five, in shirt sleeves and old felt hat, spoke in English for my benefit:

Mr. Godbout [leader of the provincial Liberal party], you know him. Well, what they are saying is, Mr. Godbout and the others with him, if they get in, they get out and Taschereau come back. [Taschereau, the long-time Liberal prime minister of Quebec, was the scapegoat in this crusade.] You know Taschereau, the one that take all the money.

Another thing. The farmer he come in here and work in the factory. Maybe he's got a farm. He hire some man to work on his farm for fifteen cents every day, and the farmer, he comes into Cantonville and work in the mill. That's not right. There are lots of men right in Cantonville who have got no work. The people from outside should not come in and take the work. We've got to have a tax like Trois Rivières and many other places; if a man come in he has to pay a tax, $25, $50, before he take a job. They are 400 men out of work here, so strangers should not be allowed to come and take jobs. The mills, you see, they hire anybody. They don't care. We must have a law to make them stop that. Then there are men who work; his wife, she work; maybe he's got some boys or girls and they work, too. That's not right, when there are men without work.

The spirit of the election arguments is further reflected in the following account from our diary:

After the afternoon train from Montreal a knot of about one hundred men stood near the bandstand (to which a platform has been added for Duplessis's speech tomorrow night), talking politics as usual. An older man was defending the Liberals. He was apparently a well-known character about town; a heavy man of about sixty. He moved around quickly and added gestures aplenty to his energetic voice. He was defending two theses: one, that a man must be pretty good to keep an office for thirty years and would be pretty poor if he didn't get something for his old age and his friends in that time; second, that the Union nationale is really Conservative and that the young people are fools if they think the party of Bennett and the trusts will do anything for *nous autres*. They never have; they never will. What do they care about the French farmer?

His chief opponent was again a slender youngish man, unshaven, coatless, and wearing an old felt hat. His chief thesis was that the old man was deceived; he has remained a Liberal so long that he is really conservative. The Taschereau government is a bunch of thieves. During his regime they built that beautiful hotel across the street there. Do we stay in it, *nous autres;* do our children ever get inside it, *hein?* And you, *fils de cultivateur*, were you ever in it? *Non.*

The young man introduced into his argument the fact that he is sick, and opened his shirt to show his flat, skinny chest. What have the Liberals done for him, *hein?* Etc.

The crowd mostly listened and laughed, and seemed disappointed when the fight momentarily slackened. But it didn't slacken for long. On the part of the old Liberal it was a good-humored affair, although he rose to the attack with energy and wit. With the younger man it was more earnest: " If they don't punish those thieves, we'll go down and put them in torture."

A more detached view of the restlessness of the youth and of the political situation in general was given by a shabby *bonhomme* of lower middle class:

Mr. Sellier, the Union candidate, is really a deep-dyed Conservative, but now he calls himself a "Nationale." Nobody wants to be called a Conservative now. Mr. Youville is an old Liberal. He and Sellier hate each other. Mr. Jobin is a staunch Conservative; he did a lot of work in the election when Bennett got in and was given a big job in Ottawa. A very big job. They say he gets maybe $5,000 a year.

They say maybe Gouin [leader of a nationalist faction which left the Liberal party and joined the Union] will get a big job in Ottawa in the library and that his right-hand man will be a senator if Duplessis wins.

The young generation; they don't want to do like the older one. They are not so fanatic. Me, my father was Conservative, so that the whole family was Conservative. Now the young people want to be for themselves. They want to change all the time. They want new shows. They want a change in politics. They want different newspapers. Give them something new and it's all right for a few days. Give them wrestling for a few days, and then they want boxing, and then something new again. And they don't play croquet the way they used to, either.

In this election the English of our town were for Mr. Duplessis, but as a Conservative, not as a leader of a French-Canadian Union nationale. They talked a good deal about the graft of the Taschereau government and about its overfriendliness to labor unions. Some were

naïve enough to imply that a Union nationale (Conservative) legislature would break French control of provincial politics.

Thus there was, in this election, support of the same candidate by
two groups who absolutely disagreed with each other on every point
supposedly at issue. The French-Canadian industrial masses, in protest against the supposed failure of the traditional French-Canadian
party to solve their problems, especially that of English domination of
industry, joined forces with the traditional Conservatism and anti-
French feeling of the industrial managing class. The real point was a
protest of both of these industrial elements against the traditional Liberal party, which was the party of farmers and of many of the old town
families of all classes.

The crusade carried the Union nationale to power. The young nationalist crusaders, quickly enough disillusioned, turned out their supposed champions at the first opportunity. The political relationship
between the French and the English remained the same.

The English never speak in public on any local political issue. As
employees of such rank as to identify their interests with those of the
companies for whom they work, but not of such rank as to make company policy, they can do nothing except stand for the position of industry in general. Even this they do privately rather than publicly. On
the smaller issues of paving streets and digging sewers they might
speak as property-owners, but they would not be heard in the louder
chorus of French voices. In the more sentimental concerns of charity
and civic spirit they are an out-group, neither interested nor wanted.
So they keep silent in public and moan in private.

As private citizens, the English must pay their taxes to French officials, are subject to arrest by French policemen, and must, if occasion
rises, be tried or pursue civil suits before French judges. A few stories
are current of trials in which English persons were unfairly treated before the courts. They are told in a complaining tone that suggests a
French cabal against the English. On the whole, English people reveal
a feeling that public administrative institutions are run by and for the
French, to the detriment of the English.

One of the common functions of politics is to give the individual the
release of participating in conflicts that mean something to him. Related to this function is that of giving the individual a sense of identification with the institutions of government. Politics do not perform
these functions for the English of our community. The zest of political
struggle belongs to the French alone, as completely as if the English
were not present.

CHAPTER X

THE CATHOLIC PARISHES

U NTIL recently our community coincided with its one parish. Its leaders, the business and professional men of the town, had as fellow-parishioners their rural neighbors and customers. As the town grew and got an industrial population, the tie between town and country was loosened. The church, even with Masses said from early morning until noon on a Sunday, could not accommodate the crowds. Eventually three new parishes were carved from the old one. The four resulting parishes are not four integral communities but are the unlike segments of a single community. Each has its own selection of classes of people as well as its own territory.

TABLE 25

POPULATION OF THE PARISHES OF CANTONVILLE, 1937

	Total Population	Catholic Population	Protestant Population	Catholic Families	Protestant Families
St. Luc (old)............	7,802	7,434	368	1,382	91
Ste Anne (city).........	3,358	2,683	675	514	158
St. Jerome (outlying)...	6,282	6,236	46	1,158	11
St. Bernard (outlying)...	1,982	1,898	84	333	21
Total.............	19,424	18,251	1,173	3,387	281

The outlying parishes of St. Jerome and St. Bernard have, almost exclusively, working-class populations. Neither includes the residence of any prominent family, old or new. Even the churchwardens, mayors, city councilors, and school commissioners are mostly factory workers; the others are small tradesmen unknown to the community at large.

Ste Anne, lying in the newer part of the town proper and including the more attractive parts of the river shore, has less than its share of the old families and more than its share of the new. Half of the Protestant population of the community, as well as a good number of the English-speaking Catholics, lives within its bounds. It is as nearly a middle-class, urban parish as could be cut from this community. Its church-wardens, except one who is a laborer, are businessmen with recently established businesses in the new Haute Ville; they are new and "progressive," rather than old, established men.

St. Luc, the mother-parish and still the largest, includes the old Basse Ville and all of the farming district as well as some newly built districts, from poorest to most expensive. The older leading merchants and professional men have their pews in St. Luc's church; many of them have been wardens. The present wardens include two businessmen of old family, although not of the first magnitude of importance, and the one dentist who was practicing in town before industry came. To these older families are added new people of all classes, from factory hands and minor clerks to the new business and professional people. By virtue of its age and commanding location, as well as its full complement of people of all classes, St. Luc remains the central parish—even the central institution—of the community. Although the pastor of one parish has no formal authority over another, the curé of St. Luc's, a titular canon, is consulted by business and industrial people as the leading representative of the church in the community. It is assumed that his word will be of weight in matters concerning the community at large.

In this old parish the urban and the rural stand in visible contrast. It alone, of the four parishes, has practicing farmers among its parishioners. They are so much in evidence at the *Grand'messe paroissiale* that it is dubbed the "farmers' Mass." Their importance does not correspond to their number. They occupy the less important pews. Business and professional families who can pay more have the favored places near the front of the center aisle. Even as in rural St. Denis, the farmers' grown sons, who cannot be accommodated in the family pews, sit in a group in the balcony nearest the hitching lot. After the Mass they and their fathers gather in close knots on the front steps of the church, on the sidewalk, and even in the middle of the street. The clothes of the older farmers, like their faces, are square-cut and deep-lined, as though of carved wood. The younger men and boys wear their clothes more like townspeople. As the farmers talk, older business and professional men stop to greet them. Often a crier will lift his voice to make some official announcement concerning the rural municipality or school district, or even to ask all to look for a steer strayed from a neighbor's farm.

Although no longer a gathering of all the families of the parish, the *Grand'messe paroissiale* remains an important community ceremonial. The pews on the main floor are reserved at this Mass for the families who rent them. The full choir sings, and younger professional men on the make vie with each other to sing the chief solo parts.[1]

January 23: This was my first mid-winter Sunday in town. As in summer, the rural people were at the ten o'clock Mass, along with many solid citizens of the town. M. Vallée stood in the choir, with an elbow resting a little possessively on the console of the organ he gave to the parish, surveying the crowds below. The shriveled little organist, whom the people still call a Belgian although he has been teaching music and playing the organ in St. Luc's for forty years, leaned over the manuals, playing without notes. The solo was sung by Dr. Dupuis, the eye specialist. Dr. Bélanger, the new bachelor dentist who is making his way in town by organizing musical affairs, was conducting the choir with more gesture than necessary.

Downstairs, M. Rolland, the merchant who formerly held an important civic position, sat with his wife and three of his eleven children in a fairly prominent pew. It is the pew left him by his father, who was a more important man than he. M. Sellier, a provincial politician, very severe in his stand-up collar, sat in his pew with his wife, one daughter, and a son; his newly married professional son sat with his bride in the south balcony, as did his daughter married to young Francœur. M. Therrien, an important town (and former provincial) politician, bitter enemy of M. Sellier and of all Tories, sat with his pretty, accomplished wife. Their two children are away at school. M. Therrien fingered the leaves of the prayer-book for a while and then dozed off during the sermon. He is distinctly not a curé's man. The Lacombe pew was empty; they are the oldest family of standing in the parish. M. Lacombe and the curé are not fond of each other. Incidentally, Lacombe never walks in any procession, although he has been churchwarden, mayor, and a leading man of the community. The Chartrand's pew was occupied only by young Chartrand's father-in-law, looking like a French provincial notary with a pointed blond beard. Old M. Chartrand is living in Ottawa, but he keeps the pew. His son, a merchant, is probably out skiing.

After Mass I counted somewhat more than thirty sleighs at the hitching rack. They were of all sorts; some light cutters, but more of the low heavy sleighs one sees in Quebec paintings. Several of the sleighs had milk cans in them. The farmers gathered on the church steps as usual. As they were breaking up, the crowd coming to the late Mass moved through them up the steps into the church. The sleighs began to move off. In the two-seaters, the women sat behind and the men in front. Some single-seaters carried four people; two on the laps of the others. Within ten or fifteen minutes after the close of the Mass, all but five sleighs were gone. A few cars were there, only one of which was the outmoded unwashed kind used by farmers. Most of the country roads are not open for cars at this season. Three or four nice big cars came in with townspeople for the later Mass.

The farmers leaving the Mass are quiet. They talk solemnly and deliberately. The only thing a little boisterous is the movement of the young men out of the north gallery a couple of minutes before dismissal. They jump the gun a little every Sunday, as though a couple of minutes talk outside were very precious.

[1] The adult choir includes the very prominent, self-made businessman who gave the church its organ; two young lawyers, fairly new to the town but prominent in the Chevaliers de Colomb; two youngish dentists and an eye specialist, also new and without kin in town; the town band leader, who is of no social importance and is probably in the choir merely because he is faithful and a good musician; one factory worker and one clerk.

July 26 (interview with one of the vicars): Vacant pews are sold at auction twice a year; when a family leaves, or the old holder dies, the seat has to be sold again. The prices vary from about $10 to $40 for six months. The amount goes to the *fabrique;* it is the *fabrique* that puts the pews up for sale. Sellier, for instance, pays $40. Rolland, Sellier, Vallée, are seat-holders. In general it is the old families, town and country people alike. Most of them are proprietors, although it may happen that a renter will buy a pew.

The seats are sold for the *Grand'messe paroissiale* only. At that Mass the curé knows that he will see the same people every Sunday. There are not enough seats for all the people; so we have several masses. The first, at 5:30, is free, so that poor people can come. At the others, except the *Grand'messe*, fifteen cents is collected for every place. We insist on children going to their own Mass, so that they can be given instruction appropriate to their age. There is only one *Grand'messe*, except on certain special days.

The farmers usually buy seats. It is an old custom of all the country parishes. In country parishes there is only one Mass, and every family comes; they all buy their own pews—perhaps two or three, if need be. The farmers of this parish hold to the old custom. Naturally, they are all proprietors, and their property is often as valuable as city properties; but they have less cash. But they buy seats. They no longer have any influence in the affairs of the *fabrique;* they are too few and are scattered in various directions from town. If you see a man of middle age smoking his pipe in the street in front of the church after the *Grand'messe*, he is almost sure to be a farmer. It is their old custom.

Many town families come and go each year. It is hard for us to know them. Each of us has his part of the city to visit at the time of the grand parochial visit and census in the fall. If the same families stay on in the same place from year to year, we get to know them; but many move on and we never know them.

Ownership of a pew is evidently regarded as a sign of stable position in the community. If, as seems the case, almost every family in a farming parish owns a pew, it is of interest to see who owns pews in this growing town parish. In 1937, only 247, or 17.9 per cent, of the 1,382 Catholic families of the parish held pews, while 55.5 per cent of the rural families did so. Seventy-four of the rural pew-owners were farmers, although by liberal estimate the farmers in the parish number little more than 100. Although only about 30 per cent of the gainfully employed male heads of families in the town are proprietors, 60.5 per cent of the town pewholders own property in the community.[2]

It is not easy, from our data, to relate the pew-holding very definitely to occupations, for our occupational data are for the town as a whole and not for the one parish only. Table 28, showing the occupations of pewholders, allows us, however, to draw some contrasts of importance. Professional people and the owners of solid businesses are disproportionately numerous among the pewholders, although less so than are

[2] Rural families are those that live outside the town limits. Only a fraction of such families live on farms.

the farmers. Conspicuously underrepresented are hired managers of businesses, agents, and employees of industry.[3]

The five physicians who own family pews all own houses also, and all hold or have held some public office. The four physicians who do not hold pews are all new, and none has held any public position; three of them are specialists. One of them, however, takes part in the High Mass as a member of the choir. One of the two older lawyers

TABLE 26

TOWN AND COUNTRY PEWHOLDERS IN ST. LUC'S PARISH, 1937

	Families	Pewholders	Pewholders (as Percentage)
Town..............	1,229	162	13.2
Country...........	153	85	55.5
Total..........	1,382	247	17.9

TABLE 27

ST. LUC'S PEWHOLDERS CLASSIFIED AS OWNERS AND TENANTS, 1937

	Owners	Tenants	Sub-tenants	Unknown	Total	Percentage of Pew-holders Who Are Owners
Town.......	98	39	25	0	162	60.5
Country.....	74	0	0	11	85	87.0
Total....	172	39	25	11	247	69.6

owns a pew. The other, although of old family, does not. The only one of the younger lawyers to own a pew is the son of a well-to-do businessman and has many kin in town; he is, in fact, a nephew of the curé. Two other young lawyers are respectively son and son-in-law of the older lawyer who does own a pew. They faithfully attend the High Mass but sit in the gallery, where the seats are not reserved. One

[3] We know of no explanation of the fact that only eight of the pew-holding industrial workers are proprietors. This is a complete reversal of the situation in other occupations. Half of them, in fact, appear as subtenants in the city directory, which means that they do not occupy dwellings of their own but are part of a larger household. A married son living in his father's house is a subtenant. A possible explanation is that it is younger men who work in industry; they may have families, yet live in the house of a retired parent who owns or rents the house.

of them attended the semiannual auction of pews, and looked on hope-
fully, but did not bid. The remaining two young lawyers, both newcomers, sing in the choir. None of the six dentists owns a pew; but one
is a churchwarden, another leads the choir, and a third sings in the
choir. A fourth one has lived in the United States, moves with a "fast
crowd," and has a non-Catholic wife and a divorced daughter in his
house. The fifth is a very poor newcomer. The sixth is a younger
brother of a businessman who owns a pew.

Of the two notaries, one is very poor and of no consequence. People
"pity" him because he has failed to get ahead. He has no pew. The

TABLE 28

OCCUPATIONS OF ST. LUC'S PEWHOLDERS, 1937

Occupations	Proprietors	Renters	Sub-tenants	Unknown	Total
Professions....................	8	1	0	1	10
Quasi-professions...............	9	2	....	....	11
Owners of businesses and services	37	11	1	2	51
Clerks, minor functionaries........	12	6	1	1	20
Laborers not in industry..........	11	4	3	5	23
Employees of industry............	8	11	17	1	37
Rentiers and housekeepers.........	13	4	3	1	21
Farmers*......................	74	....	....	....	74
Total......................	172	39	25	11	247

* The city directory did not say whether people living in the country are proprietors or not. We take local testimony and the fact that renting of farms is rare in Quebec as evidence that the farmers are proprietors.

other notary, son of a marriage between a man of old French family
and a woman of the outstanding old English family of that day,
prominent in politics and well-known throughout the district, owns a
pew.

Every living man who has been mayor of the town, the present and
past members of the provincial legislature, the four city aldermen of
the wards included in the parish, and the six members of city and
rural school commissions all own pews.

These facts suggest that participation in the High Mass—as pewholders and, for a few, as members of the choir—is associated with
stable position in the community. The younger professional men who
are still on the make seem a little less likely to own pews and a little
more likely to take part in the choir. Social class seems to have little to
do with pew-holding, except in so far as class and stability are related.
Piety also has little to do with it, for a number of the leading pew-

holders are definitely worldly and somewhat touched with the parlor free-thinking fairly common in Quebec.

The proportion of people who have a solid foot in the community has evidently decreased greatly. Those who have, and notably so the farmers, do not all have so important a place in the affairs of the community as they once did. Although the curé likes to include one farmer among his wardens, he admittedly does so only as a gesture. The farmers, he says, know too little about finance to be useful wardens of a large town parish. Both in pew-holding and in leadership in the parish, the local business and professional men have their place. They have not been displaced, and apparently most of them still think it worth their while to take some active part in the life of the parish and in the High Mass itself. The few who do not are either newcomers or failures. The parish, and its chief ceremonial, the *Grand'messe paroissiale*, is thus still well knit with the social structure of the town. The one great exception is that the managers and technical staffs of industry have no place whatever either in the leadership or the ceremonial of the parish. The parish and the *Grand'messe paroissiale* belong to the farmers and the town, not to the mill.

If the *Grand'messe paroissiale* is the most important, it is not necessarily the largest of the masses. The church is generally more nearly full at the eleven o'clock Low Mass. This is the "citified" Mass. The horse-drawn rigs are replaced in the hitching lot by shiny cars. The people are more smartly dressed. They come in quickly, find what seats they can, and clear away when the Mass is over. Although it is known as the "man's Mass," our only count showed the sexes about equal, while women are more numerous at all other Masses.

Each of the several Masses now required to accommodate the faithful has taken on a special character. At 5:30 there is a Mass for those who cannot afford the fifteen cents charged for seats at all other Masses for adults. The Masses at 7:00 and 8:30 might be called "piety Masses"; women are much more numerous than men, the worshipers come singly rather than in pairs or family groups, and many do special devotions at the side altars and stations. In the basement at 8:30 there is a special Mass for the English. Several English Catholics told us that the curé has gone so far as to stand at the door to keep French parishioners from attending this Mass. It is a doubtful story. A Low Mass for children, without much music, is held in the basement.

In addition to the several Sunday Masses, special Masses during the week and on days of obligation are held at hours to accommodate people returning from night shifts or going early to work in the factories. They are announced for this very purpose.

Thus, age and sex differences, distinctions of social class, and occupation and ethnic origin have become of importance in the scheduling of the Masses, the central feature of the cult. This process of differentiation is accentuated by the division of the community into four parishes. Ste Anne is distinctly a town parish, and predominantly of middle class. In the outlying parishes, inhabited by working-class people, the general air of the Mass is rustic. It is the rusticity of farmers at a fair, dressed up and away from home. There are no rigs, though many of the parishioners have been farmers. They are now townspeople. The problems of their parishes are the problems of working-class parishes.

The multiplication of parishes, and of the Masses in each, obviously breaks up the intimacy of the community as a whole. Only on such occasions as St. Jean-Baptiste Day are the people of the various parishes brought together in a ceremonial and festive way by an out loor Mass and a procession. Even at the *Fête-Dieu*, the most important religious communal festival of the year, each parish has its own procession. Of course, the breaking-up of a community into several parishes is nothing new. It has been necessary wherever communities have outgrown convenient parish size. In the experience of rural people, it is, nevertheless, an important thing; it breaks up a familiar relationship and creates new problems for them as well as for the community at large.

The difference between the Masses should not be exaggerated. Except for the English one, all are attended almost exclusively by French people. It is the intimacy and solidarity of the parish, rather than its ethnic character, which is injured by change and differentiation. The sermon, except at the English Mass, is always in French. As a general rule, the same sermon is preached at all the Sunday Masses. If it is the curé who preaches, he may deal, as in the following sermon, with some problem of the urban and industrial life—Sunday amusements and Sunday work, labor problems, the urban departure from modesty in speech and dress.

Today is the fête of St. Luc, patron of this parish. We are under good protection. See how Cantonville has prospered. See how it has become an asylum for those without a place to go and without bread. From being a village, it has become a city which attracts people from all over the province and even from outside it. Where not long ago there was one parish, there are now four.

In the gospel for the day, you have heard how our Lord wept over Jerusalem.

"Jerusalem, Jerusalem, that killest the prophets, and stonest them that are sent to thee, how often would I have gathered thy children as the bird doth her brood under her wings, and thou wouldest not? Behold your house shall be left to you desolate." He loved Jerusalem, but he also prophesied its destruction. There is a limit to God's mercy. So Jerusalem was destroyed, as he said; instead of defending their city the Jews divided into factions and fought with one another while the Romans destroyed their city, killing men, women, and children, until not one stone was left upon another, and the plow passed over the city that our Lord loved. It seems the same in Spain; the country whose Catholic queen, Isabella, raised the money to send out the man who discovered our beautiful country. They have killed their priests, they have torn down their cathedrals, and it looks as if God were going to let the beautiful Catholic city of Madrid be destroyed like Jerusalem. And that can happen to any city, even our beautiful parish of St. Luc at Cantonville, if we do not praise God.

I have just been to the Saguenay. It is a grand river and seems to have greater possibilities than our little river. It is majestic and creates more power. Chicoutimi is a beautiful and *coquette* city, with its cathedral, bishop's palace, its seminary, its monasteries and convents, much bigger and better organized than Cantonville, and with great industries older than ours. But for some years it has been degenerating. Its young people are growing up living on public charity, in idleness. Young men of eighteen or nineteen are on direct relief. What a tragic place it will be in a few years when these young people, trained in idleness, have grown up. And why did that happen? Because they stole Sunday! That is the greatest crime of our day. Those great industries worked seven days a week. To be sure, their directors were not Catholic, but their workers were. And today they are begging from door to door. The violation of the Sabbath did that. It is a punishment and well deserved.

And that will happen at Cantonville if Sunday is violated. Sunday business does not pay. It enriches no one. It may seem to, but the punishment comes. If you buy from those who do business on Sunday, you, too, are party to it and will suffer. Not long ago the silk mill shut down 150 looms. Suppose they shut down 150 more. Where would you be, you who have bought houses here? Where would you get your bread? The industries look solid, but factories once flourishing can shut down. Your houses would be taken for the taxes you could not pay. Your houses would be abandoned. If you violate God's day, that will happen to you. Your children will beg their bread from door to door. It will be a punishment well deserved. The Church can warn; that is Her mission. But you alone can carry out Her word. Catholic Action is up to you.

On the following Sunday, the curé pursued this theme:

I spoke last Sunday of the violation of the Sabbath. I must speak again. First, we had Sunday business; then the Sunday movies. And now it is Sunday races. There were races last Sunday, and there are races announced for next Sunday. I speak to you as Catholics. Not as to Protestants, or people of other religions, who can discuss, each for himself, what his minister says. I am not discussing. I am telling you, as your pastor and rightful moral leader and guide, the will of your Infallible Church. God reveals to His Church His will; and His rightful representative, the Pope, and your bishop, and finally we, your pastors, tell you. God's representatives know these moral questions better than you do; it is their rightful prerogative, and it is for you to listen.

So, dust is blowing over the fields of the western provinces. Generally, such things are the just punishment of God. Your children will beg their bread—if they do not live and practice what God wills. [Here reads an episcopal letter in which the bishop expressed his surprise and regret that races had been held on Sunday at Cantonville and in other places in his diocese. He commanded the clergy to read his letter of displeasure to all their parishioners this Sunday. He noted with regret the growing tendency to violate the Sabbath. Races, in themselves, are not evil; but they should be held on Saturday or some other day. The people who organized these races were doing it to make money and were therefore exploiting the *repos dominical*].

. . . . The Pope approves the Catholic syndicates of workers, of the trades and professions, of employers, of women. All must unite in Catholic organizations to meet the menace of communism. For the first time in history there is an open movement against God, to turn the whole world against Him, His Church, and the principle of private property.

There has been no change in the fundamental pattern of the sermon, which consists of praising God, exhortation to exercises of piety, instruction in doctrine and the cult, the application of doctrine to current problems, and warning of death and the wrath of God. The symbols of Christianity and the words of Holy Writ are applied with warmth and directness to whatever problems and issues arise. It was noteworthy, however, that during our stay none of the several vicars preached a sermon dealing with a current social problem; the curé alone made such pronouncements. In the outlying parishes the sermons are of the same general sort except that the language of the preachers is more homely and rural. All sermons are direct and dogmatic. None leave any loophole for a difference of interpretation by people of the various social classes, although obviously differences of practice occur. Certainly no priest was making a bid for popularity by cutting his interpretations and instructions to the tastes of more urban and worldly people.[4]

The current problems referred to in the sermons, however, were consistently and almost exclusively those of working people rather than those of the more prominent and prosperous business people. The solutions of the problems of urban and industrial life seem to be two: first, the stout adherence to the rustic virtues of piety, parsimony, and family solidarity; and, second, participation in the Church's own sponsored movements, especially the two Catholic labor organizations, the Jeunesse ouvrière catholique and the Syndicats catholiques.

[4] The young people of some of the prominent old families held a dance in the hotel on the very Sunday when the curé had expressly forbidden Sunday dancing. I twitted one of the girls at the dance about this; she replied quite directly that the curé did not mean people like those at the party.

A further significant change in parish organization is the specialization of function of the various priests. Of the several priests in the old parish, one does the work with boys; another spends a large share of his time directing the new Jeunesse ouvrière catholique, not only of the parish but of all the diocese; another is known as the "ladies' vicar"; and one, a solid peasant in appearance and speech, delivers most of the sermons not done by the curé and is known as the "farmers' vicar." A vicar in an outlying parish devotes his time to the Catholic labor unions; another is the parish leader of recreation and athletics. Although all must take their share of Masses and confessions, each has his own special class of parishioners and problems to handle.

AUXILIARY ASSOCIATIONS OF THE PARISH

All members of a Catholic parish, except young children, belong to "congregations" based on age, sex, and, in the case of women, marital state. The church recognizes that these lines are of importance in dealing with the spiritual and moral problems of the faithful. Each congregation has its place in religious processions; each has its own retreats with appropriate sermons and moral instructions.

In a simple rural parish these organizations suffice.[5] Neither the curé nor the people are likely to see the need of associations of more specific purpose, with a limited membership and a more formal organization.

In our community the parishes are more elaborately organized. The division of parishioners according to age and sex for pious exercises, ceremonial, and good works continues. In addition, there are societies which foster more intensive piety. The curé of the leading parish described the system of pious congregations thus:

Les Enfants de Marie.—The congregation of all unmarried women, under the patronage of Marie, the patron of virgins.

Les Dames de Ste Anne.—Congregation of all married women, under patronage of Ste Anne, the patron of the family.

La Ligue du Sacré Cœur.—A general society for men. Any man may belong by paying

[5] Miner (*St. Denis*, chap. iii) found in St. Denis only the following associations:

Enfants de Marie.—All unmarried women over sixteen years of age.

Enfants de St. Joseph.—All unmarried men over sixteen years of age.

Société de Tempérance.—No meetings and no specific membership.

Agricultural clubs.—One for men and one for women. Stimulated by the provincial government.

Forestiers catholiques.—A fraternal insurance order; no meetings or other activities.

Attempts of the curé and government authorities to move these organizations or to start new ones of more specialized character have met with little response.

twenty-five cents for the badge. The Sacré Cœur badge is the sign that a man is a Catholic.

La Ligue catholique feminine.—All women ought to be members, but not all are. The "Ligueuse" is supposed to be a model Catholic woman. She is supposed to forget herself in her duties. In costume she obeys strictly the Church's rules of modesty. She sets an example of Catholic womanhood. The Ligue is part of Action catholique.

Les Dames et Demoiselles tertiaires.—A religious order for lay women, founded by St. François d'Assise. They are our best Catholics; they say special prayers every day and do special religious duties. In the procession they have the place of greatest honor, in the rear, nearest the Host. (I.e., nearer than other women. All the men were nearer the Host than any women.)

Hommes tertiaires.—A corresponding piety order for men.

In a rural parochial religious procession all of the marchers would find place in the appropriate congregation. On the *Fête-Dieu*, when the greatest strictly parochial procession of the year goes through the streets, many of the parishioners of our community marched under the banners of organizations which have no integral relation to the parish. Nearly all of the women walked with their appropriate congregations. Several hundred men, however, fell in behind the banner of the Chevaliers de Colomb. In fact, the important men of the town marched either as Chevaliers de Colomb, as members of the choir, or in the escort of public officials about the Sacred Host. Some fifty older and unimportant men marched behind the banner of the Union St. Joseph, a fraternal insurance order. The banner of the Sacré Cœur, the inclusive society of men, was followed only by a nondescript residue of those who could claim no more distinguished category. The procession was embellished by numerous uniformed groups of boys, of young men, and even one of young women. The latter were the drill corps of the Filles d'Isabelle, woman's auxiliary to the Chevaliers de Colomb. All of these organizations, except the congregations, are, in the eyes of the church, profane. The curé expressed his conception of their nature quite frankly:

The Filles d'Isabelle are of American-Irish origin and are the female counterpart of the Chevaliers de Colomb. Their main function is amusement for the members; incidentally, they do some work to help girls who are in trouble. But, apart from the fact that the members are all Catholic, they play no religious role and are not an integral part of the parish. They have costumes—the costume is the honey to catch the flies. If they had no costumes, they would probably have few members. They are office girls or work in stores. If there are any girls from the industries, they work in the office and hold themselves apart from the factory girls. Factory girls do not join, perhaps because they couldn't afford it.

The Chevaliers de Colomb are on the same basis as the Filles d'Isabelle—that is, profane. Its purpose is amusement and sociability, a place to be somebody. There are few workers in it. It is very strong and getting stronger. Although it is Irish in origin, there are no Irish members in Cantonville. It also has an insurance feature which is very cheap because of the large membership. The Chevaliers are not found in country parishes.

The curé attributed the presence of some groups in the parade merely to their uniforms, music, and good marching, which made them fitting escorts for the Sacred Host. It is significant that the great body of middle-class men elected to march, on a holy occasion, not under the banner of a pious congregation but under that of a fraternal order tolerated, but not particularly encouraged, by the clergy. Indeed, some associations represented in the *Fête-Dieu* processions are devoted to aims at which the church looks rather askance, and select their members on bases that the clergy would not like to admit.

This does not mean that the church does not attempt to adjust parochial organization to the exigencies of city life. The local clergy have put great effort into the male and female sections of the Jeunesse ouvrière catholique, composed of unmarried industrial and other wage workers. Lately they have formed corresponding organizations for married workers. Special chaplains instruct the Jeunesse ouvrière catholique in doctrine on labor matters and moral problems and lead them in mass demonstrations, pilgrimages, and retreats. A special house and athletic field have been acquired and blessed for their use.

But the Jeunesse ouvrière catholique, although organized on a parochial basis, seems alien to the traditional parish, for in these groups clerical leadership is applied directly to people of the working class without the mediation of the middle-class laymen prominent in parish and community affairs. The lay officers are themselves working-class youths, picked and groomed by the clergy. The parishioners of middle class are not anxious to seem to know much concerning this movement which treats an economic class as a thing apart. Furthermore, the Jeunesse ouvrière catholique is really a product of the higher organization of the church. Special priests go about from a central headquarters to promote the organization. Young priests are sent off to get special training for the handling of local units. The local groups are in the parish, rather than of it. It is as if the central authorities of the church had taken the working class directly under its greater wing and out from under that of the integral local parish. The other church-inspired labor organizations, the Syndicats catholiques, have no parochial connections. Since the employees of a given industry are not all of one parish, the parochial framework is not suited to the needs of industrial unions. The Syndicats, moreover, sometimes go on strike. Many of the lay leaders of the local parishes are not in sympathy with unions, even though they be Catholic.

In urban communities there arise problems not amenable to treatment within the small territorial parish. Furthermore, a certain unevenness appears in the special attention of the church to the working classes. The church makes little attempt to organize the business and professional men into special groups. Our curé said of them: "They are not treated as a class by the parish. They have their own leaders and their own organizations with which the church has nothing to do." The rural parish is not only a community but a community of essentially one socioeconomic class—namely, independent farm-owners. The city parish is not a community and has a variety of classes, both economic and social. The integrity of the parish, as an institution dealing equally and effectively with all of the people within a circumscribed territory, is put to great strain.

CHAPTER XI

THE CATHOLIC SCHOOLS

THE typical Quebec school in the open country is taught by a lay teacher, generally a farmer's daughter. In the villages the school will have more rooms; in a town of some size the teaching will be done by nuns. The few boys who are to go on to higher studies are sent away, at the age of ten to twelve, to a boarding *collège*. Those who are not to go on often leave before finishing the six or seven years of instruction offered. The girls are more likely to continue to the end of the local school; a few will then go to convent boarding-schools to learn household arts or to qualify as rural teachers. Although the school district is legally unrelated to the ecclesiastical parish, it is, in the minds of the people and of the curé, a parish school.

In school administration, as in government and parish organization, the unity of our community has been broken up. The town, which includes one parish and part of another, is also a school district. The rural part of the township has its own school commission, which operates several one-room schools, some of which are attended exclusively by children of suburban settlements. The two outlying municipalities, each established as a parish, also have their own school commissions. The larger community thus comprises four school districts which coincide exactly with the four municipalities, but only two of which correspond with parishes.

The rural and the two village school districts are far below the city in value of Catholic-owned property from which a school tax may be collected. The largest working-class village, St. Jerome, with a population only a little less than that of the city, had Catholic-owned property assessed at less than one-seventh the value of that of the town. With double the school tax rate, it still offers only six years of instruction, compared with nine for the town. The other village and the rural district are in the same situation.

The school commissioners of the town are among the leading solid citizens, of the sort who become churchwardens, aldermen, and mayor. The chairman, for instance, has been churchwarden, mayor, president of the *chambre de commerce* and operates what is probably the largest individually owned business in the county. By contrast, the school commissioners of the new villages are industrial workers and very small businessmen. Unaccustomed to leadership of any kind, they get office by default.

The two villages, with their separate school systems, were, in the beginning, merely the result of a desire to escape the higher taxes of the town. Poorer newcomers settled outside the city limits to get cheap living quarters; if they were worse off as to sanitary conveniences and public services, they apparently did not mind. It was by their own will that they established separate, and poorer, jurisdictions. Eventually the multiplication of people in the outlying settlements made communi-

TABLE 29

SCHOOL FINANCES IN CANTONVILLE AND ST. JEROME, 1938*

	Cantonville	St. Jerome
Taxable property of Catholic proprietors........................	$7,188,795.00	$925,570.00
School tax rate per $100 assessed value........................	$0.90	$1.80
Estimated revenue for schools......	$64,699.00	$16,660.00
School expenditure per pupil.......	$38.71	$22.00
Years of instruction offered........	9	6
Catholic population..............	7,778	6,236

* The estimated revenue does not include that paid by the industrial corporations. Their school taxes are divided between Catholic and Protestant school boards in proportion to the children in school in each system. The industries are all in the town; hence none of their school tax goes to the outlying schools.

ties of rural aspect but of urban proportions. That is their present dilemma. Meantime, the city—with burdens enough of its own—has become accustomed to use the tax revenue from all the more valuable properties of the community. Attempts to incorporate the outlying villages into the city and its school jurisdiction have so far failed. The opposition has been led by the chairman of the city school commission, with the plain argument that it would be necessary to increase the city's very low school tax rate if the villages, with their large population and low property values, were taken in. Thus, there has become intrenched a difference of standard of education, and of other municipal services, between the various parts of the community; originally a division of the community into more and less urban parts, it continues as a difference between the working-class parts and the parts in which the working class forms a distinctly smaller, although still large, proportion of the population. Initiated by the poorer part, it is maintained by the better-off part. Ironically, the parts containing the largest proportion of industrial workers receive no school or municipal tax from the industries.

The town has several elementary schools, taught by nuns, in which boys and girls are taught together to the age of about eleven. Girls may continue above that age, but boys then go to a separate school conducted by an order of lay brothers.

The system provides for nine years of schooling, which would normally be completed at the age of fifteen. In fact, one-fourth of the

TABLE 30

SCHOOL CENSUS OF CANTONVILLE, 1936–37*

AGE (YEARS)	BOYS				GIRLS			
	In School	Not in School	Total in Town	Percentage in School	In School	Not in School	Total in Town	Percentage in School
5– 6........	6	65	71	8.5	8	65	73	11.0
6– 7........	68	14	82	82.9	68	20	88	77.3
7–11........	326	8	334	97.6	352	4	356	98.9
12–13........	153	12	165	92.7	133	14	147	90.5
14–15........	99	35	134	73.9	77	67	144	53.5
16–17........	33	93	126	26.2	27	108	135	20.0
Total.....	685	227	912	75.1	665	278	943	70.5

* Compiled from information given by the school principal.

boys and nearly one-half of the girls of fourteen to fifteen years of age are not in school. We found no evidence of any great demand that the town should furnish free schooling beyond these nine years. The upper years of the local schools, devoted to what is technically called the "commercial course," do not lead to any entrance examinations to higher schools of any kind, as do the Protestant schools.

The brother who is principal of the school would like to see the schools adapted to the needs of the community. He spoke thus of his school:

The boys come to the *Académie* at about the age of ten to eleven, after they have finished the sisters' school. The course is called a commercial course. It is not, strictly speaking, commercial; it is the course prescribed by the provincial authorities. There is a good deal of English, which is considered a requirement for commerce; also arithmetic, bookkeeping, and typing. No Latin, no Greek, and no modern language except English. It leads to no other course; a boy must go to a classical *collège* if he is to continue his studies. Not many want to continue.

The general ambition here is to get to work as soon as possible, even if it be for a wage of fifty cents a day. The parents come to town to earn money, and they want their children to earn, too, as soon as possible. The boys get the same idea. This is especially true of families recently come from the country. They left the farm because they were in debt or were losing money; Cantonville is, for them, simply a place to earn money. In the upper grades there are more boys from the older families that I have known in the town for many years. Not many boys of the newer families from the country go on into the upper grades.

If a boy does finish, there isn't much for him. He can be a clerk in a store or a bank, and that is about all. There is not much future there. I know boys from my school who have been working in banks for ten years and can't marry. An occasional one may get into the office of one of the industries and may get some real promotion, but there are not many places like that.

Some boys take no interest in academic subjects and can't learn well. Sometimes they show some aptitude for hand work. We have some woodworking apparatus, and on certain days boys can come before class and get instruction in wood work, but it is not very thorough. Furthermore, it leads to nothing except as a way of finding aptitudes and maintaining interest. There is little or no woodworking done here. There ought to be other lines of practical work, but we don't have them. Many of these boys ought to be put to apprenticeship, but there is no apprenticeship here. The lack of ambition is very discouraging to the teachers.

There is some discontent among the young men. It is not great, but it is increasing. A young man in the bank, for example, works for years without being able to marry; or a young man working in industry for $17 or $18 a week at fatiguing work in a hot, airless room for long hours. He is, let us say, twenty-one or twenty-two years old and would like to marry but can't on account of the low wages. Such people are beginning to be discontented.

The brother complained that, although there is a quite well-equipped laboratory in his school, built with provincial aid some years ago, the local school commissioners had never allowed money for effective instruction in science or for any laboratory work whatsoever. There has been something of a movement to establish a textile course, so that the youth of the town would be better prepared for work in the mills. The managers of industry show no enthusiasm for this. They contend that any looms used in the school would be so simple that the instruction would be of little use for the work in a modern textile plant; furthermore, they say that they can pick and train weavers better than any outside instructor. Whatever the reasons, the town has only a dead-end school, leading to no higher courses and fitting its best students only for minor clerical work. The tax-supported schools do not provide even the first steps toward the kind of technical education required in the middle and upper ranks of industry.

It must be remembered that the schooling leading to advancement, even of the kind traditional in Quebec, has always been paid for by the family itself. The convent for girls and the *collège* for boys is the accepted place for education above the first five or six years for the middle and upper classes and for those who wish to pursue higher studies of any kind whatsoever.

In our community, relatively small as it is and with so large a proportion of its population working for wages in industry, 124 families send 156 girls to the local convent, at their own expense, rather than to the public schools, although the teaching is done by the same house of nuns in both. Although some of the convent girls are taking the

TABLE 31

GIRLS ATTENDING THE CONVENT SCHOOL IN
CANTONVILLE, 1936–37*

Occupation of Parent	Number of Families with Daughters in Convent	Number of Girls in Convent Commercial Course	Total Number of Girls
French:			
Professions, owners of businesses, and services....................	40	11	52
Civil servants and employees of public utilities.....................	13	3	17
Clerks and independent artisans.....	15	3	19
Farmer...........................	1	0	2
Industry..........................	41	17	50
Laborer, not in industry............	6	2	6
Unknown.........................	4	2	4
English:			
Industry.........................	4	0	6
Total.....................	124	38	156

* Compiled from information given by the sister in charge. She designated as "Irish" two additional families which we know to be French in all but family name and remote ancestry. It is probable that all but one of the four families called "English" are also French in all but name. The fourth, French in name but English in fact, is the only managerial family with a child in the convent. She was later sent away to an English boarding convent.

commercial course, which prepares them for stenography, typing, and secretarial work, the convent is not primarily a school in which to learn a trade; it is the proper place in which to educate a daughter, if the parent can afford it at all. A considerable number of girls are sent to boarding convents elsewhere. A girl of any social standing in Quebec must be convent bred; and the convents are rated, informally but ruthlessly, according to the standing of the families who send their children to them. Scarcely a girl of a leading business or professional family in our community has ever attended the public school. This standard reaches even down into the working class, for forty-one workmen in industry—none above the rank of minor foreman and most classified merely as "workers"—send one or more daughters to the convent. How great an effort may be made to provide this kind of an education is indicated by the following two cases: A doctor has a daughter in the convent, although he has no car and recently lost his house by foreclosure; it is a matter of some comment that he has to send his boys to the public Academy. The undoubtedly most prosperous lawyer in town has no car; six of his nine children are still in

DIAGRAM III

SONS OF PROFESSIONAL MEN

Occupation of Father	Sons at Work	Sons at School
Lawyer..........	First, lawyer (away) Second, pharmacist (here)	
Lawyer..........	First, lawyer (here) Second, clerical (here)	Third, classical *collège* Fourth, classical *collège*
Doctor...........	First, doctor (away) Second, clerical (here)	
Doctor...........		Classical *collège*
Doctor...........		Classical *collège*
Doctor...........		Public school
Doctor...........		Public school
Notary...........		Classical *collège*
Veterinary.......		Commercial *collège*
Dentist..........	Clerical (away)	

school, but not one is in the public school. His ten-year-old son is already boarding at a classical *collège*.[1]

This is an appropriate place for further comment on the education of young men in the community. By seeing the whole educational complex, the function of the public school appears more clearly. Diagrams III and IV show the occupations and schooling of all sons of active professional men, as well as of a few leading businessmen.

The outstanding point is the fact that no boy of any leading family has received a technical education. Constant attention to the subject revealed no case of a boy either in the engineering profession, going to

[1] There is no *collège* for boys in the town. Consequently, a boy must be sent away if he is to have other than public-school training.

an engineering school, taking preparatory work of a character likely to be followed by engineering, or talking of taking engineering. Three professional men have sons following their own professions; each, it happens, has two sons at work. None of the second sons is in the profession. The second son of one lawyer is a pharmacist. Another lawyer has a second son who was given a classical *collège* course and has a clerical and semitechnical job with a power company. A physician has helped a second son with *collège* training into a clerical job which he has not been able to keep. A dentist, who has wandered from town to

DIAGRAM IV

SONS OF LEADING BUSINESSMEN

Occupation of Father	Sons at Work	Sons at School
Contractor.......	First, contractor (with father)	Second, seminary Third, commercial *collège*
General merchant.	Lawyer (here)	
Wholesale grocer..	First, business (with father) Second, business (with father)	
Accountant......	....	Medical school

town without much success, has a grown son who, after taking a commercial course, has a minor clerkship in a bank in another town. A physician in a near-by small town has two nearly middle-aged sons; one practices medicine in partnership with the father; the other is, as we were informed, "chauffeur à papa." The middle-aged sons of a prominent local businessman of the last generation are, respectively, dentist, pharmacist, and hardware dealer.

The cases on which to base judgment are few; but, so far as our community is concerned, the father's profession, like the farm of the *habitant*, goes to only one son. When the French Canadians speak of an "old professional family," they mean one in which one member of each generation has gone into the family profession.[2] In our community the other son (we find no case of more than two sons of a professional family grown and at work) has received either merely the classical course, which leads to a Bachelor of Arts degree, at the age of nineteen

[2] The French Canadians are not alone in basing their conception of the family on the character and accomplishments of a single line. It may also be that a tradition is easier to maintain if the family concentrates it in one child than if they try to make all live up to it. To train all sons equally might mean that none would get professional training, for want of resources.

or so, or the classical course followed by a brief commercial course, or only the commercial course in some *collège*.

Some of the nuances of this problem are suggested in the curé's response to our question whether there is a tendency for local upper-class families to send boys into technical professions. He did not answer directly concerning local boys:

Naturally there is a movement toward a more technical kind of education. The tradition has been for boys to take the classical course and then go on into the liberal professions—medicine, law, notarial. But these professions are bankrupt. They are overcrowded. The boy makes a brilliant record as a law student; then he perishes for want of cases. He becomes discontented. So naturally there is a demand for another type of education. The Collège Mont St. Louis in Montreal now gives a course for the baccalaureate that is more scientific than classical. After that the boy can take a couple of years of industrial chemistry, or what not. That is necessary, for the province is becoming industrial.

Of course, the ideal thing would be for boys to take the classical course and then go on to university for technical studies, but the people can't afford it. A family, even a well-to-do one, can't send three or four boys through five or six years of advanced studies. It costs too much. The family would starve. So there must be a change in the *collège* itself to give more technical training.

A very successful businessman, of no formal education, comments thus on education and success:

"Lawyer" is a beautiful title. But young lawyers like those over there [*pointing to office across the street*] can't earn enough to buy their bread. They have a few relatives, but these can't help much. . . . . A young fellow can't get ahead in the law unless he is very brilliant; and if he is very brilliant, he can get ahead without the law. . . . . The whole trouble is that a lot of young men don't know what they want. They don't want to work with their hands, and they don't want to work with their heads. They want a desk.

These facts suggest a revision of the statement, so often repeated, that "the French Canadian, who believes in the primacy of the spirit, despises business and esteems only the liberal professions."[3] The statement is undoubtedly true. But how does it work out with relation to choice of occupations and education? Evidently a French-Canadian family does love to produce a professional man. But it seems generally to be a family aim, focused on one son. The alternative is business, the supposedly despised *affaires*. In fact, the French middle classes in our town—and throughout Quebec—live by business. It is they, rather than the English, who are shopkeepers. Many of the *collèges* of the province and the two French universities offer commercial courses. But it is still almost a rule that a family which trains one son for a pro-

[3] G. Lanctot (ed.), *Les Canadiens français et leurs voisins du Sud* (Montreal, 1941), p. 288.

fession will give decidedly less training to the sons who are to go into business. No boy of our community has pursued commercial studies beyond the *collège*. The French Canadians' lack of esteem for business turns out, then, to mean only that the majority who go into business get less education than the minority (from the same families) who go into the professions. It is not an unusual situation. On the other hand, no one pretends that the French Canadians despise the technical pursuits of engineering and science; yet it is in this field that the educational system has been especially weak, and French-Canadian candidates are notoriously few.

It is also probably true that an English-speaking community in Canada or the United States would put more boys per capita, class for class, into the traditional professions than does a French-Canadian community. The difference would be that some boys would pursue higher and more intensive studies leading to advanced technical knowledge of the kinds wanted in business and industry. In short, those preparing for the liberal professions would not be the only ones to get higher technical training.

The French-Canadian boy who is to go into a liberal profession is picked out from the mass and given higher education. The others are not given anything approaching that education. So far as the middle and upper classes are concerned, they seem to expect to establish the other sons by means of family influence in positions where they can learn the techniques of business and from which they can make advancement. This means does not work in industry, and for two reasons—because the French-Canadian middle-class family has no influence with industry and because the training of their sons is not of the proper kind.

The boy who works his way through school is practically unknown in Quebec; higher education is very much a matter of effort to attain a goal agreed upon by the family rather than by the individual boy. It is almost certainly true that an educational objective decided upon by the family will be more conservative than one decided upon by the boy himself. Thus, the boy who has means and family behind him is set in traditional grooves; the boy who starts out on his own is hopelessly handicapped by the nature of his early schooling, as well as by tradition. The best he can do is to take lessons in English and a few other subjects from one of the several small, private, evening "business colleges" in the community.

CHAPTER XII

PROTESTANT CHURCHES AND SCHOOLS

FRENCH CANADIANS accord the Anglican church a special respect. It was the church of the early English governors and of the garrison society of Quebec. "At least," said a young French lawyer in our community, "the Anglicans don't hold services in a lodge hall, and they don't serve ice-cream to get the children to come." But dignity and respect do not fill the Anglican pews. For many years the local congregation consisted of the handful of farmers and tradesmen left over from the early English settlement. Recently the parish, increased by the new industrial English, has become self-supporting again—thanks, according to the rector, to guaranties made by a few leading industrial men. A new floor, a new organ, a raised pulpit, candles for the altar, and a new parish hall have been donated by individuals or groups, all of the new industrial element.

But on several summer Sundays never as many as fifty people came to morning prayer. While across the park the curé was telling his thousands firmly that, if they violated the Lord's Day, their children would certainly have to beg bread in the street, the rector was weakly pleading with his handful not to leave the church out of their Sunday plans.

It is rather in its auxiliary activities that the old Anglican church has been revived. It has become the center for a new social life. In winter, badminton, benefit bridges, rummage sales, and Women's Guild meetings keep the hall and the English women busy. The new social life, however, does not include the few remaining rural English families. The rector and the socially prominent industrial English women complain that the old families oppose "progress," such as the putting-in of new altar fittings and the adoption of High Church practices. The old-town English are not too pleased at the new tone of the Women's Guild, where the women smoke cigarettes while playing bridge for prizes. To these rural people, who think of themselves as the faithful who kept the church alive during the long decades of decline of English population, the revived church is no longer theirs. The parish hall and new organ are unwanted gifts from strangers.

115

Factional differences appear even among the industrial constituency of the church. Two sections of the Women's Guild meet separately. Interviews show clearly that one group consists of people better placed socially and in the industrial hierarchy, while the other smacks of the old-country skilled worker, the clerk, and the foreman. The bridges and teas of the socially prominent faction are attended by a few French women of similar class. Some young French women and the English-Catholic women of higher social standing play badminton in the parish hall with a socially select group of Protestant women.

The rector is quite aware of these divisions. For financial support, he has to count on the prominent English, who rarely come to church; for attendance, he has to count on the few poor English farming families and some of the old-country English of working-class origin. It was this that he had in mind when he said that the old-country English come to church but have no thought of supporting it, while the Canadians and Americans don't come at all. At another time he said, regretfully but not bitterly, that, since the leading industrial managers do not come to church except for occasions like the coronation services, the lesser people think they don't have to come either. This was accompanied by the remark that such snobbery should have nothing to do with coming to church but that, since the lesser do follow their leaders, the latter should set them a good example.

The Anglican church has, then, a congregation of village size, split into three factions but serving as the center for the social life and class-grading of the English population. The whole is so small, and the social differences so great, that the parish, like the small English community it represents, lacks real liveliness and solidarity.

The United church has no such history. Established by old-country industrial people of the "Chapel" tradition, it was later affiliated with the United Church of Canada and gathered in a number of the Canadian and American people of some standing. Some people have moved from one of the Protestant churches to the other. A considerable number of English of other denominational origins went to the Anglican church when they first came to town, because it was the only one for a time; most of them remained Anglican.

We have already noticed that the French have more respect for the Anglican church than for the United. But that does not mean that the Anglican rector has any more contact with the Catholic world than does the pastor of the United church. Both of them say they never meet the Catholic priests; both of them feel the isolation of their positions. Each church has, however, a handful of French members. The rector has a number of stories, from the past, of French who married Protestants, became Anglican, and were persecuted bitterly by Catholic relatives. One of these stories tells of French-Catholic women who came to the door of the Anglican church to curse and physically attack a woman of their family who turned Protestant; others tell about efforts to get converts to turn back to Catholicism on their deathbeds. There are some more recent stories of mixed marriages resulting in conversions to Protestantism. But such cases are few; the Protestant churches are and will remain English. They constitute no threat to Catholicism in the community.

THE PROTESTANT SCHOOL

The Protestant school has no official connection with either church, although it stands on the same grounds as the Anglican church and is historically thought of as closely related to it. Before the industrial population came, it was a one-room school presided over by a teacher from one of the local families. It now has more than two hundred pupils housed in a new building of several rooms, and it carries its pupils through ten grades.

Its support comes from a tax paid on Protestant-owned real estate, plus a share of the taxes paid by corporations. The school board gives English people their only chance at public office. The school principal and leaders of the Protestant group complain that it is difficult to get good school commissioners without undue burden upon a mere handful of people. Some of the more prominent English people live in houses owned by the companies or by Catholics and are therefore ineligible to serve on the school board, for school board members must be proprietors. Of eight persons who were school commissioners in the period of our study, two were American citizens. It was not legal for them to serve, but no one seemed concerned about it. Indeed, the principal commented that Americans show more lively interest in the school than do old-country English. As in the church, the nonindustrial English families have been pushed into the background. Two school commissioners, one an unlettered horse-trader, are of this group; but they are, as in the church, considered backward and obstructive. Leadership is in the hands of industrial people of high rank.

The difficulty of getting school commissioners makes the English complain that the French ignore them in politics seem a little silly. For the school board is the one thing of a public nature which the English have to themselves, and they cannot get up any enthusiasm about its election or operation.

The Protestant school is generally called the "English school"; some English-speaking Catholics always so speak of it, with the obvious intent of emphasizing the school's and their own ethnic, rather than religious, affiliation. In fact, it is the school of the English Catholics, of the Jews, of the few families of French Protestants, of a few rather anglicized French Catholics, and of families resulting from marriages of English Protestants with French Catholics. The marginal people choose the legally Protestant, *de facto* English school.[1]

There is no corresponding group of English Catholics in the Catholic (French) schools. One such family has a small girl in the French convent kindergarten but seems very uncomfortable about it. It is something they have to defend before their social companions, who are all English and of some social standing. The defense is that they want the children to stay there just long enough to learn French. Another Catholic family, of British colonial origin, sends two children to English-Catholic boarding-schools outside the district. Since a number of English-Protestant families of social standing also send children away to school, this is an easy solution of the problem for English Catholics who can afford it.

Some further consideration of the English Catholics and other religiously and ethnically marginal people will show more clearly the essentially ethnic nature of the division of the community. The Quebec system would operate at its best if the population contained only English Protestants and French Catholics. For such persons have clearly a sort of citizenship in one or the other of the two systems of religious and educational institutions and in the constellation of organizations and activities which revolve about churches and schools.

---

[1] To get this information we went through the school rolls with the principal and other teachers. They were able to identify the families and to name the employment of the father, the religion, and the language of the family in all except a few cases. From this information we compiled the following table of children in school:

Protestant	136
Catholic	46
Jewish	6
Doubtful	17
Total	205

At least seven of the Catholic children are known to be of mixed Protestant-Catholic marriages; two of these, of mixed English-French marriages. Thirteen are known to be of French families. Of the English-Protestant children, only six are of old English families of the town and district. The doubt about a few seemed to emanate merely from the insignificance of their families.

The marginal people participate in these systems of institutions only partially and on sufferance. The English Catholics present the perfect contradiction to the system. The ethnically right system of schools, churches, and associations is of the wrong religion for them. Ethnic affiliation proves the stronger, so far as school is concerned. Not the least function of a school is the social orientation of the child. It gives him a large part of his social personality by determining the groups with which he identifies himself and with which others identify him. In our community, ethnic identification is crucial. Class feeling also enters the matter, for, while there are French Catholics of all classes, the English Catholics of some standing could not enter the French social world without loss. The upper classes of French are divided into cliques of families which no English family could get into. The English world of informal social activity is more open; no one has been in the community long, and things are in flux. The English Catholics of managerial rank are, it is fair to say, definitely "on the make" in the English world. There would be no gain for them in leaving their present standing and their hope of advancement in the social world of the economically advantaged group, whose ethnic sentiments they share, for a hopeless excursion into the economically disadvantaged, but socially more close, French society. The upper-class French do not send their children to the local schools in any case. That the English Catholics should send their children to an English school, even though Protestant, is not astonishing.

For similar reasons, it is not surprising that English-Catholic women should have their social life about the Anglican church hall in winter, when the golf club is closed, or that they should be familiar with all the factional gossip of the organizations affiliated with the Anglican church.

In religion these marginal people remain Catholics—one-dimensional Catholics, communicants but not parishioners. They are not an integral part of the parish. The English Catholics complain that the churches do not offer them the services of a real English priest. The large central parish church offered an English Mass in the basement at 9:30 on Sundays. The Mass and sermon were taken by an old priest who spoke English fluently, although with a marked French accent and many of the characteristic French errors. It was a Low Mass, held in the unattractive church basement. Yet, in spite of the smallness of the English-Catholic group, 180 attended this Mass on an ordinary summer Sunday, while only 35 were at the Anglican church, and a similar number at the United church. The English-Catholic minority which has no church of its own attends religious services more than do the English Protestants who do have churches. But it does not follow that the English Catholics have a church life apart from this Mass; they do not.

Even the English Mass is a stepchild. The priest who celebrated it was old, rather cross, and without other functions in the parish. The English did not regard him as their priest, even though he was there because of their presence. They complained of the curé's lack of interest in them and of his failure to provide a good priest and facilities. The curé's story is that the Irish (his name for English Catholics in general) lack zeal and are a complaining lot; in spite of their relatively well-off position, they will not pay enough to keep a priest in food and clothes.

The curé's testimony is corroborated by a family of English Catholics from another Quebec city but now living in our community. They support the curé in his statement that the English won't get together and pay enough for a priest. They even had an argument as to the proper hour for their Mass; some men wanted it at 11:30, so they could get in a game of golf first. Some women wanted it at 9:30, to allow time for preparing dinner afterward. It is held at 9:30, and the men play golf anyway.

In sum, the English people can practice their Catholicism so far as sacraments and formal piety is concerned. They have no outlet for any other social energies through the church. They are disenfranchised in this respect, as in others—whether by their own will or by their lack of consensus. Many of them find adequate outlets for leadership in secular neighborly life in the English group and perhaps would not take much interest in parish affairs anyway. At least one Catholic family complained of the frustration of the local situation. The mother, a widow, was accustomed to lead parish women's affairs. Her son, a young man in the late twenties, had also been active. They missed such activities in our community. A sharper edge is given their disappointment by what they term the "exclusiveness" of the old-country English and others in larger industries. Such Catholics are entirely without outlets for group activity of a sort that would seem, to them, significant.

All of the English Catholics are effectively disenfranchised in school matters. The Catholic classrooms are full of signs glorifying the French language and admonishing pupils to preserve their French-Canadian

traditions. The English school is Protestant; Catholics have no right
to vote or lift voices in any way about its affairs. They have to pay
special tuition to send their children to it.

There is a wealth of Catholic auxiliary organizations in the town;
the outstanding organization of Catholic men is the Chevaliers de
Colomb. No English Catholics belong to it, so far as we could discover. A couple of minor officers with English names turned out to be
French Canadians with a remote Irish ancestor. Although upper-class
French men belong to it, to such an extent that practically every man
prominent in local affairs has held some high office in the organization,
such men do not characteristically have their club life in it. They belong to it to lead and prove their public interest. English-Catholic industrial men have no such motive; they take no interest in civic affairs. They find their club life with their colleagues of industry in the
golf club. In any case, they make no secret of the fact that they do not
care to be in the Chevaliers de Colomb here, where the members are
all French and are mostly "factory hands of a poor type." One young
man, an American of French-Canadian ancestry and very fond of
sports, was thought by us to be the perfect type of prospective member
of the Chevaliers. Inquiry brought out his complete contempt for the
local Chevaliers, probably sharpened by his determination never to be
identified as French.

The rest of the story of the local English Catholics is not a thing by
itself, for it is simply the story of the English population of the town.
The life they lead is that of the golf club and such other associations as
their position in town puts them into on other considerations than
their Catholicism.

If any French Canadian were to leave his own world to become
English, these are the formal institutions in which he would have to
find his place. He would, to put it mildly, become a member of a local
social order of much less richness than his own. To do so at all, he
would have to turn his back on family, kin, friends, and all the fulness
of life. The reward would be doubtful and small. That this is so will
be even more apparent when we describe the associations and the informal social life of the community.

CHAPTER XIII

VOLUNTARY ASSOCIATIONS

I N A stable rural community the French Canadian, like other people so placed, need not and does not actively seek companions and collaborators. They are his by virtue of birth into a family and a community. In Cantonville, where many people are newcomers, where many are engaged in new pursuits, and where new problems are arising, the business of finding associates and of creating instruments for collective action is more active and conscious. The clergy find their task of mobilizing the faithful for piety and social action along the lines of "age, sex, and social condition" more complicated and more delicate as occupations and economic interests become more varied. The multiplication of parish organizations is evidence that the clergy have attacked this problem vigorously. But laymen have far outstripped the clergy in the sorting and mobilizing of people for action and sociability. Analysis of the many voluntary associations should give some notion of the effective "estates" into which the population is being sorted. Also, if there be any knitting of the French social structure with the English, it should appear on the lively margins where people are establishing new voluntary groups, where the individual is seeking new companions, and where, sometimes, the groups seek the adherence of the individual.

The most voluntary association is an interest group which serves simply as an instrument by which the several members seek to gain, by common effort, some conscious secular aim which they individually share but could not separately attain. But people may also voluntarily set up and maintain an association to cultivate sentiments, to attain some goal of moral or religious character, or merely to find themselves in agreeable company. Most associations, whatever their stated purposes, combine these features in varying proportions.

One would expect the mixing of people of different ethnic and religious affiliations to be more common in associations which pursue secular interests than in those devoted to sentiments. Where the very basis of organization is consensus as to the sacred values, mixing with strangers is scarcely to be thought of. But it is not comfortable to mix

122

sociably, except on those rare and brief occasions when strangeness adds zest, with people whose sentiments run counter to one's own. Easy sociability requires a common sense of what is to be said and what is to be left unsaid; in the absence of this consensus of discretion a burden of restraint rests upon the company. Even when pursuing secular interests—for which conscious agreement is wanted—it is safer to have some consensus about basic sentiments.[1] These general remarks are designed to indicate the sort of analysis which we shall make of the associations of Cantonville.

Our first concern is to determine the ethnic and religious composition of associations of various kinds. Diagram V, accordingly, shows how French or English, and how Catholic or Protestant, the various associations are. At the edges of the diagram are those which are most purely Catholic, French, Protestant, or English, respectively; toward and in the center are those which are mixed in membership.

Certain facts appear at first glance. First, as might be expected from the relative number of the French and English population, French-Catholic organizations predominate. Second, there are no English-Catholic or French-Protestant organizations. French Protestants are too few to form associations. But there are English Catholics in considerable number, and their failure to form associations and their absence from French-Catholic organizations are facts of some significance. The third, rather obvious, point is that the mixed associations are concerned with the secular matters of sports, entertainment, and business.

While many of the French-Catholic organizations are statedly Catholic, only four—and they, minor ones—are statedly French. Only two of the four have a distinct nationalistic bent. One of the two was a short-lived political movement. The other was a fraternal order—also of short life—established as a French-Canadian counterpart to the Irish-tainted Chevaliers de Colomb.

The great majority of associations, and the important ones, are French in fact rather than by definition and stated policy. The language and culture of the members is French. A few are definitely nationalistic. The retail merchants association, for instance, states its

[1] Max Weber was, I believe, the first to point to the study of voluntary associations as a device for analysis of the structure of a society. W. Lloyd Warner, however, has been the pioneer in effective use of this device. See P. Lunt and W. L. Warner, *The Social Life of a Modern Community* (New Haven, 1941), and other volumes to appear as the "Yankee City Series." Most study of voluntary associations has been focused on overtly stated purposes rather than upon their functions in the social structure.

purpose merely as defense of the independent retail merchant, but its propaganda is openly directed against non-French competitors. Similarly, organizations without a specifically stated Catholic purpose may be completely Catholic in membership. Even in the more secular organizations, Catholicism and French-Canadian culture are taken for granted. In general, people do not say: "Go to, let us form an associa-

DIAGRAM V

TYPES OF VOLUNTARY ASSOCIATIONS BY RELIGIOUS AND ETHNIC AFFILIATION

RELIGIOUS AFFILIATION	ETHNIC AFFILIATION						
	French by Definition	French in Fact	Mostly French	Mixed	Mostly English	English in Fact	English by Definition
Catholic by definition	Insurance* (1) Fraternal (1)	Church† Savings and loan† Drill corps (1) Insurance (1) Fraternal (1) Charity† Youth (3) Labor (1)					
Catholic in fact	Political (1) Insurance (1)	Business (2) Drama and music (3) Political (1) Insurance (1) Drill corps (1) Fraternal (2) Sports (3)					
Mostly Catholic			Sports (3) Musical (2)				
Mixed				Business (1) First-aid (1) Sports (1)			
Mostly Protestant					Business (1) Sports (1)		
Protestant in fact						Sports (1) Drama (1) Boys (1)	Fraternal (2)
Protestant by definition						Church	

* The insurance associations are all fraternal insurance orders.
† Parochial organizations found in some or all of the Catholic parishes.

tion of French-Canadian and Catholic membership and purposes." They simply form associations for various purposes among their fellows, who are French and Catholic. If they have occasion to express patriotic or religious sentiments, they express those which are common in the society in which they live.[2]

[2] We labor this point because Americans and English Canadians constantly betray the impression that French-Canadian society results from some sort of conscious cabal. This kind of ethnocentrism is betrayed even by people who have studied French-Canadian life a good deal.

Some of these associations would probably accept English, or even Protestant, members. The associations affiliated with the parishes would certainly accept English Catholics, as would also the Chevaliers de Colomb and the Catholic labor unions; yet they have no such members.

Diagram VI shows in what kinds of associations English and French sometimes mix and in what kinds they do not. There are no mixed church auxiliaries, charity and mutual-aid societies, boys and youth organizations, fraternal insurance or purely fraternal orders, marching and drill corps, or political clubs. Mixed, as well as unmixed, groups put on plays and concerts, organize sports, and pursue business and property interests. One small, mixed organization trains a first-aid corps. The two ethnic groups have separately pursued aims imbued with sentiment; they sometimes unite for entertainment and pursuit of economic interests. The facts thus correspond to a sociological truism. But to appreciate the significance of the mixing or failure to mix, one must see them in relation to the social structure of the community, for the selection of members of voluntary associations reflects the class positions of people. The obvious differences in the class structure of the English and French populations account for at least part of the failure of the ethnic groups to mix, and—paradoxical as it may seem—for some of their mixing as well.

The English Catholics could presumably join in the auxiliary activities of the local parishes; they do not do so. Certain of these associations have functions which limit participation to classes of people among whom the English Catholics are represented either not at all or in insignificant number. This is obviously true of the Jeunesse ouvrière catholique. It is equally, if less obviously, true of the parish mutual savings banks, in which a person may deposit any amount of money, however small, at the church door after Mass. This is a working-class way of saving.

The case is not clear in the parish charitable organization (St. Vincent de Paul) and the boys' and youth organizations. One must remember that social classes are not merely separate groups of people; they constitute a system of related groups. In the charitable organization the donors and workers tend to come from one class; the recipients, from another. The English Catholics in Cantonville, although a few of them are of the lower-middle class ordinarily active in

DIAGRAM VI

VOLUNTARY ASSOCIATIONS

I. KINDS OF WHICH NONE ARE MIXED

TYPE OF ASSOCIATION	ETHNIC AFFILIATION	
	French	English
Church auxiliaries	Catholic	Protestant
Charity and mutual aid	Caisse populaire St. Vincent de Paul	
Boys and youth	Scouts catholique Action catholique de la Jeunesse canadienne Jeunesse ouvrière catholique Jeunesse ouvrière catholique féminine	Boy Scouts Girl Guides
Insurance fraternal orders	Artisans canadiens-français Association canado-americaine Union St. Joseph Maccabées	
Fraternal	Chevaliers de Colomb Chevaliers de Dollard Club Rendezvous Filles d'Isabelle	Masons Sons of England
Drill and parade	La Garde d'Honneur Les Zouaves	
Politics	Jeunesse nationale Club liberal	

II. KINDS OF WHICH SOME ARE MIXED

TYPE OF ASSOCIATION	ETHNIC AFFILIATION		
	French	Mixed	English
Musical and dramatic	Cercle Luc Hamel Jeunes Amateurs Harmonie (band)	Symphonie Philharmonic	Associated Players
Sports	Les Raquetteurs (snowshoe) Les Coureurs (snowshoe) Ligue de Balle molle	Baseball club (F*) Hockey club (F) Tennis club (F) Mill A sports club Good Fellows club Golf club (E)	Badminton
Interest groups	Syndicats (labor) Marchands détaillants Les Proprietaires	Chambre de commerce (F) Canadian Manufacturers' Association (E)	
First-aid		St. John's Ambulance Corps	

* "F" indicates predominantly French; "E," English.

St. Vincent de Paul societies here and elsewhere, have not, like French
of the same class, any web of relationships or any sense of identification
with the poor of this community. The poor of Cantonville are not the
poor of the English people, Protestant or Catholic.[3] The local counterpart of the Boy Scouts, organized and led by an undertaker of lower-
middle class and composed of boys of the same standing, is equally outside the system of obligations felt by the English Catholics. Their distribution among the classes conspires with ethnic separateness to keep
English Catholics out of parochial associations.

FRATERNAL ORDERS

Fraternal orders, just when they are becoming *passé* in the United
States, are coming into their own in the growing towns of Quebec.
The Chevaliers de Colomb lodge of Cantonville was recently reported
to be among the most rapidly growing units in the whole order. The
tide is stemmed neither by the jibes of French-Canadian intellectuals
at what they regard as the last word in Irish-American vulgarity nor
by the attacks of nationalists on what they consider an alien and essentially non-Catholic institution. The local lodge has become the great
inclusive men's association of the French community. In it men may
grow into the larger magnitudes of popularity and leadership. Those
of lesser standing and more modest ambitions may document their
identification and solidarity with the leaders of their community. No
French-Canadian citizen is too exalted to belong. Although those of
most prestige in the community are not among the more active members, some of them were among its founders and have held the higher
offices. The present leaders are young professional men on the make.
The lesser officers, the faithful doorkeepers and secretaries, are small
businessmen and clerical workers, as is generally the case in fraternal
orders. The membership of several hundred reaches down into the
uncertain margins of the lower-middle class and perhaps beyond. Its
clubrooms, bowling alleys, and billard tables are frequented by the
members of less prestige. In summer it is people of this group who
hold croquet matches on the lodge's special courts. Aided by com-

[3] Another example of the feeling of the English middle classes that they have no obligation to the French in poor circumstances is found in a common complaint concerning the
disposition of school funds. As previously noted, the school tax collected from corporations
is allocated to the Catholic and Protestant schools in proportion to the children in each
system of schools. The English accept the principle that their own poor should be educated
with taxes paid by better-off people. But they complain that "their money," the money
of Protestant-controlled corporations, goes to the education of the numerous children of
poor French people.

forting beer, they play far into the night, amid mutual chaffing about what their respective "old women" will say when they get home.

Local English Catholics, when asked why they do not belong to the local lodge, do not say that it is because the members are French but that "many of them are of a low class," that they are "mostly factory hands of a poor type," or that "it is not a good lodge here." While these may be the true reasons, there are others which are probably more cogent. The English Catholics constantly lean over backward to avoid that identification with the French to which their Catholicism makes them liable. In fact, they make a good many defensive statements to dissociate themselves from certain features of Quebec Catholicism. Most of them are moving up in the world, occupationally and in social connections; they might not even belong to the organization any longer if they lived in English communities, for there is every reason to believe that there is a good deal of social graduation from the Chevaliers de Colomb throughout North America. Certainly, the Cantonville English Catholics have nothing to gain among their English-Protestant colleagues and social companions by associating themselves with so French and so Catholic a group. On the other hand, since their careers depend in no way upon public popularity among the French, there is no positive motive to lead them into the order. If they did join, they have neither the language nor the understanding of the local mentality to win positions of leadership in the lodge in competition with local French citizens.

The Rendezvous Club, the second fraternal order of current importance, grew out of a clique of young men who loafed in and about a soft-drink parlor. The owner, a Greek, organized them into a sports club, of which he remained president for some years. Eventually the club acquired the use of a lot upon which they kept an outdoor hockey rink; a shack used as a warming-house for hockey-players became a place for passing the time and playing cards. None of the members had social prestige. Its list of officers and leading members did not, at the time of our visit, include any man important in other organizations. About that time, however, it became affiliated with a similar club in another city and adopted a ritual. It has since grown to such proportions that men seeking popularity pay attention to it. The mayor and a number of other fairly prominent men have been initiated into it at large festive meetings. The club has also begun to play a part in charitable activities, has officially conducted the sports on St. Jean-Baptiste

Day, and its uniformed marching corps appears in sacred and secular processions.

The promoters and members of the Rendezvous Club are young men of a class whose very existence the church authorities would like to avoid—young men of no great ambition, who play pool, loaf, go to the movies, like to drive about in cars for the fun of it, and engage in sports as players, spectators, and petty gamblers. Yet, while the full encouragement of the church is required to keep the Jeunesse ouvrière catholique going, this undesired estate has established a lively and growing organization. It gives promise of following the familiar line of development from informal loafing clique, to sports club, to an organization of such political importance as to force itself upon the attention of people who would prefer to ignore its existence.

The development of this town-minded association, whose leading promoters were of the lower-middle class, indicates a most significant change in the social structure. The people whom it musters for sociability and action constitute an unpremeditated and unwanted new class which has its social life about that ubiquitous American institution, the Greek soft-drink parlor. If the Greek brought the hangout and the club, the local society had its revenge in his marriage to a French girl, conversion to the Roman church, and the changing of his name from Alexis to Alexandre. He slipped into French-Canadian society at its probably most easy port of entry—the town lower-middle class. By furnishing a pleasant and purposeless hangout he became a popular personage; he also brought a little sophistication to the organizing of local sports. The trophy cups which he donated gave an example of a kind of generosity to which the frugal rural French Canadian is not accustomed but to which his town-bred children—to whom parental frugality is beginning to appear restrictive—may be attracted. Free of all sense of mission and of pretension, the Greek became the center of a group likewise free of these meritorious but often resented qualities. In spite of its growth in numbers and importance, the Rendezvous Club is still a somewhat free and open place in the close-knit local society; not a portal for the entrance of new doctrines, but simply a place where young men may declare their freedom from rural tradition and family control by loafing, by small spending, and by engaging in recreation for its own sake and without the patronage of their elders or betters. The pattern is one familiar wherever—in North America at least—people of rural cast have been drawn into cities.

The sports organizations are of the two familiar kinds—those which maintain teams which play before the people or provide facilities for public use and those which provide facilities for a closed group of members.

Cantonville, like other Canadian towns, supports a hockey team in winter and a baseball team in summer. The town French Canadian plays at and watches these games from early boyhood. If the taste for them is new to anyone in Cantonville, it is because he came from England. The English Canadian and French Canadian, being equally devoted to these sports, can co-operate to maintain the teams. The city council grants some money for them. One industry gives the use of land for a ball field; the others give jobs to support the players. The managers of industries serve on the committees who organize and promote the town sports. The various soft-ball, croquet, and bowling leagues are supported and participated in by French people only. An outlying working-class parish has tennis courts and other recreational facilities for its people, who are all French. A large industry has its own sports club. Its curling rink and bowling green are patronized by homesick, old-country English clerks and foremen. The tennis courts of this industrial club are frequented mainly, although not entirely, by English staff members, clerks, and the families of executives. Not much mixing of English and French takes place about them. All of the sports enterprises thus far mentioned require a supporting patron. Where the whole community is concerned, as in maintaining the hockey and baseball teams, the managers of industries share this role with French townspeople. People of the two ethnic groups sit side by side to watch the games. The lesser teams, which engage in local tournaments, are supported by French people; and only French participate.

The closed sports associations include two snowshoe clubs, a tennis club, a small badminton club, and a golf club. The snowshoe clubs, an established feature of Quebec town life, do more sociable parading and drinking than snowshoeing. They require little equipment except the gay costumes in which the members occasionally parade. The two snowshoe clubs in our community are simply rival cliques of French businessmen of moderate importance or less. One of them has elected a couple of English industrial managers to honorary membership.

Tennis, badminton, and golf require more equipment. They are also games of the classes rather than of the masses. The tennis club consists of the young adult sons and daughters of the better families, of young business and professional men and their wives, who probably could not afford to join the golf club, and of a few unattached white-collar young men and women who are socially presentable. Two English members, designers in smaller industries without sports facilities, came to the courts only for quick matches. The French members fore-gathered of an evening to chat and to pass the time sociably as well as to play tennis. From time to time, clubs came from other towns for a Sunday-afternoon tournament, a picnic on the river shore, and a dance in the best hotel. The courts were the rendezvous of the more select young people of the community.

The tennis club has a hidden subsidy, for its courts were built and are maintained by the power company on the latter's property. About the time of our visit, a strong movement arose among local taxpayers to reduce or remove the company's tax concessions. Whether to counteract this movement or not, the company about that time allowed the Chevaliers de Colomb to build croquet courts on ground near the tennis courts, and there was talk of the town's being allowed to use the company's whole tract near the river as a public park. Pressure from somewhere forced the tennis club to extend its membership to a large number of the Chevaliers de Colomb the following season. These moves brought a large number of players of a lower class to the courts. All of this was much resented by the members of the club, some of whom stopped playing on this account. It was a frequent sight to see the former members of the club come to the courts and shortly go away muttering because they were crowded with people "who won't take their turns" or "who can't play tennis anyway." These young people wanted not merely to play tennis but to play with people of their own class. Since they were dependent upon a sort of subsidy from the English officials of the power company, they could not protect their club when those officials felt it expedient to make gestures for public good will by offering recreational facilities to a larger number of local people. The parents of the club members, some of whom have a stake in the power company (as professional men sometimes retained by it and as political figures who must bend to the wind of local movements), were helpless to prevent the ruin of their own children's club. The point of this is that the economic dominance of an English corporation in this case was felt in a matter affecting the relationship of the social classes of the French society. The people adversely affected were of such position that they could not openly express resentment against what they regarded as outside interference.

The golf club is the recreational center for the leading English industrial managers and for those of their staffs who can afford it. Its members also include most of the leading French Canadians, although many of the latter play but little.

The overhead costs of the golf club are so heavy that English and French—if they are to play at all—must support a common club. Even so, something like a subsidy is required. A nonresident English representative of the power company bought the one suitable piece of ground, organized the golf club, sold them the land, and took a mortgage on the property. The good golf links then became one of the inducements to bring industries to the community. The mortgage has since been taken over by one of the industries; the treasurer of the industry is the permanent secretary-treasurer of the club. Some of the members think the club has paid too dearly for its ground and is too much controlled by the mortgagor. It is, however, apparent that a golf club was made possible only by these operations, initiated by the financial backers of the power company. The resulting financial condition sets the membership policy of the club.

The club must have as many members as there are moderately presentable people who can pay the fees. The people who can, and do, include practically all of the English industrial people above the rank of foreman and a number of minor office workers who mingle socially with the staff. They include those of the French population who are minded to play golf and to take part in the social life that goes with it. The result is a mixed group from the top ranks of the local society down to a point fading off into minor white-collar workers. The golf club makes a mingling place for the upper part of the two ethnic groups. The women's golf-bridge parties bring together women of the same class. French and English meet as formally equal members. Each member is presumably in the club because he himself wants to play and to have such associations as the club offers. The English are not in it, as they are on the committee of the baseball club, patrons of a worthy civic cause, although they fill the offices and are the prime movers. They play more avidly; some go from work to golf to bed, altering the schedule only on Sunday, when they don't work. Their wives play during the day and attend golf-club bridge-teas.

Golf is not so important as this to the French. They enter less into the fiercely competitive fraternity of golfers. For one thing, they have more family and other local connections. The English, practically without civic interests, find in the golf club their only antidote to work. Among the French, membership in the golf club and participation in the life of what is regarded as the most sophisticated group of the community is apparently sought by those who are less devoted to the traditional local concerns. They are the town's "smart set" of French Canadians. They must find this life with the English for the simple reason that the town could not support two golf clubs. But the mixing is not complete. At golf-club dances there was a tendency for the cliques to separate for supper and for the drinking, done in private rooms of the hotel. It was a pretty complete separation of French from English. At bridge-teas of the women's golf club the conversation tended to be English. The French women were a little out of the main conversation. In both the men's and the women's groups the French are a minority—24 French among 101 men, and 12 French among 56 women.

Some of the English group who play golf in summer have formed a club to play badminton, a very English sport, in winter. It requires a hall. The hall is that of the Anglican church. The badminton club thus gets a certain attachment to the Anglican church. Yet the same French women who are among the more active at the golf club turn out to play badminton under these very English and Protestant auspices. These women, French and English, are the young to middle-aged "smart set." That this group should be predominantly English and that the sports engaged in should be those of the English upper classes in Canadian towns is some indication of what happens when there is ethnic mixing at this social level.

INTEREST GROUPS

The voluntary associations openly and primarily devoted to economic interests reflect, in their memberships, the places of French and English in economic life. The Canadian Manufacturers' Association includes only people who can speak with authority for some industry and some who will and can be of influence in promoting public measures favorable to industry. In Cantonville such people—few in number—are nearly all English. The proprietors' league, the retail merchants' association, and the Catholic labor unions are French for the simple reason that the people of proper interests to join them are nearly all French. The only really ethnically mixed interest group, the chamber of commerce, is so by virtue of having a membership of diverse occupations. It includes, along with the leading business and professional men, many representatives of industry.

Although the composition of these groups may be due primarily to the distribution of French and English among the economic positions, people generally regard the relation between ethnic affiliation and economic interest as more than an incident of an impersonal process of competition. Some of the associations openly—and others, implicitly—identify their economic interests with their ethnic group and traditions.

The Canadian Manufacturers' Association represents the most powerful economic force of the community. Given the necessity of culti-

DIAGRAM VII

ETHNIC COMPOSITION OF INTEREST GROUPS*

	English	French
Canadian Manufacturers' Association............		
Chamber of commerce.....	17	64
Retail merchants' association..................		
Proprietors' league.......		
National Catholic labor unions..............		

* The chart does not compare the size of membership of one organization with another, but only the English with the French membership within each organization. The proprietors' league and the labor unions both have some hundreds of members. We are reasonably sure that there are no English members whatsoever in the retail merchants' association and the labor unions. Perhaps as many as four or five people of the old nonindustrial English families belong to the proprietors' league. The French members of the Canadian Manufacturers' Association include the managers of the smaller industries and a few leading men of commercial interests who had a hand in bringing industry to the town.

vating the good will of a French public, it is not to be expected that the English leaders of this association would allow themselves any official expression of a conflict of interest between the ethnic elements.[4] The theme of the public pronouncements of the Manufacturers' Association is that what is good for industry is good for all. In the chamber of commerce, where English industrial managers join with French businessmen, any expression of ethnic sentiment would jeopardize the

[4] The Board of Trade of Montreal, which represents the larger businesses and is predominantly English, likewise avoids any reference to ethnic difference. In private, however, the members express themselves on the subject rather bitterly. A French *chambre de commerce*, composed, in the main, of representatives of smaller concerns, does make use of ethnic symbols in speaking of economic interests.

unity of the association. In private, English people of the kind who belong to one or both of these associations do speak of their problems in ethnic terms.

Every interest which has formed the basis of an association in our community is, in fact, publicly or privately, talked of in ethnic terms. Only French organizations, however, publicly identify the interests of job, property, and business with their ethnic group. The retail merchants' association makes this identification most explicitly.

The French Canadians consider that retail business is their special and rightful domain which chain stores, department stores, and mail-order houses unjustly invade. The retail merchants' association accordingly directs against these intruders the slogan: *Achetez chez nous* ("Buy from our own"). The leading spirits of the local association also were active promoters of a nationalistic fraternal order designed to wean French Canadians from the Chevaliers de Colomb. The connections of attitude are revealed in the following note from our diary:

Mr. Raimbault, a small merchant, talked of the *Achat chez nous* movement, of the problem of the small merchant as against the chain stores, how race should be put above small savings at chain stores, and how, in the long run, you don't save at the chain stores anyway. "The Chevaliers de Dollard split off from the Chevaliers de Colomb because they take anyone at all who is a Catholic; he could be a Chinaman or a Negro. But we Chevaliers de Dollard are French as well as Catholic. It is a question of race. For me, it is a little *outrancé*. . . . ." [Shrug.] He then went straight back to the chain-store question.

Although this interview does not mention Jews, the general movement, of which *Achetez chez nous* is a slogan, is also strongly anti-Semitic. Not only are the chain stores called Jewish; but the Jew is, in fact, the only kind of outsider who, in this and similar communities, has successfully invaded the field of small retail trade itself. The local Jewish merchants do not belong to the retail merchants' association.

A milder degree of the same spirit prevails in the proprietors' leagues in Quebec towns. The members are, in the main, people whose real property is their chief possession. In Cantonville the small owners think that they pay out of their small purses what the "millionaire" industries save by reduced assessments and outright exemption from municipal taxes. The few English industrial people who own houses would not belong to an organization whose definition of interest expresses some conflict with industry. A very few English nonindustrial people do belong. The ethnic feeling is perhaps milder than in the retail merchants' association, but it is undeniably present.

The National Catholic Labor Syndicates of Canada use the term "national" in their formal propaganda to distinguish themselvés from the international American Federation of Labor and Congress of Industrial Organizations. Freedom of international taint figures about equally with their conformity to papal encyclicals on the labor problem. Although the leaders do not define the syndicates as definitely French-Canadian, the movement is so thought of both by its members and by its opponents. Executives of industry call the syndicates "nationalistic," a phrase which they sometimes preface with "red."[5] The attitude of organizers and members appears in the following notes, taken from a speech at a syndicate rally in Cantonville:

If the syndicates are inferior to the other unions, it lies not in the syndicates but in the members. The chaplains give sufficient moral guaranty [that the unions will stay within bounds of religious rule], but the real work lies with the laymen. Three hundred completely organized workers of other nationalities recently proved themselves stronger than 3,000 unorganized French Canadians in the Montreal dress strike. When we are organized 100 per cent, we can make the employers recognize us as the sole union.

A priest from another town was more explicit:

The syndicates in Allouette now have 1,200 members; one must be in the syndicate to work in Allouette. [*Applause.*] The Catholic workers should be in a union with Catholics. The *Canadien* should be in a union with *Canadiens* only. [*Great applause.*] There are three stages:

1. The employer allows syndicate members to work for him.
2. The employer recognizes the syndicate, and the workers must belong; but the employer chooses the workers.
3. Syndicate chooses the workers. [*Great applause, but note that it came right after the emphasis on "Canadien." The national references were less frequent but more applauded than the Catholic ones.*]

The conception of the completely closed shop developed at this rally was that of one closed to workers other than French-Canadian Catholics. At other such meetings reference was made to "foreign" employers. Many French working people feel that they have something of an enemy both in the non-French employer and in the competing non-French worker.

The mediating organization of the town is the *chambre de commerce.* Founded in 1901 by French people, it has a long tradition in the town. After a period of somnolence, it was eventually revived by an English bank manager. He said of it:

[5] The phrases "red priests," "anti-English," "Fascist," and "Catholic communists" were all used by English people in Montreal in referring to French strikers and their leaders in a Canadian aluminum plant in 1941.

I called a meeting to see whether the members wanted to continue the chamber; headquarters had threatened to revoke the charter. We revamped the whole thing and started having a monthly 6:30 dinner meeting at the hotel instead of the old evening meeting. It used to meet in a little smoky hall and talk to all hours of the night. It was deadly dull. We close the dinner meeting now at 8:00 or 8:30, so that the members can keep evening engagements. It is hard to keep discussion down. There are a few soreheads and spiteful members who oppose anything proposed by their enemies. I have insisted that the president be changed every year and that every second one be French. It is important to have the right president. Talon is the best man possible, but there may not always be enough good men to fill the job.

We allow no politics in the meetings; sometimes we send a resolution to the mayor. We have discussed roads, streets, street signs, railway service, phone service, and mail delivery. It was our chamber that first took up the matter of getting new phone equipment, and now we have it.

After this revival, the minutes were recorded in English for the first time. The English industrial people who are active in the chamber speak with something of a patronizing air of it and of the French members.

Early minutes show the chamber encouraging the people of the county to trade in Cantonville. Later it became interested in getting industry to come to town, supported tax concessions to new industries, and helped form a syndicate to buy the large hotel which the power company also helped to procure. It now promotes more urban services in the town and attempts to keep the peace between town and industry. In this new role it has, for the first time in its history, a considerable English membership—17 out of a total of 64 in 1937. Of the 17 English, 16 are executives of industries or other concerns representing outside capital, while only 9 of the French—and not the more important of them—represent outside interests. This fact and the alternating of English and French presidents suggest the essentially diplomatic role of the organization. It does not so much pursue a clear line of action as foster a feeling of common interest between the English industrial managers, speaking for their employing corporations, and the French local businessmen, speaking for themselves.

The role of French and English in these groups suggests the alignment which one might expect in the case of an open conflict of interest. In our community there have been three strikes, all led by the syndicates against English managements. One of them we observed. The curés tacitly blessed it by holding prayers for peaceful conduct and a "just" solution. English people, so far as we could observe, all opposed the workers' claims and were inclined to tell much more harrowing versions of the few riotous incidents than did even those French who were opposed. Although we could not take a census on the matter, it seemed that the French people of larger business interests were against the strikers, on the grounds that strikes would keep new industries from establishing plants there. Some smaller merchants favored the strikers, with the argument that better wages meant more money to spend.

A more recent and severe strike has occurred since the war started. We did not observe it, but the ethnic rift seems to have been sharper than in the first. At least one French Canadian of some standing, and of a clique opposed to the strikers, is said to have lost a profitable connection with industry for his failure to support the company vigorously. While many French thought that the strike was a great mistake, others of business and professional class thought it was justified and that the company had acted unfairly. The strikers and their supporters certainly thought of their struggle in ethnic terms; the management did likewise. But at least some French people apparently acted more on a basis of class position than of ethnic affiliation.

THE FRATERNITY OF SUCCESSFUL MEN

In American towns one generally finds associations which—whatever their overt purposes and activities—muster and delimit the fraternity of successful men. The golf club and the chamber of commerce do this in Cantonville. Membership in these two associations is a matter of civic class. Civic class is a male affair; the wives of the men who have it need not call on each other. In addition to some basic consensus as to economic and other public matters, the members must have something in the way of personal accomplishment, must show an interest in affairs somewhat beyond the limits of their own trades, and must be moderately presentable.

Every important layman in Cantonville—whether English industrial man or French man of the town—belongs to one or both of these associations. In many of the town organizations the more influential men participate only as patrons who, by virtue of their positions, assist in the provision of services for other classes of people or for the community at large. In the golf club and the chamber of commerce they appear, formally at least, as peers of the other members. The two associations bring together, nominally as equals, men from the highest ranks down to an undefined margin somewhere above the bottom of the business class and also somewhere above the industrial working class. Both are ethnically mixed. We propose to analyze the memberships of these associations and their overlapping with those of other associations. The purpose is to get a closer view of the nature and extent of the knitting of the French and English elements.

The chamber of commerce serves as the instrument of civic action for the leading men of affairs. Its monthly dinners furnish men of this kind their only opportunity to eat and talk together with common class interests taken for granted.[6] The economically most powerful men may engage in the talk and festivity with that condescension which men exhibit when keeping smaller businessmen properly oriented. And somewhere down the scale one finds the men who, although flattered to eat and smoke a cigar in the company of the biggest men in town, must be annually persuaded that the money and effort spent in the association redound to their individual advantage.

The golf club provides the community's most expensive and exclusive sport. The players, if not social equals, must at least be mutually acceptable companions at the nineteenth hole and at the annual dinner, where the club champion fills his trophy cup with champagne for the assembled company. The golf club has no place for men who would ruin the game by expression of undiplomatic national or religious sentiments or of unorthodox views concerning business, labor, or the future of the country.

Of the 157 men in the two organizations, 77 are French and 80 are English. Seventy-five are men of business and professional occupations; 82 are employed in industry. The golf club had 95 members; the chamber of commerce, 89. The near equality of the two ends of these several dichotomies, of no significance in itself, makes certain contrasts apparent. The 80 English are, of course, a much larger fraction of all English in the community than are the 77 French of their group. Naturally, most of the French (68) are of nonindustrial occupations, while most of the English (73) are industrial. And it was to be expected that the French businessmen would predominate in number in the chamber of commerce and that many of them would belong to this association but not to the golf club, while the English industrial men would constitute the majority in the golf club and many of them would belong to it alone. These things are so. Each organization is a mustering ground for one of the two kinds of successful men most common in the community.

Twenty-seven men, of whom 14 are French and 13 are English, belong to both associations. Five of the English are nonindustrial, but

[6] There are no service or luncheon clubs in the community. The Canadian Manufacturers' Association is too limited in membership and too specialized in its interests to serve as a fraternity of successful men.

they are like the industrial men in that they are hired managers, responsible for keeping local good will for their employers. Twelve of the 14 French are business or professional men; one is the most important French industrial man of the community. The last is a minor clerk. With the exception of the clerk, the 27 who belong to both organizations are important men. Most of them are the most important men in their fields of endeavor. Each organization roots in its own system of things, but their tops are intertwined.

The 46 French business and professional men who belong to the chamber of commerce alone include a few men of great importance

TABLE 32

MEMBERS OF THE GOLF CLUB AND THE CHAMBER OF COMMERCE
OF CANTONVILLE BY ETHNIC GROUP AND OCCUPATION, 1937

| OCCUPATIONS | MEMBERS OF— | | | TOTAL |
	Chamber Only	Both	Golf Club Only	
French nonindustrial...........	46	12	10	68
French industrial...............	3	2	4	9
English nonindustrial..........	2	5	0	7
English industrial.............	11	8	54	73
Total....................	62	27	68	157

and influence. One of them is a lawyer and politician whose recreational life centers about his large family. Others among them are French men of some importance in local life who live very much according to the quieter French-Canadian standards. They include, however, a much larger number of less prominent people who would naturally identify themselves with a civic body such as the chamber of commerce but who would neither aspire to, nor think they could afford, the kind of sport and fellowship found in the golf club.

The 54 English industrial men in the golf club alone include, likewise, men of some importance. But there is some difference between their positions in industry and those of the men who belong to both. In a large industry a man may be in an important position and in charge of a large number of employees without having the responsibility for maintaining the public good will of the company. That falls to the general manager or to someone delegated by him. Thus, a chief engineer may not belong to the chamber of commerce, while the less important office or personnel manager will. This is shown, in reverse, by the fact that three managers of small industries belong to the chamber of commerce but not to the golf club. In each such case the industry is too small to have a group of English colleagues in the higher positions; the manager himself keeps contact with the community through the chamber of commerce but is a little outside the fraternity of English industrial men. These managers are thought of as "queer ducks" by the other English industrial men. The golf club reaches below such men, however, into the lower managerial and white-collar ranks of the larger industries. Some men make a considerable financial sacrifice to identify themselves, through the golf club, with those higher in the industrial hierarchy. They would have no mandate to speak in the councils of the chamber of commerce.

No lawyer belongs to the golf club. The lawyers in our community still depend for their living upon local business and politics rather than upon industry. On the other hand, no physician belongs to the chamber of commerce alone; one, who has political aspirations and is physician to an industry, belongs to both the chamber of commerce and the golf club. Three specialized physicians, new to the community, belong to the golf club alone. No dentist belongs to the chamber of commerce, but two belong to the golf club. The specialized physician and the dentist have not so solid a place in the traditional system of things as does the family physician. In Cantonville, at least, the older physicians with connections in the community are not found in either the golf club or the chamber of commerce. The newer men—specialists and dentists—identify themselves, through the golf club, with the new, more urban order of things. Few as they are in number, their behavior suggests that French Canadians who take up more urban and specialized occupations, even of the nonindustrial type, may find their social and recreational life less in the old Quebec system of family gatherings and salon and more in the formal clubs of the English type.

Our community is too small for the various types of successful people each to establish a separate and exclusive association. Only by some formal co-operation and mixing can they provide the facilities for recreation and an instrument for civic action. At the upper levels of success they are disposed so to co-operate. Our observations indicate that the formal co-operation is greater than the informal mixing, even in recreation.[7]

[7] In the text we have, in the interest of brevity, omitted a detailed analysis of the persons in each of the more or less unexpected positions in Table 32. For instance, there are 10 nonindustrial French who, contrary to expectation, belong only to the golf club. In the

If, in these two associations, there seems to be some intertwining of the upper ranks of the two ethnic elements, it still remains true that the French of the upper ranks have many more connections in other associations of the town. The 14 French who belong both to the golf club and to the chamber of commerce hold 39 offices in other local organizations; the corresponding 13 English hold only 19. In only 5 of the 23 organizations so linked were there both French and English officers. These leading French Canadians appear both as directing patrons and as active members in many organizations. The English participate in other community organizations only as patrons who lend their names and influence, except in the Protestant churches and a few small purely English associations. The French have won leadership in competition with their fellows. The English have only such leadership as comes ex officio to men of authority. The mixing of successful English with successful French in these two associations does not presage any tendency for English to take an active role in the general associational life of the community.

---

text we noted that 5 of them are dentists or medical specialists. Of the remaining 5, 2 are students, sons of a member of the golf club. They are too young to be in the chamber of commerce and have no occupations. One is simply the steward of the golf club, who is hardly an equal member. There remain the only two cases of successful local French businessmen who belong to the golf club but not to the chamber of commerce.

Similarly, there are 11 English industrial men who belong only to the chamber of commerce. We mentioned in the text that some are managers of the smaller industries. All but 2 of these are, in fact, people regarded as queer by the industrial fraternity. Two, for instance, are thought to be Jewish. Another is European in birth and education. Of the 2 English nonindustrial men who belong to the chamber of commerce only, one is a railroad agent who does not have a place in the industrial fraternity but who promotes the interests of his employers by dealing with the chamber of commerce on matters of transportation services. The other is one of the few English entrepreneurs of the community.

We offer this kind of analysis with trepidation, because of the danger of finding good reasons which might fit our conception of what is happening in the community. Yet it is not without significance that a good reason meets the eye for almost every case in which an individual seems to be behaving in a way somewhat out of line with his ethnic and occupational connections.

CHAPTER XIV

RELIGIOUS AND PATRIOTIC CEREMONY

THE French Canadians and their English compatriots are citizens of one country. Both follow the Christian calendar. Yet on no great day do they celebrate in common ceremony an equal and unaffected loyalty to symbols whose meaning is the same for both. They are ceremonially separate peoples.

This point, significant because ceremonial marks the line between "us" and "them," is one of the themes of the following pages. The other theme follows from the frequently attested fact that urban ceremonial differs from that of rural folk.[1] The two themes run together in our community and in Quebec generally because "they," the English, are the most active agents of urbanization and are the people in authority in the large industries which bring "us," the French Canadians, to town.

The Catholic religious calendar, always richer than the Protestant, is especially so in Quebec. The English are each year astonished anew to see the French carry the Sacred Host through the streets in their *Fête-Dieu* procession. The French are sometimes shocked that the eve of their two days of devotion to the dead, All Saints' Day and the Day of the Dead, should be for the English merely a night for practical joking and masquerade parties. Several days of obligation, completely unknown to Protestants, fill the Catholic churches. Every year organized pilgrimages take hundreds of Cantonville people to Ste Anne de Beaupré and to a lesser shrine on a day devoted to blessing vehicles. Even lowly bicycles, gaily decorated, are ridden in a procession which becomes a race across country to be blessed at the door of a church.

The religious occasions common to both elements are separately and differently observed. No sanctions, except those of the capricious individual conscience, enforce Lenten deprivation among even the Anglicans; other Protestant denominations are unfriendly to such practice. Among the French, clerical authority combines with family and general opinion to enforce specific rules of fast and the cessation of public social events. As Easter approaches, a French town is heavy with the

[1] See Robert Redfield, "Folkways and City Ways," in Herring and Weinstock (eds.), *Renascent Mexico* (New York, 1935).

odor of sanctity. The premature elation of Palm Sunday is quickly extinguished by the approaching blackness of Good Friday. On Saturday people come to town to shop for Easter feasting, spruce themselves up, and fill the taverns, which have been half-deserted during Lent. Food stores are decorated; and hams, the special meat for breaking the fast, are decked with paper rosettes and bright ribbons. The churches are full of people coming to confess, to pray, and to carry away holy water from tubs placed in the vestibules.

On Easter Day itself the whole community is alive with pious elation. In the city of Quebec, the religious capital of the province, the feeling is more intense than an American Protestant can imagine.

All of this the English Protestants view with detached interest. Their own Easter is very tame in comparison. After Easter the social festivities are more gay and numerous among the French. One has also the impression that the custom of wearing smart new clothes on Easter is even more marked among French than among English. Certainly the Easter High Mass, as well as the coming and going before and after it, impresses one much more both as religious festivity and as a parade of people dressed in their best than does the Protestant counterpart.[2]

The central feature of the French-Canadian Christmas is the midnight Mass. In the great Notre Dame Church of Montreal, the near-great of the city arrive in state and, as they make their way down the long aisles to their family pews, nod to acquaintances and even stop to shake hands. In our community, families occupy their pews, and the leaders of the community seem to be more conspicuous than at regular parochial High Mass. The hundreds upon hundreds who receive communion keep busy at the rail as many priests as can be spared from the singing of the Mass. But the mood is of public festivity rather than of private piety. After the Mass the people greet each other. The local newspaper reports the affair with loving enthusiasm, referring to the ideally clear and cold starry night, to the fulness of the church, to the presence of distinguished persons, to the brilliancy of the Mass itself, the music, the candles, the crèche, and finally to the merry exchange of greetings in the small hours. "The *fête du Noël* was celebrated in our churches with *éclat*," is the appropriate beginning of every such account.

Christmas is essentially a religious fete, and the church does its best

[2] Part of the impression may be due to relative number. The English are, after all, too few to make much of a procession to and from church. Furthermore, they come to church in cars and do not walk about the streets much.

to keep it so. Pulpit and newspaper homilies warn the people against the American commercial Christmas, competitive gift-giving, against using the day for secular amusements, and even against that "dirty old graybeard, Santa Claus, to whom are attributed powers belonging only to the Christ-child." Town and city French Canadians give their leaders some reason for such warnings. The stores advertise holiday gifts and enjoin people to buy early, but from their own people rather than from strangers. But there is, in our community at least, no suggestion of the decline of the festive midnight Mass. And New Year's Day remains, as in the past, the day for exchanging greeting cards and gifts. It, too, is given religious solemnity by the traditional return of children to their paternal home to receive, on bended knee, the father's formal blessing. This custom is likewise idealized, and people are warned against its evident decline. New Year's Eve carousal is especially attacked as an alien custom which leaves people in no fit state for a paternal religious blessing.

The French-Canadian holiday season shows a closer relation between secular gaiety and public religious festivity than does the English Protestant. It is this connection that clergy and national leaders seek to preserve. While the English pattern seems to be making some headway, the publicly religious character of the holiday season does not seem, in our community, to have waned.

All the public ceremonies which we observed or of which we read reports brought together religious and civil authorities, as well as organizations of both religious and secular character. The configuration varies somewhat, but the central features remain the same, as may be seen in the diagram of functionaries and organizations who appeared in four public processions.

The central figure in all such processions is a group of clergy, usually including the curé, and of city officials, always including the mayor. This group appears at the point of greatest honor, near the rear of the procession, followed only by a rear guard of lesser people. If the Host is carried through the streets, this group will be gathered about it. At a Eucharistic Congress in the city of Quebec the pattern was the same, but the dignitaries were of greater magnitude. The Cardinal Archbishop of Quebec, primate of all Canada, carried the Sacred Host, accompanied by a papal guard, by members of the provincial cabinet and of the dominion parliament, as well as by the mayor and other prominent citizens. When a new bishop made his first official visit to our community, the mayor and the local member of the provincial legislature escorted him from the outskirts of town to the presbytery, where a great crowd had gathered to receive him. Although these two officials were political and personal enemies, they were bound, as the

DIAGRAM VIII

FUNCTIONARIES AND ORGANIZATIONS IN PUBLIC PROCESSIONS

	Visit of New Bishop	Fête-Dieu	St. Jean-Baptiste	Funeral of Young Man
Officials:				
Clergy	X	X	X	X
Mayor	X	X	X	X
Member of legislature	X			X
City councilors		X	X	X
Musical and uniformed corps:				
Church choir		X		X
Town band	X		X	X
School boys' band	X		X	
Garde d'Honneur	X	X	X	
Rendezvous Drum Corps	X	X		
Filles d'Isabelle (drill corps)	X	X		
Church- and school-sponsored youth groups:				
School boys		X		
School girls		X		
Scouts catholique		X		X
Parish youth	X			
Action catholique de la Jeunesse canadienne			X	
Jeunesse ouvrière catholique	X			
Jeunesse ouvrière catholique féminine	X			
Piety organizations:				
Ligue catholique féminine	X	X		
Femmes tertiaires		X		
Sacré Cœur (men)	X	X		
Fraternal orders:				
Chevaliers de Colomb	X	X	X	
Union St. Joseph	X	X	X	
Club Rendezvous			X	X
Labor:				
Catholic workers unions	X		X	
Business firms (floats)			X	

highest civil dignitaries of the community, to appear together to greet the new religious authority. On these occasions it is the civil authorities who do the religious authority honor, but at the same time they are claiming their own recognized place in relation to the religious hierarchy and religious symbols.

The following account, taken from diary notes, gives something of the flavor of a public religious festival.

The Fête-Dieu

This is the big outdoor religious festival of the year. The houses are hung with bunting and flags—the Union Jack, the French tricolor, the Sacred Heart, the Cross and Fleur-de-lis of the old regime. Large banners hung across the street read: "Jesus the Host, give us peace," "Be favorable to our people." One on the hospital asks: "Jesus the Host, Bless our work, Bless our houses."

After a brief High Mass without sermon, the Garde d'Honneur marched into church and blared a trumpet salute before escorting the Sacred Host to the street. Meanwhile the marching groups were gathering in the streets; and the spectators, in the park and along the curbs. Finally the procession moved south from the church. The onlookers knelt as the Host approached and passed: it was like a gentle breeze dipping the heads of grain across a field in a slow wave. The piety was unaffected, but people clicked their cameras even as they prayed aloud. To a Protestant the procession seems a queer mixture of showy parade and deep piety. Pride in smart uniforms and marching was evident among the young men. Drum majors strutted with high steps and twirled their sticks dangerously. Marshals gave orders sharply and officiously.

As the procession turned west, it passed under an archway of evergreen, surmounted by a motto. Birch boughs were planted along the route.

At the Academy the organized groups were deployed about the grounds and massed, leaving a way open for the Host and escort to reach the altar on the school steps. The women were put off into the corners, while the men's organizations massed in the more central places. The massing took some time. Meanwhile women knelt and prayed hard and fast, fingering their rosaries. Old, poorly dressed women in black knelt longer and prayed harder.

The lay brother, principal of the Academy, led the schoolboys in prayers, which were responded to by all near enough to hear him. "Marie, pleine de grâce ... ." Other persons led out in other parts of the grounds, until there was a continual sound of high, strong voices leading and an unbroken lower-pitched murmur of response. Greetings and chatting could be heard, too. Finally the Garde and the Sacred Host reached the altar. The mayor and councilors awaited near by as a sort of reception committee for the Body of Christ.

The altar, erected on the steps, was surmounted by a red crown with a gold cross. High above on a small gallery stood six girls, like angels, with white robes and crowns, each with a silvered star in front. They stood silent and motionless throughout the ceremony.

The crowd massed before the altar looked very impressive. In one corner was a patch of white, the veils of school girls; in the center, the blue, maroon, and white hats of uniformed groups. Across the street a couple of three-story apartment houses were decked with bunting and flags from top to bottom, and every gallery was full of people who looked both gay and pious.

After a benediction with chanting, the Host was elevated and the trumpets blared a triumphant salute while the multitude knelt. The parade slowly formed again, the women and children first under the firm marshaling nuns, and the Host at the rear. As God the Host was carried through the streets to His temple, the bells of the church pealed continually in full sound.

The whole affair gives one a sense of what a Catholic community is. Mr. Vallée, "the richest man" in town, with rosary in hand, marched and sang. The mayor and councilors were there. Yet I felt that certain important people were not there. Mr. Genest and Mr. Jonquière, the most nearly aristocratic men of the community, were almost certainly not there. I am sure I would have noticed them pass me in the procession. Nor did I notice any of the people of the sporty golf-club set. I wonder if they would feel self-conscious. Interestingly enough, the organizations in the parade included none representing trades, occupations, and estates. The Catholic labor unions, the Jeunesse ouvrière catholique, and the chamber of commerce were not there as labeled groups, although, of course, many of their members marched. The people marched as the faithful of various ages and of the two sexes and under the devices of special piety groups and fraternal orders.

Some English young people who drove out from Montreal for tennis matches were two hours late. The processions in every country parish had delayed them. They were a little annoyed at being late, but also somewhat curious. Otherwise the local English knew little of this. They were not in the procession or among the spectators. They hardly knew it was to happen, although the local paper had been full of instructions in advance. It was nothing to the English, and they weren't missed.

PATRIOTIC HOLIDAYS

For French Canadians, no patriotic holiday approaches in significance the twenty-fourth of June, the day of their patron, St. Jean-Baptiste. It is a saint's day, but not one of religious importance in itself. St. Jean-Baptiste is not a favorite object of personal devotion, nor is Mass obligatory on his day. Although Quebec farmers leave their planting on St. Mark's Day to attend Mass and walk in the procession at which seeds are blessed, they pay little attention to St. Jean-Baptiste.[3] The latter is important chiefly as a symbol of the unity and historic continuity of the French-Canadian people. His day is a patriotic holiday celebrated in town and cities. If the ceremonies are somewhat religious in character, it is because of the close connection of religious and national sentiment expressed in the very fact that the master-symbol of the French Canadians is a saint.

The curé stated the relation of the church to the occasion thus in a sermon: "This week we celebrate our patron, St. Jean-Baptiste. Re-

[3] Miner, *St. Denis*, chap. viii, "The Yearly Round." This chapter, which goes carefully through the rural calendar of work and festivity, does not mention Jean-Baptiste Day. Our own informants agree that farmers work in their fields as usual on Jean-Baptiste Day. There does seem to be some survival among rural children of a custom of lighting bonfires on St. Jean's Eve, but without special reference to its national meaning.

member it is the great fete of our race. The clergy and the church lead you in celebrating it. The church is the center of the fete and of the race."

The newspaper is full of the plans for tomorrow's celebration and for the bonfire (Feu de St. Jean) to be lighted in the Academy grounds this evening. We saw the English school principal and his wife today. They knew nothing of the plans for the celebration. According to him, St. Jean-Baptiste means nothing to the English except that they have to be careful to lay in a supply of groceries the day before, because the stores are to be closed.

At 8:00 P.M. the benches in the park were full—of women and children, which is unusual—and gradually the streets filled with people, also mostly children. About 8:30 the school boys' band marched around the square and took up a position in front of the presbytery. A car then drove up near by, and from it emerged two city aldermen, who proceeded to distribute flags to the children. The flags were of blue, with a white cross in the center and a white fleur-de-lis in each corner. The children had been lined up, without much order, to receive the flags and to march to the academy grounds. The smiling aldermen, besieged by reaching hands, gave out the flags with a magnanimous air. The curé and a couple of city officials stood on the porch of the presbytery to receive the homage of the children. Before the last of the flags were given away, the band played and marched away, followed by several hundred children with flags more or less intact.

At the school grounds a crowd of both adults and children waited for the parade to come. They milled about, not quite knowing where the festivities would center. When the band appeared, the crowd surged toward it and almost blocked its way. After some difficulty the band came to rest and, under the leadership of a little lay brother, played a couple of selections featured by a very unsteady alto solo with trombone obligato. Shortly afterward singing was heard from a little eminence near the pile of evergreen which had been prepared for burning. The disorderly crowd of children, attracted by the singing, rushed to get to the place where something was going on. One little lady of ten or so, in white hat, coat, and gloves, forgot herself and with head down butted her way straight through the ranks of the band.

The singing was a prelude to the lighting of the bonfire. The singers were schoolboys led by lay brothers, some of whom appeared little older than their charges. The songs were not the folk songs of rural Quebec but the formal patriotic songs of school songbooks. The crowd didn't join in even when the boys sang "O Canada." Sometimes even the boys seemed not to know the last verses, and only the brothers sang faithfully to the end. Presently the fire was lighted and flames shot high from the dried evergreen branches. There was a rush of those too close to get away from heat and sparks, and another rush of those too far away to gather in a circle about the fire. Older people stood farther back. On little rises several hundred yards distant sat little groups of workmen calmly smoking their pipes. On an ordinary evening they would have been smoking in similar silence, but on their front porches.

As the fire dwindled, so did the crowd. But groups of boys remained to sing, shout,

[4] Diary account.

and shoot off firecrackers. The lay brothers chatted and laughed with the boys, and finally led a final verse of "O Canada," about "notre patron," St. Jean-Baptiste—a verse that does not appear in the English version sung elsewhere in Canada.

The whole was a rollicking children's affair, led by the official guardians of boys, the lay brothers, and patronized by city officials and the curé. After it was over, an old resident told us this was the first time there had been a St. Jean's Eve fire and celebration of this kind in the town. He didn't know any particular story or legend about the bonfire; it is just to celebrate St. Jean-Baptiste. He said that only larger towns celebrate St. Jean-Baptiste Day at all. In his native rural parish, a few miles away, the farmers pay little attention to the day. It isn't a day of obligation; so they don't have to go to church.

St. Jean-Baptiste Day

The festivities began with a preliminary parade which started from the mother parish church about 9:30 A.M. in this order:

1. The school boys' band.

2. The Catholic labor unions, behind a gold and white banner with a maple-leaf design. The twenty or so men were not smart looking; they were workingmen dressed up for a holiday.

3. Canadian Catholic Youth (A.C.J.C.) banner with a contingent of five men.

4. The Chevaliers de Colomb. Only a few men, and none of the important men of the town.

5. The town band.

6. The Union St. Joseph. The few men were old and rather shabby looking.

7. The banner of the Club Rendezvous, with no followers.

8. The Garde d'Honneur, in uniform.

9. The curé, the mayor, and three aldermen.

The director of the parade, a clerk in a leading drug store, dashed up and down on a horse with a red, white, and blue ribbon in its tail. There were only a few spectators along the route to the village of St. Jerome. At the St. Jerome school ground an altar was set up, with a reredos in white with red and green maple leaves and fleurs-de-lis. In the center was a gold panel with the figure of St. Jean-Baptiste, as a curly headed boy holding a cross. In fact, the St. Jean-Baptiste of French Canada is generally the pleasant shepherd boy with a pet lamb at his heels, not the fanatical. prophet denouncing the license of Herod's court. Streamers of red and gold reached up to the cross on the cornice of the building. A cross of firs capped a canopy of evergreen over the altar. A streamer bore the words: "Ecce Agnus Dei." The nuns, always a little removed from the center of things, watched from the windows of the school building, along with many little girls.

The Garde d'Honneur and the banners were arranged before the altar. An organ and choir were ready near by. The curé and the mayor, with other clergy and aldermen, took front seats.

The crowd, spreading far out over the field, was gay and colorful. The day was bright and just warm enough for the women to appear in summer dresses. As the Mass began, some women who were without hats covered their heads with handkerchiefs. The place had become a church. Most of them had hats and white gloves, for care in such matters reaches down to the poor and humble in French Canada. The kneeling was uneven, except at the Elevation, when it was as deep and silent as in church.

Some women laid down handkerchiefs to protect their stockings when they knelt on the sand.

The Mass was sung by three priests. The celebrant was the curé of a new outlying parish. The curé of the still newer town parish of Ste Anne preached thus:

"Patriotism is a virtue of many nuances. We do not want Bolshevism as in Russia, or imperialism as in Britain, but a true Catholic-French patriotism, centered in the church. True patriotism begins with faith.

"We owe respect to England, our constitutional *patrie;* justice to our compatriots, the English Canadians; but we must insist that they recognize our right to be at home anywhere in Canada. But to the province of Quebec we owe tenderness. Here the blood of our dead has established our true *patrie.*

"Imagine a *petite* parish with a *petite* church at its center, a presbytery hard by with a *petit* curé[5] in it, a *petite* school, a cemetery, a church steeple. An Uncle Jean sits on his front porch and looks up and down the road. He knows the people, his relatives and friends, in every house. But that is not enough in these days. We have new problems to face.

"The patriotic way for the true French Canadian to live is to save and become a small proprietor. English methods are not ours. The French became great by small savings and small business. Don't borrow the commercial ways of others. The prosperity of this community lies with us, not with the industries of England and the United States, but in the number of small proprietors. Our country is not just any place where we make our living, as in the United States.

"Shun United States extravagances—radios, newspapers, and other expensive things and ways. Love your priests, go to Mass, and observe the feasts. It will be a great day when we have a real Catholic patriotism—a patriotism which not only makes every French Canadian ready to die for his country but ready to vote independently of parties."

At the end of the Mass, the crowd sang "O Canada." The parade then took form, but it was much bigger this time. Crowds of men fell in behind the organization banners.

A number of floats joined the procession. One, sponsored by a hardware store, gave homage to "The Patriots of 1837," who led a rebellion which, although condemned by the church at the time, has become an event symbolizing the struggle of the French for their rights in Canada.

The Canadian Catholic Youth float showed the death of a Dr. Chenier at the hands of treacherous redcoats. The municipality of St. Jerome showed a country school, with small boys and girls reciting to a lay girl-teacher and a religious brother; a banner read: "Preserve our French heritage." The most elegant float of all, that of the Catholic labor unions, showed Jean-Baptiste denouncing Herod and his licentious court who were drinking and spilling a red liquid from trophy cups. Salome, in jewels and draperies more than adequate to the rules of modesty, drank with them.

The parade moved back to town with many more spectators than before. Houses were decorated with flags: the blue one with the cross in the center and the fleur-de-

---

[5] This priest is known for his homely language and wit. At a regular Sunday sermon he moves his people to smile and even to laugh. On the present occasion the smiles of the crowd showed that they recognized the half-humorous affection in the repetition of the adjective *petit.*

lis in the four corners, the papal flag of gold and white with miter and keys, and the tricolor of the French Republic. In the city park there were a few Union Jacks. At the Academy there was a stop for a brief ceremony. Schoolboys took an oath to preserve their *patrie*, Christian patriotism, their language and traditions. Again "O Canada" was sung, and the parade went on down through the main streets of town. The only burlesque touch was the driving of a very ancient Ford through the streets by a group of clowning young men. They got into the way of traffic, called out to people, and generally amused themselves and the crowd.

In the afternoon the Club Rendezvous held an athletic field-day for all comers at the ball grounds, but the town was rather quiet.

At night there was a great gathering in the town park. The band played. A grocer distributed candy to a mob of children. Speeches were made. Finally fireworks, furnished by the city, were displayed down by the river. As is usual at band concerts, quite a lot of English people sat in parked cars around the edge of the park, and some watched from the veranda of the large hotel across the street. A few even milled about the crowd in the park.

The evening speakers were a priest, a college boy who delivered himself of an oration which had won him a prize in a school contest, and finally the most nationalistic of the young lawyers of the town. The latter's speech was the *pièce de résistance* of the occasion:

"What are the aspirations of French-Canadian youth? Not to curse the Jews and avoid the English, but to develop *our* talents and to resist their trespassing on our rights. We have many things to be proud of: the memory of our fathers and great men— Dollard, Jeanne Mance, and others. Our fathers came from the *petite noblesse* and peasants of France; they were not convicts and adventurers, as in Australia, the United States, and the rest of Canada. Our province has saved Canada from American invasion and from Communism. But we lack pride in ourselves. We lack orientation and knowledge of our history. We fear the English.

"We have accepted an inferior position in our own country. Our policitians have sold out to foreign financiers. Though our town is nine-tenths French, our main streets are named Sinclair, Bridges, Holmes, etc. We need a good name for this park and for the new park on the river. Our city council is too busy with "important" things to change this. They will hear of it again.

"We do business with the A and P, the Central, Regent, and People's chain stores, which are foreign or Jewish. No French Canadian has the right to buy at the stores of nonpatriots. The Jews have a right to live if they obey the laws and respect Catholicism [*applause*], but they should be our servants, not our masters. The right place for them is down over the hill at the edge of town, like Schwartz, the man who deals in hides and junk, not in the best stores on the main street. [*Laughter.*]

"Is it just that a small minority should dominate our finance and government and hold us in poverty? We are not revolutionaries. But beware, you blind, who have not heeded the lesson of Ireland. There is a man running the big hotel right over there [*pointing at the hotel*] who does not speak French. That is an insult to us.

"Buy at the Bazar Adrien, a real French enterprise, and avoid other stores that sell such goods. Resist the seductions of the United States. Speak our language in buying. Use our flags. A pessimist has said that within fifty years our race will have disappeared. Young Canadians, it is up to you."

After this feast of music and oratory the crowd moved down the hill toward the river to see the fireworks. We went to the back veranda of the hotel and found ourselves in a crowd of English people and some French of the better-off classes. No mention was made of the speeches. Simpson, the manager, the object of the most direct attack of the evening, apparently had not yet heard what was said, although he had been in earshot of the loudspeakers at the time. The next day our old farmer-friend, M. Marquand, laughed about the speeches and said the young lawyer was a little extreme.

All of this was the ambitiously staged celebration of a town that is becoming a city. The bonfire on the eve was no simple folk custom but the consciously organized revival of one. The celebrating crowds, although devoted to the symbols elevated for view, were townspeople enjoying the leisure of a day away from work, not farmers electing to do honor to God and country on a day when the fields cried for their labor. The presence of labor unions, albeit Catholic ones, indicated that a new estate and a new institution have their rightful place among patriots.

The speeches emphasized the problems of an urban and industrial civilization. The priests did so with nostalgic reference to the simpler life and with insistence on the continued efficacy of rural virtues. The young lawyer demanded of his people a more concerted economic and political action to win their proper place in the new order of things.

Yet relations between the sacred and the secular symbols and functionaries is as strong in this celebration as in any. Although the grandiose scale of the affair may be new to recent arrivals from the country and the day itself may be new in their calendar of festivity, the familiar symbols and authorities remain in their accustomed places.

Exactly one week after St. Jean-Baptiste comes Dominion Day, July 1, the greatest of all Canadian national holidays. In the year of which we speak the larger industries were closed on St. Jean-Baptiste Day and remained open on Dominion Day.[6] No public celebration of Dominion Day was undertaken. In some years an unsuccessful attempt had been made to warm up the St. Jean-Baptiste parade for Dominion Day. The French, although Quebec was a consenting party to the Confederation which Dominion Day recalls, are as indifferent to that day as are the English to St. Jean-Baptiste.

Canada's other important holiday is Empire Day, the birthday of Queen Victoria, first British monarch to bear the imperial title. This

[6] The Protestant managers of industries in the German Rhineland were not so wise in the middle nineteenth century. Their insistence on work on Catholic holidays brought on strikes among Catholic workers whom the Socialists had not previously been able to move.

day, May 24, is also the anniversary of the heroic death of one Dollard des Ormeaux, a symbolic French-Canadian figure. At a parade and celebration in the French district of Montreal the speeches were all in honor of Dollard. Our community celebrated the occasion in 1937 with a parade of youth organizations followed by an assembly at which clergy and lay leaders did honor to Dollard and French-Canadian traditions. The leading speaker wound up with the pronouncement that Canadian youth would not fight for the British Empire in Europe or elsewhere.[7]

It is in keeping with modern mentality that the English of Quebec should resent the French attitude to national holidays more than differences in the religious calendar. In Montreal the immense St. Jean-Baptiste parade marches into the section of the city where English people do their business. The latter, starting with a complaint about interruption of traffic and the difficulty of getting to appointments, warm to the subject and call up all the supposed vices and impudence of the French and occasionally suggest that it is time for a Second Conquest.[8] The basic complaint, however, is that the symbols held up for reverence are not those of Canada at large, although a few war veterans and Union Jacks are in the parade, and that, on the holidays of all Canada, the French are—presumably by intent—completely wanting.

In our community the English—many of whom are really old-country English and American, to whom Canadian patriotism means little or nothing—do little except play golf and go on picnics on Empire Day and Dominion Day. Canadians are only slightly more, if at all, addicted to public ceremony than are Americans generally. But the death of King George V and the coronation of George VI brought them to church, and especially to the Anglican church, which is so intimately associated with the crown. Always there is a solid body of sentiment of distinctly religious quality for the crown, for the Empire, and especially for Canada. It is perhaps the awareness that their own

[7] Many English-Canadian students said the same thing in that period. But, for the English, it was pacifism; for the French, it was the expression of a determination to retain their cultural independence.

[8] One must not, however, overlook that many of the English enjoy the parade and even pursue, as a cult, the collection of French-Canadian antiques, build country houses in the old French style, and are generally sentimental about the antiquities of Quebec, which they accuse the French of not appreciating. The tolerance of each other is really very great in Quebec. The St. Patrick's Day parade by the ancient Montreal enemy of French Canadians would be as nothing without French bands and the French mayor and aldermen. Even the Orangemen hold a small, but defiant parade without being molested—or even much noticed.

religiously held patriotic sentiments do not coincide either as to symbols or meaning with those of the French that underlies the very real resentment of French conduct with respect to patriotic holidays. The *petite patrie* of French Canadians seems a threat to the spiritual unity of the large dominion.[9]

The ceremonies which attend birth, marriage, and death show additional evidence of the richness of local French community life, the closeness of weave of the society, and the remoteness of the English from events of great moment to the French.

Baptism musters kin and friends of kin into special roles as godparents and attendants who will be of importance throughout the life of the newborn French-Canadian child. Godparents are usually fairly close kin, and often the priest who officiates is himself a relative. We heard of no case in which an English person assumed the role of godparent for a French child. The religious difference alone could account for this. Every Saturday, except in forbidden seasons, several wedding parties ride noisily through the streets in beribboned cars. English people have no part in French wedding festivities, except for the few cases of mixed marriage. Even then the party is French, for the bride is characteristically a local girl with numerous kin about, while the English groom is alone in the community.[10] One popular English manager was asked to the wedding party of a daughter of one of his French foremen. He was asked and went in the role of kindly patron. It was an unusual role for a man in his position to play in this community.

These are family ceremonials. Funerals, however, often assume the proportions of community events in our town. The evidence lies before the eye in Diagram IX, showing the attendance and tributes at three funerals.[11]

The threads of kinship and other connections reached from these

[9] English people who are meticulous concerning patriotic etiquette especially resent the very cavalier attitude of French Canadians toward national anthems and flags. Even in France we noted that French people didn't stand at attention for the "Marseillaise." In Canada the French pay little attention either to "God Save the King" or to their own "O Canada." It just isn't in their folkways to be silent and stand at attention for national anthems. And they don't care in the least whether the United States flag they put up to attract tourists is above or below the Union Jack or tricolor.

[10] An exceptional case was the marriage of a French girl to an English man in a Protestant church. This was, of course, in defiance of the girl's family. The minister got up a little party for the couple.

[11] The data are from newspaper accounts. We observed two large funerals and many smaller ones.

three deceased persons and their families far out in the web of social relations but not far enough to more than touch the English world. None of these deaths, in fact, touched any English individual in a personal way.

DIAGRAM IX

THREE FUNERALS

	ALBERT (Twenty-eight-Year-Old Son of a Hotel Proprietor)	BERTHIER (Seventeen-Year-Old Seminarian, Son of Prominent Businessman)	COLLETTE (Small Daughter of Mayor, Merchant)
Procession	Police, band, uniformed marching corps, Scouts, 19 priests, choir, 11 members of family, mayor, 4 aldermen, member of legislature, pallbearers, honorary pallbearers	Provincial police, town police, band, 18 priests, choir of priests and laymen, 35 members of family, pallbearers, mayor, council, member of legislature, mayor of seminary town	No account
		Named as Present or Sending Messages	
Public officials	*Local:* Mayor, 4 aldermen, member of legislature, 3 other city officials	*Local:* Mayor, council, member of legislature, Catholic school commission *Nonlocal:* Mayor of seminary town, senator, member of parliament, provincial premier, member of provincial cabinet, member of legislature	*Local:* Town council, police, firemen *Nonlocal:* Mayor
Religious	*Local:* 17 clergy, 2 religious orders *Nonlocal:* 59 clergy, 8 religious orders	*Local:* Clergy not accounted for, 4 religious orders *Nonlocal:* Clergy not accounted for, 3 religious orders	*Local:* Clergy not accounted for, 5 religious orders *Nonlocal:* Clergy not accounted for, 2 religious orders
Organizations and groups	*Local:* Club Rendezvous, proprietors' league, 4 parish organizations, 1 musical society, 1 school group, employees and residents of father's hotel *Nonlocal:* Hotelkeepers' association, Scouts	*Local:* 2 school groups, 4 local musical societies, Chevaliers de Colomb *Nonlocal:* 5 higher school groups, 1 club	*Local:* 4 leading fraternal orders, proprietors' league, 3 sports clubs, Catholic labor unions, 4 other associations *Nonlocal:* 1 college group, retail merchants' association
Professionals	*Local:* 19; *nonlocal:* 16	*Local:* 11; *nonlocal:* 13	*Local:* 15; *nonlocal:* 3
French business and industry	*Local:* 10 businesses	*Local:* 3 businesses,* 1 industry *Nonlocal:* 1 business	*Local:* 11 businesses†
English persons, English institutions, and English-managed industries	*Local:* 1 industrial manager, 1 bank manager, 2 minor industrial executives *Nonlocal:* 5 businesses, 3 persons	*Local:* 1 utility company, 4 minor industrial and utility executives, 1 "old English" *Nonlocal:* 4 wholesale companies, 1 hotel, 6 persons	*Local:* 3 industries, 3 industrial managers, 7 minor industrial and utility executives, 3 women, Anglican minister, women's association of United church *Nonlocal:* 12 wholesalers, 3 businesses, 1 utility executive, 11 persons
Total number of messages‡	*Local:* 246; *nonlocal:* 254	*Local:* 88; *nonlocal:* 102	*Local:* 313; *nonlocal:* 135

* One of the three businesses is a French-managed local branch of a large English company.

† Two of the eleven businesses are French-managed branches of large English companies.

‡ Includes telegrams, floral tributes, Masses, condolence cards.

THE ALBERT FUNERAL

Albert was an unmarried man of twenty-eight, a popular member of the lower middle-class Club Rendezvous and son of the proprietor of the most popular locally owned hotel and beer tavern. Although widely known, the young man and his father were not important. Their circle of kinship was extensive, spreading from the "cradle" parish of the family some six miles away.

Young Albert's funeral was accompanied by a public procession on foot, not unlike that of a religious or patriotic holiday, except for the mood. The mayor and councilors, police, the band, schoolboys and Scouts, uniformed marching corps, and numerous citizens marched, as well as the immediate family, relatives, choir, clergy, and honorary and active pallbearers.

In addition to those who honored the defunct and his family by their presence, five hundred persons and institutions—246 from the community and 254 from forty-five other places in Quebec and from five cities in New England—sent messages, floral tributes, or "spiritual bouquets." The latter are cards of sympathy with a promise of prayers or Masses for the soul of the deceased. These persons and institutions were all mobilized in the space of a couple of days by the death of a not very notable young man.

Kin.—The deceased and his father and mother were all born in a near-by rural parish. Residents of the parish turned out *en masse* to the funeral. The Albert family name and the names of two other intermarried families of the native parish appeared with great frequency among those present and those who sent messages. People of these names sent messages from many communities in Quebec and from Woonsocket, Rhode Island, a French-Canadian center.

Priests and nuns.—Nineteen priests, including the curés of the four local parishes, attended this funeral of a young man without a reputation for piety and without public accomplishments to his credit. Four of the priests, including one local curé, were known kin of the defunct. Ten religious houses, one from distant Alberta, sent spiritual bouquets. Most of them were from houses of an order in which a sister of the defunct is a nun. A total of 76 priests noticed this funeral in some formal way.

The evidence suggests that this phenomenal mobilization of religious functionaries was due to kinship, extended further through the ties between fellow-priests and nuns.[12] This is a significant feature of French-Canadian society. The clergy is drawn from farming and town families of moderate circumstances. The church is within the bosom of the family, just as the family is in the bosom of the church. The priest, always God's emissary, is kinsman as well. At family reunions, baptisms, weddings, and funerals the kinsman priest or nun brings a warmer and perhaps more effective blessing than could a stranger.

Personal associates.—Young Albert's associates were, like himself, young men of sporting tastes and no great accomplishment. They appeared at his funeral as members of the Club Rendezvous. They are the young men who hang out in the taverns and poolrooms. Of all elements in the town, the church likes them least, for they use their leisure in ways that are farthest from rural traditions and from the church's ideals. But they are all French, and there is no evidence that any of them has any English connections, although twenty of them who were named as present are employees of English-managed industries. However incompatible some of the ways of these young men may be with the traditional elements of their culture, they could and did appear in this important ceremonial with priests and civil dignitaries.

Dignitaries.—The public officials present were doing homage to a fairly prominent local man, a property-owner and voter, for such is the elder Mr. Albert. After listing

[12] One must keep in mind the familial symbols used to denote relationships within religious orders, as well as the preoccupation of the church, and especially of nuns, with death.

the names of 119 local citizens who were present, the report added: "and most of our prominent citizens."

Business firms and professional men.—Ten local business firms and five from outside sent tributes. The majority were firms such as supply hotels with goods or services. Nineteen local professional men and 16 from elsewhere noticed the occasion.

This impressive array of persons and institutions from a wide area and from all classes of French-Canadian society included but seven English names. Three messages came from persons of English name from other communities. The only local English people named were two minor executives from one of the industries, a bank manager, and the manager of a small industry. The latter is an Alsatian Catholic who speaks French and mixes little with the English, although he is a naturalized citizen of the United States. The English managerial class, so crucial to the community's economic life, was untouched by this community event.

The Berthier Funeral

Mr. Berthier is, of all local French businessmen, the one of whom the English population knows most and who has had most to do with the industries. In the French community he is known as a powerful and wealthy self-made man and former mayor, a large donor to the church and right-hand man of the curé and the bishop.

His son died while preparing for the priesthood in the seminary in the cathedral town some forty miles distant. It goes without saying that the church, public dignitaries, and the community at large took note of his death. Yet, in spite of Mr. Berthier's great connection with the English world, only 11 English persons are named in the extensive report of the funeral. All were named as representing industries and businesses. The local English people named are not of particular importance in the industrial hierarchy.

The Collette Funeral

This was the funeral of the small daughter of the mayor, who is the respected but not powerful owner of a business which he inherited from his father. Several of the industries did send messages, as did also three members of old English nonindustrial families, the Anglican minister, and an organization of women of the United church. While no doubt real sympathy was expressed in these messages, the list suggests that honor was being done the public official rather than the man as friend or neighbor.

The social world that is reflected in these public ceremonials is one that is warm, which gathers closely about the individual and the family; yet it is a world rich in formal ceremony and recognizant of degrees of deference. The individual within it may, at various times in his life but especially in death, become the point about which a far-reaching mobilization of people gathers. Many people are, of course, not of sufficient importance to be noticed in this way. Some are loosened from the web by mobility and by the individualizing forces of urban life. But the web of society is intact. The English have and want no place in it; nor does the English society have any such close-knit and spreading web into which a French Canadian could be drawn even if he wished. The English are outside the system of relationships which are expressed in the funeral ceremonies—outside in both dimensions. While certain English people are important and powerful, theirs is not importance and power which would make them objects of ceremonial and popular recognition either in life or in death. Neither are they in such position of intimate connection with French persons or families as to make them participate warmly in such ceremonial in deference and honor to French Canadians.

At the beginning of this chapter we took up two themes: the separateness of the French and English and the effect of urbanization upon French ceremonial. The first theme stands out clearly enough; the second is more obscure. At least, it is clear that the English urban society offers little or no ceremonial. Industry has not become the object of ceremonial fetes; nor does it, through its functionaries, take part in existing ones. The English-Protestant churches are wretched affairs to the eyes of people accustomed to the rich calendar and pageantry of Catholicism.

Since there is no substitute system of ceremonies, there remains the possibility that French Canadians may be weaned from significant ceremonial altogether by city life and contact with the English. In our community we see no reason to believe that this will be so. The ceremonies we have described do show certain differences from those described by Miner in his account of the yearly round in rural St. Denis. The fetes relating to the rural life are gone. Patriotic holidays seem more important, and ceremonies are staged in a more pretentious way. There is more of a division between spectators and active participants. Certain new organizations, indicative of a new order, have a place in public festivities. There are new festive occasions which mobilize only some one class of people, such as the Labor Day fete conducted by the Jeunesse ouvrière catholique. And, not least among the changes, a holiday of any kind has a new significance as a welcomed day of leisure from wage-work. Whatever these changes presage, they do not of themselves indicate any weakening of French-Canadian love of ceremonial, any *rapprochement* between French and English, or any decline of the honor in which the historic and religious symbols of French Canada are held.

CHAPTER XV

SOCIAL CONTACTS

A LARGE proportion of the people of our community meet some of the opposite ethnic group at work every day. Rarely, however, are they equal fellows at the same kind of work. People of the two groups also meet and greet one another on the streets and in places of business. At theaters, concerts, and athletic events they sit amicably side by side. Categorical and casual relations abound. Intimate and prolonged contacts are few.

Of all social contacts between two cultural groups, the most compromising are those which might lead to courtship, marriage, and children of divided loyalties. Visiting in each other's houses, especially at table, is perhaps the next most compromising. Less crucial is association in recreation—games, dances, and small social gatherings; but, even when adults meet in gay and irresponsible mood, the more serious game of jockeying for social favor goes on. It is a game which requires sensitivity to the expressed or implied canons of social prestige of the others present. Contacts of these kinds depend upon the sex, age, clique, and class structure of the two groups, as well as upon their relative number and upon other circumstances which may bring people together or keep them apart.

At the opening of the industrial revival of the community a small group of families—French, English, and mixed—were acknowledged to be the socially élite. The English among them were nearly all middle-aged or elderly persons of moderate means, no longer active in business and with no children in town. The French were active, both as reproducing families and in affairs. The money of all had been made through ownership of land, independent businesses, and professional practice.

The new era brought new English people, who took the places of greatest power and income in the industries, and others, who filled nearly all positions down to the ranks of the skilled workmen. The French in industry were factory hands; they were not people who could claim higher social ranking. The many French who came to establish new businesses or professional practices were, however, potential candidates for higher social position.

The middle- and upper-income groups of both French and English thus include many who are new to the community. But there are important differences in their social ranking. The English are new not only in person but in kind. Hired managers and technicians in industry have no accustomed place in the Quebec social hierarchy. The independent business and the profession have a place, and an honored one.[1] Even those French who are dubbed *arrivistes* have some of the valued symbols. For the *habitant* family has often occupied the same land for many generations and has a long memory, which may be referred to when, after business or professional success, its members seek higher ranking in town society. Even so, the French of our growing community have not yet settled into a stable social ranking.

The English are not only new in person and in kind but are heterogeneous in social background. Only three managerial families have clearly been used to anything like upper-class position in other communities. Nearly all the American families have evidently improved their incomes, their degree of authority in the industrial hierarchy, and their social standing by moving to this smaller and growing town.[2] The old-country English of higher income include a number who have risen from the working class. The move to Canada, followed by quick promotion in a growing plant, has made the break from one style of life to another much easier for them. Although such people belong to the golf club and live in nice houses, their previous condition is not forgotten even by native Canadians and Americans, who claim not to believe in such distinctions.

Here [said an American woman who is something of a social arbiter] there are all sorts of ways to do things and all sorts of [English] people. It is not homogeneous. For example: Word came that a child in school had had head lice, and we were warned to watch out for it. We were all talking of it at a tea. Mrs. Small, a Lancashire woman, said: "That would never happen in England. We have to show our fingers and necks every day in school there, and they are inspected, aren't they, Mrs. Harper?" Mrs. Harper simply answered: "I never went to a school where I was asked to show my nails and head to anyone."

[1] It has been found that the girls in the French Ligue de la Jeunesse of Montreal were much more frequently daughters of professional men and higher civil servants than were the members of the English Junior League of that city. The latter are decidedly the daughters of men important in the financial and industrial world. See Aileen Ross, "The French and English Social Elites of Montreal" (unpublished Master's thesis, University of Chicago, 1941). Throughout the history of Quebec the up-and-coming English man in industry and finance has often found a mate among the daughters of French families whose names have been of standing through many generations.

[2] The Americans have nearly all been sent from large home plants to smaller branch plants here.

The whole English community is mobile as to social rating but is settling down to a sort of order. While nearly all the men of staff rank in industry and their wives are in the golf club, social mingling at the club itself, and especially in private houses, reveals significant differences of rating, expressed through small cliques.[3]

The social ranks of the new English population appears thus, in descending order:

1. One family which keeps aloof. The wife does not try to play the role of social arbiter.

2. Three or four families who lead a "quiet life": they do not take part in the gayer affairs of the golf club but are of influence in church and other affairs. The wives play the role of social arbiters.

3. Several cliques who lead a gayer life, take active part in golf-club dances, and hold frequent smaller gatherings in each other's houses. One group is known as the "American crowd"; another, as the "Company A clique." They accuse each other of cliquishness.

4. Some younger people who are socially acceptable and will probably enter the above cliques as they grow older and as the men get higher positions.

5. Old-country English middle and higher executives and their families with the marks of working-class origin still upon them. Accent, manners, too much devotion to "chapel" religion, and the knowledge others have of their past are against them.

6. The English foremen, skilled workers, and minor clerks. They are an isolated group. They dislike the French, complain of the snobbishness of the English of higher ranking, and—if from England—are bitter about Canada.

The French society appears thus:

1. Two old families recognized as of highest standing. One is the family of a professional man whose father was a French businessman and whose mother was of an old-English family of high standing. The second is a family who had large holdings of land and also owned a sawmill. Both these families are said to have lost in land speculation since industries began to come to the town. They are also declining in political influence.

2. A group of six, and perhaps a few more, families of business and professional men, who live in big—and generally, old—houses at the bottom of the town. They, too, lead a "quiet life." Their wives are practically unknown to the English. Their daughters go to better convents, play the piano very well, dress with charm, and speak English fairly well. Their sons are in *collège*, or professional schools, or are in professions elsewhere or in business with their fathers in the community.

3. The "sporty" clique of recognized good social standing. They are "young middle-aged people" who incline to the life of the golf-club dances, bridge, and other activities in which a corresponding group of English share. Many of the English peo-

[3] Before a large golf-club dance the various cliques meet in private houses for drinks and do not go to the dance until about eleven o'clock. Only people who do not belong to cliques go earlier. At the hotel where the dance is held, each clique rents a room to which its members retire for drinking and private hilarity.

ple would place them at the top of the French society. The older French families and the remaining old English of some standing regard them as a little "cheap."

4. A group of several families of recent rise to influence and relative wealth but very conservative in their social life. They are "very narrow." The daughters are closely guarded from the gayer social life.

5. A large middle class of the families of merchants. The English speak of the men as "good, solid men," "honest Frenchmen," etc. Their wives are unknown to the English.

6. A lower-middle class in small business, trades, etc. Some of the younger men follow city ways in a rather noisy, unsophisticated way.

7. The masses of working-class families without social pretensions.

8. A group of shack-dwellers around the outskirts of the town and villages.

The French society is marked by very strong factional feuds, which run through extended kin-groups. For the French, unlike the English, are in the midst of their kin. The first, second, and third groups mentioned are not much involved with kin; but the fourth group, the *arrivistes*, present a maze of kinship and intermarriage, reaching down into the lower ranks and out into the surrounding rural counties. Diagram X shows the chief connections between the families of this group.

This one web of kinship, intermarriage, partnership, and close friendships includes four of the seven lawyers, two physicians, several of the most prominent businessmen, as well as some of less importance. The whole is tied with several bonds to the curé of the leading parish. Six of the men now hold public office, and others have done so; all are Conservative in politics, although they vary from extremely nationalistic to moderate and compromising in their attitude to the English. While several of the men belong to the golf club and have important diplomatic relations with English people concerning matters of industry, business, and politics, no family of the group has any social contacts with English families.

The years in which the larger industries were being planned and their plants built are referred to as a sort of "honeymoon." The French were expecting their businesses to boom and their land to become more valuable. The staff and workmen sent from England and the United States to open the new plants were in an expansive pioneering mood. For many of them this seemed an opportunity to get ahead faster than in the larger mother-organization. Many of the men had no wives; and those who did, did not immediately bring them. Houses were scarce. So the newcomers boarded with French families. They now complain of the crowding and of the food and the prices they paid for it, but they speak of that period as a time when they all had a good

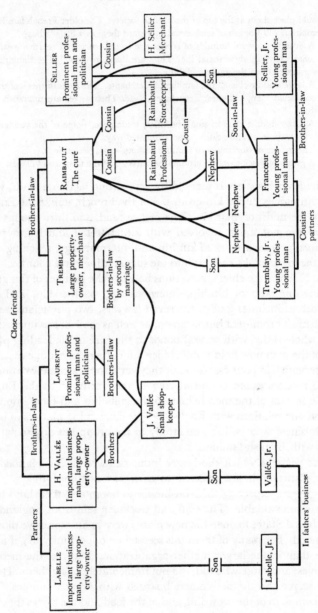

DIAGRAM X

KIN AND OTHER CONNECTIONS BETWEEN A GROUP OF LEADING MEN

time. It seemed strange and amusing to have to get along with people of another language. Sports furnished occasion for *camaraderie* of men of the various ranks in industry and of French with English. One of the most important men in a large industry spoke with mild nostalgia of those early days.

The English crowd who came out ten years ago took up hockey. We divided the staff into teams. We had a wonderful game that everyone still talks about, played by men who had never learned to skate. They fell down all the time. Or they could not turn and kept going until they hit the fence. They would be within a yard of the puck and could not hit it.

I was the only one who knew how to play. I had learned as a boy in the West, and it came back easily. They wouldn't let me play with the plant boys, who were beginners. But I played with the town team. I was the only English-speaking one on the team, and I don't know why, but they made me captain. They knew just enough English for me to get along with them.

Then the plant took over the town hockey team and began to be angel to sports. But it costs too much, and the plant is abandoning it. You see, you have to pay the players, and the gate receipts are not enough. We were giving men jobs in the plant o that they could play on the town hockey and baseball teams. The baseball players would be given $100-per-month jobs, just to keep them here to play ball.

People say that in the same period the leading new English families mixed somewhat with the leading local French families. The most cynically objective observer of such things in the community was probably right in accounting for the passing of the honeymoon by the coming of more English women and the growth of the English Protestant churches to such size that their subsidiary organizations, especially those of the Anglican church, made the occasion for most of the English teas and informal gatherings. Finally, a growing realization by the French of the lower ranks in industry that the good jobs were all held by English people led to a growth of nationalistic feeling. Some of the French leaders, fearful of being accused of selling out to the English, became cautious about associating with them. Several strikes gave the coup de grâce to the hopeful good feeling.

At present French and English mix little except at the golf-club affairs, held either at the club or in the large hotel. English people say that a few of the French are above "national and religious prejudice." They always name the same people—and they are few, indeed—as those of whom this is true. We saw the same three, four, or five couples of French at parties with the same few English couples, all of them dancing and engaging in badinage. They flirted, as the faithful fiancé does with the girl from out of town who will go back to her own town and her own man after the party. These people, French and English, compose a "sporty" set.

We met with a few other occasions of mixing. An unmarried daughter of a French "first-family" came to a small tea at the house of a high industrial executive; it was a tea held after tennis matches in which she had played on the company team. Another French girl of similar standing often turned up informally at an English house which is the rendezvous from which some of the unmarried English men of the minor executive class start off on swimming parties and canoeing and skiing expeditions. An English couple once went to this girl's house for cocktails before a dance. Another French girl was there with a young American college man who was playing on the town baseball team for the summer. A total of perhaps four girls of this type have some social life with English people. They are charming, accomplished girls of the best social connections but of such an age that their prospects of marriage dwindle each day. The town contains no unmarried French Canadians of the age, social standing, and prospects to be suitable mates for them.

When English and French women meet socially, there is something of a barrier between them. Golf club and other semipublic bridge parties furnish the chief occasions for female mixing. Most of the English women cannot converse in French and accuse the French of chattering away among themselves: "The French are much freer. They laugh and giggle, while we [English] sit quietly and talk. Some of them play bridge, but they like to cheat, bid high, and set each other. Only four or five really play seriously, as we do, and like to play a really good game." These apparently trivial complaints reveal a wide and deep gulf between French and English manners. It is a difference which appears in men's sports as well. English tennis players play deep and drive hard; the chopping, tricky, bantering play of the French annoys them to distraction and often beats them. Similar complaints are made about golf. For the French, games and sports are always the occasion for lively social interplay. For the English, they are serious business.

It is also agreed that there is more mixing of men than of women. A group of men, whose wives rarely meet, play poker and drink together. Their meeting place used to be a Chinese restaurant. During our residence they rented an old house in the Basse Ville to use as a club. The French members included some from the very top social ranks right down to a lower-middle-class "regular fellow" who is thought to drink and gamble too much. The English are of the "sporty" set. An English member of this set said that he had only once been invited to a French house for any hilarity. The crowd—men and women, English and French—were on the way home from a golf-club dance in the early morning. They found the Chinese restaurant closed; so "Mme St. Jacques took pity on us and invited us to her house." This was regarded as a rare thing. That the men should mix more than the women is to be expected; it is generally so. It is so among the English themselves. But even this mixing of men is said to be declining. Some of the English men have "settled down"; others, French and English, have become disgruntled. A feud between two French factions over politics has taken some of the French out of the all-night poker and drinking set. In fact, the whole community is set-tling down as does a boom town after wives and churches appear.

Intermarriage is perhaps the most significant indication of intimate social connections between two elements of a population. People speak as though there had been a good many mixed marriages in Cantonville and as though they are increasingly frequent. Neither seems to be true. We were told of the same few couples over and over again. The Angli-can rector's cases were mainly from a previous generation. The minis-ter of the United church gave details of five cases of industrial working-class men who married French girls of similar standing. The priest told mainly of upper-class French girls who married young English white-collar men because there were no French boys of proper stand-ing and because they were "quite naturally attracted by tall, athletic men."

Of the many possible combinations of French and English—man and woman, Catholic and Protestant—and of social classes, only two appear in any number at all, and they are really very few. Four Eng-lish men of the executive and white-collar type in industry have mar-ried local French girls. One of the men was really here to play ball on the town team but, of course, had some sort of job in industry. The other men are more permanent, but only one has a really important and well-paying job. He, interestingly enough, is of English working-class origin and is married to a local girl of not much standing. The other two are young men of more breeding but with relatively unim-portant and unpromising jobs. Their wives are girls of very good pro-fessional families. One of the French families involved is perhaps the first-family in the district. These couples lead the social life of the golf club. Their children will, in all probability, go to the English Protestant school, although they will be Catholic, for all of these couples were married by priests and hence must have agreed in writing to Catholic rearing of the children.

There are very few English candidates for such marriages left. In the early days the industries brought many young English-Protestant men. In those days the leading families, it happens, had several daughters of marriageable age. At the same time, French youths of the professional class were leaving town, and eventually they married away from Cantonville. But this temporary supply of unmarried English men of white-collar class is gone; more English girls came, and the sexes were balanced.

The other type of marriage is that of old-country English-Protestant workingmen, mostly of Methodist-chapel upbringing, with girls of similar class whom they met in the factories. One such couple was married by the Protestant minister, and the wife drawn over into the English-Protestant pious group. The family will be English. Others will have Catholic children; some are in French-Catholic school. Incidentally, this is the old story of Quebec. Upper-class intermarriage leads to English or mixed social connections; lower class, to a French life from which the husband himself is partially excluded.

We venture to predict that intermarriage of both these types will be rare in the immediate future. The industries are not bringing young English men to town any more. Those who do come will find a more settled English social life. No English workingmen are being hired, and those who came in the past have passed the marrying age. The young English people who are brought up in town have almost no contact with the French. They seem to be more aloof than their elders, who came to town from outside the province. Their elders, in fact, keep them separate in school, and in social life as well. It seems probable that most of the English young people will leave town to work. A small group of English working-class young people may stay in the industries. The example of the working classes in Montreal and other old meeting places of the two elements would suggest that they will keep strictly apart.

The French of the lower and middle classes, who, of course, far outnumber the few people who participate in the golf club and the hotel social affairs, could not mix with the English even if they wanted to. There simply are no English of any class they can aspire to. They probably do not even think of it. They may have English employers or

bosses; they may see American ways portrayed in the movies and pick
up a few words of slang. But no English-speaking world is present and
open to them. A few girls from the country work as servants in English
houses. Some confide in their mistresses concerning the apparent ease
and freedom of the English wife's life as compared with the burden of
piety and frequent child-bearing imposed on the French woman of the
poorer classes. But no evidence exists to suggest that they marry any
the less willingly on that account or that they take English ways into
their families. The French may be affected by the presence of the
English; but, if they are, it is not by intimate and informal social
contacts repeated over a long time and touching diverse classes and
elements of the population.

CHAPTER XVI

THE RURAL ECONOMY IN TOWN

THIS chapter will deal with the effects of town life, and especially of wage-work, upon the spirit and organization characteristic of the economic life of rural Quebec. The distinctive feature of the rural life is close co-operation of the family in a common enterprise. Its obverse side is stubborn independence of the family and a certain distrust of communal effort. The following chapter will concentrate on fashions and the urban means of communication and amusements. The last two chapters will treat of the collective discontents which so often accompany realization that a new way of life puts old sentiments, values, and life-objectives in jeopardy.

The New York or Ontario farmer who goes to a city to work and live thereby makes a change less drastic than the Quebec farmer who does likewise, for the former's material condition and his general view of life are more "urbanized."[1] In addition, the position of his own, the English, language and ethnic group in the cities of his region is such that there will not be the slightest temptation for him to change them. On the other hand, the changes faced by the Quebec *habitant* are far less drastic than those met by the Mayan village-dweller of Yucatán who goes to a city in his own state. The latter will have come from a life in which techniques, material conditions, mentality, and even language are not those of the city.[2] The Yucatecan villager is not only far more rustic than the French-Canadian *habitant;* he also is of another ethnic affiliation than city people. As he enters city life, he changes his language and his dress, as well as his occupation. He has to adapt himself to ethnically alien models of life.

The French Canadian participates in some degree in the culture which prevails in cities. He speaks and reads the language of the majority of people in all Quebec cities. There are before him models of city behavior which are thoroughly French and of long standing. It is, in fact, possible for a rural French-Canadian boy to go, in one lifetime, from an *habitant* farm to the Latin Quarter of Paris without any con-

[1] See Table 1 (p. 6).

[2] See Robert Redfield, *The Folk Culture of Yucatan* (Chicago: University of Chicago Press, 1941).

170

siderable contact with people who are ethnically or linguistically strange to him. It would be a long road to travel so quickly, and the Parisian destination is not often reached by one born to the *habitant* life. But it could happen, and it does happen in two generations not too infrequently.

The Yucatecan could enter only the lowest social and economic ranks of the city and would have to change his language and ethnic identification to rise. The French Canadian, like the Ontario farmer, can enter urban society at one of several ranks and can move up without ceasing to be French Canadian. The French Canadian can go to the city by several routes. Nearly all of the priests of Cantonville are farmers' sons who, at an early age, were sent off, at their family's expense, to a *collège* and then to a seminary. A few of the professional men are also farmers' sons. With this training and the badge of their professions they enter urban society in the middle classes. Other French Canadians, of less schooling, come to town with some capital and set up small businesses; it is significant, however, that no important businessman of Cantonville was born on a farm. It apparently takes longer than one generation to get established in the middle and upper ranks of business. By far the majority come to town without any particular skill to exploit and find their places at the bottom of the social and the economic ladders. It is of these people that French-Canadian leaders seem to be talking when they express concern lest town-dwellers lose their rural virtues.

It also happens that the majority of the French Canadians enter, when they come to Cantonville, occupations which bring them under the authority of English persons. To rise in the industrial order they would perhaps have to become less French than they are. Furthermore, while there is a long-established traditional French-Canadian town life, English-American models are given force by the dominant position of English people in the economic realm and by the fact that the French-Canadian world, both rural and urban, is but a small one surrounded by a pervasive, expansive English-speaking world. Thus it comes about that French culture is constantly threatened by American influences—fashions, popular literature, radio, motion pictures, and ideas. On the other hand, the French Canadian finds himself inescapably among his own people and institutions. He lives, in short, in a French-Canadian urban society; and he only rarely ceases to be fully identified with it. But urban French-Canadian institutions—the newspaper, the French radio, etc.—are themselves strongly influenced by American models and so bring to him, although in his own language and through his own fellows, much that emanates from the English-American world.

Before proceeding, we suggest a hypothesis—namely, that the chief features of the economic life of the *habitant* persist and operate with effectiveness not so much among the more recent and rustic townspeople, who came directly from farm to factory, as among the French-Canadian business and professional classes who, generally speaking, are not of recent rural origin. The latter are not in any sense rustic; they may, in fact, have traveled, speak English fluently, and be urbane intellectually and in their manners. It may be of some psychological significance that people of this class are perhaps more concerned than others lest their recently arrived rural fellow-countrymen lose their rural orientation.

Let us recall the chief characteristics of the *habitant* economy. First, the farm is a family enterprise. The work is done by members of the family, who thereby produce a living for all. The head of the family generally owns the land and equipment. Because the farm is a producing plant, and of such size that to divide it would be to destroy it, the children must be dispersed when they grow up. To this end the head of the house enforces upon himself and upon the rest of the family an extreme frugality. A corollary of this frugality is an extreme distrust of public expenditure, even for education which might help the emigrating children. The family itself expects to pay for the higher and specialized education of such of its children as are thought to require it. Only the basic elementary education is provided by local taxation of land.[3]

This insistence of the individual family on attaining its objectives by its own efforts appears as the proverbial "individualism" of the Quebec farmer. It is not "individualism" of the individual, but—if the inconsistency of phrase be allowed—of the family. The family does not want to yield its fate into the hands of others, nor to help pay for the education of others. It wants to conserve its resources for objectives agreed upon by the family itself.

What happens to this economy of effort and objectives in towns and cities? Let us first consider the feature of family enterprise. The bulk

[3] This trait of the French Canadian is remarked by Solomon Vineberg in *Provincial and Local Taxation in Canada* (New York: Columbia University Press, 1912). There was some opposition to the establishment of local government in Quebec a century ago, partly on the ground that it would require taxation of the *habitant*. I do not suggest that this trait is due entirely to the factors I mention—only that it is functionally related to the struggle of the family to keep its land intact.

of the French Canadians in Cantonville work for wages in factories owned by large corporations. The situation of the worker in industry is the complete antithesis of that of the independent farmer working with his family upon his own land. While an industry may hire several members of the same family, each does his own work for his own wage. It may be that a father can persuade his children to put their wages into a common family fund, but this is not the same thing as a common living from a group enterprise. It is evident to any observer that the industrial workers of Cantonville, who are not engaged in family enterprise, are of more recent rural provenance than are the more successful businessmen, many of whom do live by a family enterprise.

It is, in fact, the middle-class entrepreneur who adheres closest to this feature of the rural life. The family business is very common in Cantonville. The family enterprise is indeed thought of as the foundation of the French-Canadian middle class. Our data have shown that in Cantonville the French middle class actually sticks closely to this ideal.

The desire to have a family enterprise has led to the establishment of a plethora of small businesses, many of which are run by families some of whose members are at work in industry. The old solid middle class, many of whom decry the loss of the rural virtue of independent enterprise, are concerned over its very persistence in these poor businesses which bring "disloyal" competition. The thing that is regarded as "disloyal" about the small business people is that they do not depend upon the businesses alone for their living and that they threaten the security of the more substantial business people who do.

The second cardinal virtue of the rural French Canadian is that he owns his farm and, of course, the house upon it. The house, as is usual in the country, contains but a single household, albeit a large one.

In town the French Canadian turns quickly into a flat-dweller. Even in Quebec towns of less than 30,000 inhabitants more than one-third of all dwellings are apartments.[4] In cities above 30,000, 86 per cent of the dwellings are apartments. These conditions prevail in Cantonville. Only 22 per cent of the buildings contain but one dwelling. The percentage of families who have a house to themselves is, of course, much smaller. The typical building contains from two to four dwellings. Even in the outlying villages, where space is plentiful, the single house is rarer than the multiple dwelling.

It follows from the above facts that, under the prevailing system of

[4] A dwelling is the self-contained space housing a household. Each apartment in an apartment house is a dwelling.

individual ownership, only a small proportion of the householders of
Cantonville own their houses. The Quebec farmer is more likely to
own his farm than is his English compatriot in Ontario, but in towns

TABLE 33

APARTMENTS AND HOUSES AS A PERCENTAGE OF ALL DWELLINGS IN
RURAL AND URBAN LOCALITIES IN QUEBEC AND ONTARIO, 1931*

	APARTMENTS AS A PERCENTAGE OF ALL DWELLINGS		HOUSES † AS A PERCENTAGE OF ALL DWELLINGS	
	Quebec	Ontario	Quebec	Ontario
Total..................	42.4	7.6	57.2‡	92.1‡
Rural.....................	1.5	1.2	98.2	98.7
Urban.....................	62.9	11.8	36.6	88.3
Localities under 1,000......	5.3	2.4	93.5	97.1
Localities 1,000–30,000.....	33.5	7.2	65.7	92.4
Localities over 30,000......	85.7	16.6	13.9	83.2

* Census of Canada, 1931, V, 965, Table 54, and p. 978, Table 56.
† Includes houses, rows of houses, and semidetached houses.
‡ The very small percentage of nonspecified have been omitted.

TABLE 34

DISTRIBUTION OF PERCENTAGES OF BUILDINGS BY
NUMBER OF DWELLINGS, CANTONVILLE, 1937*

	PERCENTAGE OF BUILDINGS		
	Cantonville	Villages	Total
One dwelling.................	18	26	22
Two dwellings................	37	42	40
Three or four dwellings........	25	23	24
Five or more dwellings........	20	9	14
Total..................	100	100	100

* Data gathered by a house-to-house canvass.

of all sizes the Ontario householder is more likely to be an owner. In
cities of more than 30,000 the Ontario householder is nearly three
times as likely to own his house as is the Quebec householder.

Other facts indicate that the French-Canadian conception of the
function of real property is not that expressed in the American and
English-Canadian slogan: "Own your own home." Ownership of

property is, to the French Canadian, an income-producing investment rather than a way of coming by the luxury of being alone under his own roof in the right neighborhood. In the former sense, the proprietor ideal is far from dead among town and city French Canadians. Ownership of real property is, in Cantonville, widespread within the limits of the possibilities created by the large numbers of multiple dwellings. The majority of the owners occupy some part of their property and have rent-paying tenants as well. The few English owners,

TABLE 35

OWNERS AS A PERCENTAGE OF ALL HOUSEHOLDERS IN RURAL
DISTRICTS, TOWNS, AND CITIES IN QUEBEC
AND ONTARIO, 1931*

	PERCENTAGE OF OWNERS	
	Quebec	Ontario
Total............................	47.9	61.4
Rural...............................	84.4†	75.6
Urban.............................	29.7	52.6
Localities under 1,000...............	67.7	70.5
Localities 1,000–30,000..............	45.8	58.5
Localities over 30,000..............	16.2	46.2

* Calculated from *Census of Canada, 1931*, V, 1016–20, Table 63.
† This percentage is lower than that given in Table 1 (p. 6) because it includes all rural households, not just "occupied farms."

with the exception of the few old-English families of the town, conform to the "own-your-own-home" pattern; they own only the rather nice houses they live in. All English who rent—and the great majority do so—have French landlords.[5]

This pattern appears more clearly in the details of ownership and tenancy in four sample districts of Cantonville. The districts are: (1) the old business street in the lower town, (2) two new streets occupied largely by industrial workers, (3) a new street near a large industry and inhabited by lesser English industrial people as well as by a good many French, (4) the Boulevard, a newer residential district which contains many of the houses owned and occupied by English higher executives. Of the 189 parcels of land in these four districts, 165 are owned by local residents. The remaining 24 are owned by companies who do business

[5] We do not here consider the property of corporations. The industrial corporations own the property on which their plants are built. One owns several large houses which it rents to members of its higher staff; another owns a large house in which its manager lives.

on the premises, by the city, by the parish, or by outside individuals. The few outside individual owners are, without exception, French people who live in the region. Of the 152 occupied parcels, 97 are occupied by the owners. Twelve of the occupying owners are English; the others are French. (See Table 37.)[6]

The property of the old business street is almost entirely in the hands of older families and of well-established business people. While some of the proprietors are *rentiers*, the majority do business on their premises. Several individuals or families own as much as $30,000 worth of property each on this street; one widow owns apartments and stores assessed at more than $50,000. The magnitude of the estates of the larger owners—all of them local people—is indicated in Table 36.

TABLE 36

ASSESSED VALUE OF REAL ESTATE HOLDINGS OF THE 12 LARGEST
INDIVIDUAL TAXPAYERS OF CANTONVILLE, 1937*

Assessed Value	Number of Owners with Property of Each Value	Assessed Value	Number of Owners with Property of Each Value
Over $100,000..........	1	$25,000–50,000.........	4
$75,000–100,000........	0	$20,000–25,000.........	6
$50,000–75,000..........	1		

* These are values of property owned anywhere in the city, not merely in the old business streets.

Downtown property and the associated enterprises are the solid stake of the more prosperous residents of the community. Very few of their properties are without some apartments or business space to rent. The impression is of property, locally owned, stubbornly held by individuals and families, and devoted to as great a variety of purposes as is found profitable. Little of it is property acquired and built upon for a specialized purpose. The French Canadians who own this property exhibit the ideal of proprietorship in land and of family enterprise in full form. Their conception of property stands in contrast both to the "homes" of the English, which are, in fact, a kind of conspicuous expenditure paid for out of salaries, and the property and buildings

[6] From inspection of the tax rolls and from our knowledge of the community, we are certain that our sample contains at least half of the English owners of the town. It contains only about one-tenth of all owners and none of the several hundred owners in the outlying villages. A fair estimate is that there are about 25 English owners and something more than 2,000 French owners in the larger community.

which corporations acquire and design for a particular business or kind of industrial production.

In the working-class streets selected for study the buildings are nearly all new and are better than the average in the outlying villages. The typical building is owned by a French factory worker who occupies one flat and rents out one or more to other families. The 24 owners, all French, who live in their buildings, have 11 English tenants.

The third section, of new apartment houses of greater average value, shows the same consistent local French ownership, although a slightly smaller proportion of the owners are of the industrial working class. Even on the Boulevard, the owners, except for the few houses owned by English of the managerial class, are equally local and French.

The facts show, then, that while only a small proportion of French families own real property the proprietor ideal remains vigorous in its original and pure form. The property is owned by local residents. The bankers and city clerk testify, further, that most of the mortgages on local property are held in the community. The owners generally live on their property, but they either make use of part of it for their own businesses or rent part of it to others. Many do both. While the more valuable properties are in the hands of old families or of business people, ownership extends down among the workers in industry. It is, in fact, almost the rule for English industrial families to rent their living quarters from French people who have jobs of much lower rating and income than their own. As a group, the French Canadians of Cantonville are not yielding ownership of land to others except to such English families and corporations as acquire property for their own occupancy.[7]

In Montreal the situation appears to be the same. In the working-class suburb of Verdun, old-country English artisans live in flats owned by French Canadians, many of whom inhabit the basements or the poorer parts of their own buildings. In the eastern central part of the city, where small apartments and rooming-houses abound, the French buy the property from under the English tenants.

On the other hand, with every increase in the proportion of French Canadians who live in towns and cities, the number and proportion of

[7] The English of Cantonville reveal that they buy for occupancy only by the fact that they invariably build single houses; by the fact that, when they leave town, they make a desperate effort to sell their houses; and by the frequent statement of English people that they do not build or buy a house because it would be hard to sell if they were to leave town.

them who do not own property also increase. And as the proportion of those who work for wages increases, so also does the number who, though they own property, depend in part upon their wages to pay for it and keep it up. The curé of St. Luc's told his people so in a ser-

TABLE 37

OWNERSHIP AND EVALUATION OF PROPERTIES IN FOUR SAMPLE
AREAS OF CANTONVILLE, 1937

LOCALITY	ALL PROPERTIES	INDIVIDUAL OWNERS				OWNED BY COMPANIES	OWNED BY CITY OR PARISHES
		Occupied by Owners	Not Occupied by Owners				
			Local Owner		Outside Owner		
			Improved	Vacant	Improved		
I. Old business street:							
Parcels........	56	28	18	....	1	9*	....
Evaluation....	$ 680,000	$278,000	$217,500	....	$ 4,000	$180,500	....
II. New working-class streets:							
Parcels........	34	19	5	2	3	....	5†
Evaluation....	$ 138,150	$ 67,350	$ 21,550	$ 1,050	$11,300	....	$36,900
III. New apartment area:							
Parcels........	30	10	6	11‡	3	....	....
Evaluation....	$ 100,550	$ 53,100	$ 25,850	$ 6,100	$15,500	....	....
IV. The Boulevard:							
Parcels........	69	40	7	19	1	....	2§
Evaluation....	$ 186,375	$142,300	$ 24,500	$ 9,075	$ 6,000	....	4,500
Total number of parcels........	189	97	36	32	8	9	7
Total evaluation	$1,105,075	$540,750	$289,400	$16,225	$36,800	$180,500	$41,400

* All but 2 parcels used by companies for conducting their business. Of the exceptions, one is owned by a manufacturing company for the manager's residence (evaluation, $10,000); the other is owned by a fraternal insurance order (evaluation, $4,500).

† All are vacant lots owned by the city of Cantonville.

‡ This includes 1 parcel owned by an outsider. As it was the only exception, it was included here.

§ Both parcels are owned by parishes. One is vacant and assessed at $300; the other, improved and assessed at $4,200.

mon: "Not long ago the mill shut down 150 looms. Suppose they shut down 150 more. Where would you be, you who have bought houses here? Where would you get your bread? Your houses would be taken for the taxes you could not pay." Further, as the proportion of the income of a town which derives from industrial wages increases, so also does the prosperity of the property-owner depend upon the course of industrial prosperity, for rent is ultimately paid from wages. In Cantonville, the anxieties and passions of politics already reflect awareness that the French-Canadian property-owners' prosperity is contingent upon the state of industry.

What of the "individualism" of the *habitant?* One small indication is contained in the rather bitter comment of a French-Canadian architect that his people's chief contribution to architecture is a winding and, in winter, exceedingly dangerous outside stairway. As nearly as is feasible, there is a separate stairway to each flat. On the several back

TABLE 38

NATIONALITY AND OCCUPATION OF INDIVIDUAL PROPERTY-OWNERS IN
FOUR SAMPLE AREAS OF CANTONVILLE, 1937

LOCALITY	FRENCH							ENGLISH						To-TAL
	To-tal	Busi-ness	Pro-fes-sional	Ren-*tier*	In-dus-trial	Arti-sans or Clerks	Un-known	To-tal	Busi-ness	Pro-fes-sional	Ren-*tier*	In-dus-trial	Un-known	
I. Old business street*	42	22	9	9	....	......	2	4	....	....	3†	1†	......	46
II. New working-class streets‡	24	3	1	2	18	......	......	....	....	....	....	....	......	24
III. New apartment area§	15	3	.....	2	10	......	......	1	....	....	....	1†	......	16
IV. The Boulevard‖	36	9	.....	5	15	4	3	11	....	....	....	11	......	47

* Only 2 of the 46 buildings included in this group serve as residences for only one family. In all others there are either other residential tenants, business tenants, or both; or the owner, himself, does business on the premises.
† The English owning these properties are all of "old" local families.
‡ Of the 24 owners in this group, all but 7 have tenants. The 11 English tenants have French landlords.
§ Of the 16 owners, 15 have tenants. The 13 English tenants have French landlords in every case but one.
‖ Eighteen out of 47 in this group rent to tenants. Of the remainder, there are 11 privately owned by French and 11 privately owned by new industrial English. Eighteen English have French landlords.

porches of many of Cantonville's most modern three-story apartment buildings there stand little woodsheds of corrugated iron, one for each tenant. Several English people report that landlords hesitate to instal common heating plants in their buildings because their French tenants will not stand for it. By keeping the common hallways and services of the building to the minimum, each family guards its control over its own expenditure. None becomes the dupe of some other family who might, by prodigal use of heat and hot water, increase the cost for all.

A more significant picture of this "individualism" and frugality in town may be had from a description of the course of public affairs in the largest of Cantonville's outlying working-class villages. As noted earlier, so much of the increase of population has occurred outside the city limits that, at present, the outlying population is greater than that of the city. A large proportion of the outlying population lives in the village of St. Jerome. The street which forms the boundary between Cantonville and St. Jerome is almost completely occupied on the St. Jerome side and almost completely vacant on the Cantonville side. The villages were settled by distinctly rural people who wanted to build cheaply on inexpensive land. They wanted freedom from city taxes and building regulations more than they wanted the public services for which the taxes would pay. It is of some significance to see what elements of the rural existence they have preserved and to note the dilemmas created by preserving them under town, wage-working conditions.

Both the industrial and the nonindustrial workers of the outlying villages are proprietors in greater proportion than the corresponding

TABLE 39

OWNERS AND RENTERS AMONG THE GAINFULLY EMPLOYED
MALE HEADS OF FAMILIES IN CANTONVILLE, 1938*

	Town	Villages	Total
Industrial employees:			
Owners.............	109	326	435
Renters.............	332	484	816
Total............	441	810	1,251
Other occupations:			
Owners.............	178	223	401
Renters.............	348	275	623
Total............	526	498	1,024

* Data from the Cantonville city directory, 1938.

groups within the town. This is the more striking when one recalls that the villages have scarcely any people above the lower- and lower-middle-class level.

The settlements outside the town had become quite large before any of them were incorporated. Each family, for and by itself, elected to live outside. By so doing, they put themselves outside the area served by the town schools, sewers, water system, fire department, streets, and sidewalks. They planted their houses and small flat buildings where the sand blows and where odors and mosquitoes rise from swampy spots and open drainage ditches. The lacking public services were scarcely necessary on the farm. But as the settlements grew, certain basic public services became necessary. The village and school district of St. Jerome were organized, but the inhabitants stubbornly strove to keep taxes down. The school building was scarcely large enough even when finished. The limits of the village were so set that, very shortly, settlements extended far beyond them. For these settlements—twice removed from Cantonville—one-room rural schools were built.

The village buildings are flimsy in construction; the typical structure is a wooden frame covered with cheap unpainted siding or with one of several kinds of tar paper. A favorite covering is of a composition paper with a design imitating the appearance of brick. Eventually the number and proximity of such structures created a fire hazard. Insurance rates rose above those of the town, where certain under-

TABLE 40

PERCENTAGES OF BUILDINGS CONSTRUCTED WITH
VARIOUS MATERIALS IN CANTONVILLE, 1937*

MATERIAL	PERCENTAGE		
	Town	Villages	Total
Brick or stone..........	49	11	28
Frame.................	30.	54	43
Patent covering........	21	35	29
Total.............	100	100	100

* Data from house to-house canvass. Most of the buildings listed as being of brick have a wooden frame and a mere facing of brick. Such a facing, however, reduces insurance rates considerably.

writers' restrictions are enforced and where there is a fairly adequate fire department. A growing fear of fire, together with pressure from fire underwriters, led the village to provide a small chemical engine. Its purchase became a major issue of village politics.

The disposal of wastes became an even more troublesome issue. Finally unemployed men, paid by the government, were put to digging sewers. The town was to furnish equipment. A small outfit for treating sewage was bought. The provincial health authorities found, however, that the machine was much too small to make the sewage fit for discharge, as planned, into a near-by stream. The voters then refused, in a referendum, to allow expenditure of the few thousands of dollars necessary for the prescribed outfit. This impasse between province and village continued for a year or more, during which the sewers could not be used. Meanwhile, no street has been paved, no public water system has been installed, and only recently has the council passed an ordinance requiring people to pay for the building of side-walks past their property.

These problems are made more acute by the fact that all the more valuable taxable properties of the community are inside the town of Cantonville. The per capita value of property in St. Jerome is only about one-seventh that of Cantonville. Hence, while the town fur-nishes nine years of schooling and the village but six, the village's school tax rate is already double that of the town. The burden of pub-lic services in the villages falls entirely upon small proprietors. These frugal people have, by their insistence on a rural way of living under urban conditions, created a dilemma. They live so close to one another

TABLE 41

TAXES AND PUBLIC EXPENDITURE IN CANTONVILLE AND ST. JEROME*

	Town of Cantonville	Village of St. Jerome
Value of taxable property (1938)............	$7,936,995.00	$925,570.00
Per capita valuation (1938).................	$906.87	$147.33
Municipal tax rate per $100 (1938)..........	2.10	0.65
School tax rate per $100 (1938).............	0.90	1.80
School and municipal tax rate (1938)........	3.00	2.45
Municipal expenditure per capita (1936).....	$21.93	$2.42
School expenditure per pupil (1937–38)......	$38.71	$22.00
Years of instruction offered (1937–38).......	9	6
Annual salary of lay teachers, female (1937–38)	$360.00	$300.00

* Sources: city directory, 1938; report of Catholic school commission, local paper, January 26, 1939; *Statistical Year Book* (Quebec, 1937).

that they must have more public services. But they cannot pay for them without a burden of municipal debt which they could hardly bear and which would be the greater because they live outside the town of Cantonville.

Meanwhile, the town has acquired a vested interest in the difference of standards between itself and the villages. If the town were to annex the villages, it would have to share the taxes from its more valuable business and industrial properties with 8,000 poor relations who bear no gifts for the city treasury—poor relations for whom even the begin-nings of proper public services would require an immense capital out-lay. A recent mayor of Cantonville attempted to have the villages in-corporated with the town. He stated that it would have to be done eventually and that every year made a bad situation worse. His pro-posal was defeated by the town voters. The opposition was led by the largest individual taxpayer, who argued correctly that Cantonville's school costs would have been nearly doubled by the change. The private attitude of English industrial managers is that the people of the villages, having made their holes, should be allowed to wallow in them; they sense that, if the population of the town were increased by all of the outlying population, the murmur for increased taxation of the industries would swell to a roar. The village people, however, are beginning to point out what they consider the injustice of the situation, namely, that more than half the employees of the industries and the customers of the larger businesses reside outside the municipality which receives all of the taxes from these institutions.

The villages have no leading businessmen or large property-owners who might see in the improvement of the village a corresponding increase in their own prosperity. As noted earlier, even the mayor of St. Jerome is an industrial worker—not a labor leader who might speak for a class, but just a small, faithful workman who is not a leader at all. Most of the village officers are elected *faute de mieux;* they are, like their constituents, little people trying to make an adjustment—as little as necessary—to the changes going on about them and realizing, bit by bit and with some resentment, that the standards of their native rural parishes do not work well here.

The villagers do some gardening, but not in a large way. Many families, since they rent apartments, have no ground to cultivate. There is nothing to suggest that gardening takes on the proportions of a major auxiliary occupation. The characteristic yard in St. Jerome is a bare plot, with perhaps a few flowers set in a bed surrounded by a white-washed box, an old automobile tire, or bits of ornamental pottery. It is the rural yard brought to town.

In town and villages alike, the people have completely abandoned the outward form of the traditional rural Quebec house, with its steep roof whose ridge runs parallel to the road. Such a house is the symbol of Quebec, precious to artist and antiquarian. But the *habitant* who builds anew, in country or town, puts up a square box with a nearly flat roof. This newer form allows more room upstairs and is obviously better suited for flats. Such box-shaped houses—they are the majority in St. Jerome—are often decorated with ornate false fronts and cornices. Occasionally the owner will stucco his house and insert glittering colored glass in the stucco. The acme of this departure from the dignified *habitant* house is a certain small, one-story box, dingy in spite of its newness, but decorated with a high false front with many curves; a large washing machine stands by the dining-table, both visible through a tremendous window with an encircling row of small panes of colored glass. The numerous family eats in unashamed public splendor, not dimmed by curtains.

The inner arrangement of the house is not so easily abandoned. In a large proportion of the village buildings, and in many of the town itself, the kitchen is the front room, entered by the main front door. An immense kitchen range, gloriously enameled in various colors and adorned with mirrors, may be seen from the street like the high altar through an open church door. The range, made to burn wood, furnishes most of the heat for the house. This feature of the rural economy is stubbornly maintained. Even when the kitchen is put at the back of the house, as is increasingly the case in the town and, of course, in all buildings designed for middle-class families, the kitchen may still be large. The other rooms are quite small and often without stoves.

We dwell upon the physical features of the houses because they seem to indicate that it is not sentiment for a traditional form so much as the attachment to an economy of family life that persists among the rural people who have come to Cantonville to live.

Part of the rural system of life in Quebec has been the retirement of the father when he gives the land to the son who is to succeed him. In the contract drawn up between father and son, the son guarantees to care for the parents and sometimes agrees to complete the education of younger children and to give them sums of money to start them on their way in the world. In the district surrounding Cantonville, according to local lawyers and notaries, this custom has fallen into desuetude. The reasons given are that the land is rather poor, so that often no son will undertake the burden of looking after his parents. The standard of living has come to include more professional medical care, which can make the declining years of the parents expensive. Furthermore, clothing is purchased, not made at home. In the towns these things are the more true. More crucial, however, is the fact that the children are no longer part of a common family working-force. They work, each for himself, as soon as they arrive at the legal age. This makes family planning for each child more difficult. The industrial family has no enterprise to hand over to a son. It can give education if it can muster the money. But the money must be got from the cash wages of the several working children, which is quite a different matter from taking it from the common income of a farm.

The curé thinks this change in economy has an effect on the number of boys who go into the priesthood:

The girls go into religion about as much as in the country—about a dozen a year from this community. But the boys don't. The reason is that a girl, without money, can enter the teaching or nursing orders and pay only for her habit. Her life is one of service and devotion, and that pays her way. But to have a boy become a priest costs $200 or $300 a year, and it takes eight years. Our people are too poor.

Of course, there is a certain loss of religious fervor. But it is not a thing of the town. It is so all over. As a matter of fact, our people perform their religious duties better in town than in the country. Why? Well, in the country there is just one Mass. If you miss that, you miss all. But here we have five Masses a Sunday and Masses throughout the week, and seven priests in the presbytery to serve the people whenever they wish. It is made easier for them to perform their duties.

If the priest's analysis is correct, an increase in general religious activity is accompanied by a drop in vocations to the priesthood. Of course, increase in religious activities does not necessarily mean a corresponding increase in depth of piety. It may mean the opposite. That question aside, a key factor in the vocation is its function for the family and the kind of family effort which brings it to fruition. The testimony of priests in general is that the urban working class does not produce priests. The few cases of vocation which came to our attention in the community were those of sons of smaller businessmen, fairly successful in their enterprises, but not of the first rank in their social position. None of the distinctly high-ranking families, new or old, has produced a priest in the memory of any of the older residents. One may suggest, although the data are not adequate for proof,[8] that the deeper piety of the rural people and lower-middle classes of urban people, along with the family solidarity engendered by maintenance of a family enterprise, is the condition most favorable to directing sons toward the priesthood. Gaining a living from individual wages and salaries is not favorable; nor is the more secular spirit, expressed in a more sophisticated set of social ambitions, of the middle and upper classes favorable to vocations, even though such families may conduct successful enterprises.

Of similar import is the trend—alleged by the priests of our community to be true—toward earlier marriage among the industrial working classes. It is attributed to the fact that the young people need not wait for a farm. Full wage-earning capacity comes early. The church, for its part, rather encourages early marriage, to take girls out of industry. This seems to mean that marriage is less a family affair

[8] There seem to be no data available on the sources from which priests come. A Montreal priest says the time has passed when vocations may be expected in the families of professional men.

than in the country, and precisely because the industrial family has no family enterprise which might be affected by the marriage.

While the data of this chapter indicate that the more rural of the inhabitants of the Cantonville community, who are at the same time industrial workers, strive in various ways to maintain their rural values, it is actually the middle classes who can and do maintain the tradition of family co-operation in an enterprise, of developing a family property, and of determining the careers of their children by co-ordinated family effort. Perhaps this is a way of saying that the values of the *habitant* are essentially of middle-class character, while his economic position in Cantonville is that of a wage-worker.

CHAPTER XVII

BY-PRODUCTS OF TOWN LIFE: FASHIONS, POPULAR LITERATURE, AND AMUSEMENTS

I N ADDITION to changing the economic organization of the family, town life brings people into touch with many new ways and ideas. And it gives them leisure in which to be tempted by the new ways. Some of the city ways are condemned on moral grounds; others are frowned upon simply because they cost money which might have been devoted to better purposes. Condemned or not, they make headway even among people of recent rural origin. We shall discuss the progress of certain of these city ways in Cantonville.

Of the phenomena attributed to city influences, fashion is perhaps the most notorious. The French Canadians adopt city fashions in dress without any hesitation. The stylish dress, the permanent wave, cosmetics, and all the accoutrement of the city girl appear in Quebec small towns and even in the country. Newspaper advertisements and fashion magazines bring changes in fashion promptly. Local hairdressers think that the country girl is even more likely than the town girl to have a permanent wave. She has less leisure in which to look after her appearance.

In the poorer outlying districts of the community young girls evidently try as hard as anyone to follow the fashions; sometimes the results show a little lack of sophistication. In these parts of town the older women are likely to wear the same drab, unfashionable clothes as do country women; the number of them who wear mourning increases this effect. In short, all girls and young women dress in the fashion; older women of rustic or working-class background often do not. But older women of the middle and upper classes of the town dress smartly, with the usual differences found in the dress of their age groups. If there is a difference between the dress of French and English middle-class women it is only that the former are more meticulous and chic.

The church deals with fashion in dress only to insist on modesty. In Cantonville, as in other Quebec towns, the wearing of shorts and bathing suits on the streets, even by little girls and for walks of only a block or so to the water, is strictly forbidden. But the bathing suits worn by the French girls and women are just as "daring" as American fashions decree.

The men follow the fashions in clothing in much the same way as women. Young men of all classes buy the clothes that are in fashion. Older rural and working-class men wear ready-made suits, but without much attention to neatness of fit or pressing. The young men affect sideburns and thin-line moustaches. Their suits and ties are perhaps darker than those of the English. These features, along with slighter figures and darker coloring, give the impression of a somewhat distinct French type of well-dressed young man. Light tweeds and bright ties, common among the English of Cantonville as among English-Canadian men generally, are seen among the French Canadians who play golf and who belong to the tennis club. This is perhaps a matter of social class. Incidentally, the most nationalistic young French lawyer of the town goes about in a very English-looking ensemble of yellow tweed coat and flannel trousers. Nor does one hear the nationalists complain of the fact that their suits bear the trade-names of well-known American-Jewish manufacturers.

Mechanical conveniences are not subject to any particular moral condemnation. The telephone is much less common in rural Quebec than in rural Ontario. The 1,002 telephones in Cantonville are few for a North American community of this size. In the town itself, there are 9.2 telephones per hundred people, and in the villages only 1.9; the corresponding numbers of strictly residential phones are 6.3 and 1.5. These figures indicate that the telephone is scarcely found at all among the working-class French of the community.[1]

The automobile is spoken of as a luxury upon which some people needlessly waste their money and as an occasion of instalment buying. So expensive an item is said to divert money from the buying of real property. The largest local dealer in automobiles and house furnishings stated—in a general complaint that people are losing their rural virtues and want too many material comforts—that many of his customers spend more than they earn. He continues, however, to keep his salesmen energetically selling cars. The curé also deprecates the spending of hard-earned wages upon indulgences, including gasoline for the car. The preachments are probably of no importance; but only 19 per cent of the French gainfully employed males of the community

---

[1] Calculated from directories and the parish censuses.

have cars, while 52 per cent of the English do.[2] That this difference is mainly a matter of economic position is evident from Table 42, which relates ownership of cars to occupation. Car-owners are more common among the occupations of higher income and social ranking; and in the outlying villages, where businesses are small, ownership of cars by owners and managers of businesses is only half as frequent as among the larger owners and managers of the town itself. And, in another

TABLE 42

FRENCH MALES OWNING CARS BY OCCUPATIONS IN CANTONVILLE, 1937

	TOWN			VILLAGES			TOTAL		
	Number of Persons	Number of Cars	Percentage of Persons Owning Cars	Number of Persons	Number of Cars	Percentage of Persons Owning Cars	Number of Persons	Number of Cars	Percentage of Persons Owning Cars
Professional and quasi-professional..........	60	40	66.7	14	11	78.6	74	51	68.9
Managers or proprietors of businesses..........	135	67	49.6	87	23	26.4	222	90	40.5
Agents and clerks.......	231	36	15.6	100	16	16.0	331	52	15.7
Services and trades......	169	55	32.5	224	41	18.3	393	96	24.4
Day laborers and janitors	238	17	7.1	379	21	5.5	617	38	6.2
Industrial employees.....	1,002	202	20.2	1,412	214	15.2	2,414	416	17.2
Miscellaneous, *rentiers,* and public officers........	67	8	11.9	29	2	6.9	96	10	10.4
Total.............	1,902	425	22.3	2,245	328	14.6	4,147	753*	18.2

* This total does not include 42 cars owned by people listed in the city directory without occupations. Thirty-two were in the town; the remaining 10 were from the villages.

tabulation which we have not included, it appears that in every occupational category car-ownership is more frequent among those who own the houses they live in than among those who rent. Some changes in fundamental values may lie in the fact that, while in the villages 50 per cent more of the industrial workers own houses than own cars, in the town proper twice as many own cars as houses.

The telephone, the automobile, and the radio all are less frequent in Quebec, rural and urban, than in Ontario; all three are also much more frequent in Quebec cities than in the Quebec countryside. The disparity of frequency is, likewise for all three, less marked between the cities of the two provinces than between the rural districts. City life

[2] The data concerning automobiles were gathered from the lists in the local licensing office.

reduces, but does not eliminate, the French Canadian's relative lack of use of these modern devices for travel, communication, and pleasure.

The radio is more than a mechanical convenience. It is, like the newspaper and the motion pictures, a medium of communication. It may be tuned to English programs broadcast from Montreal or New York. Even the French stations broadcast some programs from outside. We have no data on the amount of listening to English programs. The objection to them is not a moral one, as in the case of the movies, but rather that they are not French in language. The French

TABLE 43

PERCENTAGES OF HOUSEHOLDS REPORTING
RADIOS IN QUEBEC AND ONTARIO, 1931*

	Quebec	Ontario
Total...................	27.8	44:7
Rural.......................	8.4	30.3
Urban.......................	37.5	53.6
Localities under 1,000.........	23.5	37.1
Localities 1,000–30,000........	34.5	49.4
Localities over 30,000.........	40.9	58.5

* Calculated from *Census of Canada, 1931*, V, 979, Table 57.

programs are of the type usual in America, except that there is more use of "small-time" talent and more speech-making on religious and cultural problems. Café songs and entertainment of Parisian type are presented in commercial programs. A few programs stick to the traditional songs of Quebec.

In the years just before our visit the county received daily more than 3,800 newspapers from Montreal and Quebec. Of these, close to 500 were English; the rest were French.[3] Most of these papers undoubtedly came to Cantonville. The number of English papers is so high in relation to the English population of the town and county that one must assume that a considerable number of French people read English papers. The practice of reading an English paper is fairly common among French business people.

Of the French papers, about one-fourth were of the type known as "la bonne presse," papers definitely devoted to the Catholic cause. Subscriptions to one of the more widely circulated of these, *Action catholique* of Quebec, is openly solicited by the church. More than one

[3] The data are from the reports of the Audit Bureau of Circulation for 1935–36.

solid citizen remarked that *Action catholique* is more subscribed to than read. The other papers are commercial newspapers. The largest of them, *La Presse* of Montreal, is the most widely circulated paper in Canada. It prints news from the standard news services, along with advertising, cartoons, and all the usual features of American papers. Two of the dailies which circulate in the community are Montreal tabloid.

The commercial papers are not only sources of news and popular literature; they are advertising media used by national advertisers and by all of the large department stores of Montreal. The latter are English-owned. The goods advertised in French and English papers are the same. Many of the advertisements are merely translated from English into French; few attempt any adaptation to French tastes or mentality. The social types portrayed and idealized are, in the main, American: new clothes bring success to men; girls get or keep their man by washing their clothes two shades whiter, taking the proper pain-killer on the night of the big party, and by getting rid of "B.O." French Canadians are thoroughly familiar with the Canadian and American nationally advertised brands. The volume of distinctly French-Canadian advertising is relatively small. It is mostly advertisement of retail firms rather than of brands. In the more nationalistic papers some advertisers announce themselves as French-Canadian and ask patronage on this ground.

The newspapers also keep people posted concerning the sporting events of the United States and Canada, the movies being made and shown, crime, and many of the banalities of life in the United States.

American movie and confession magazines are found at the newsstands and drug stores of Cantonville, although the circulations, as gauged by statements of the salespeople and in some cases by publishers' reports, are smaller than in English-speaking towns. The vendors say that many French girls, who speak but little English, regularly buy English-language magazines. This is especially so of movie magazines, which have pictures, and of the fashion magazines, which contain dress patterns. Even English detective and true-story magazines are bought by some French people. That these readers may be mainly people of longer urban experience is suggested by the absence of English magazines from the one drug store in an outlying village.

Montreal has its own cheap French magazines with pictures of actresses and the lore of Hollywood. The number of such publications is small; the more popular of them have large over-the-counter circulations in Cantonville. Another type of weekly very common in the province of Quebec combines cartoons and jokes of the type *esprit gaulois* with articles of semiscandalous character and obscure political gossip. All of these circulate in the community.

The priests have a good deal to say about the evils of such *mauvaise lecture*, and the intellectuals decry the banality of the American newspaper and magazine, as of most things American. Beyond the evident acquaintance of French-Canadian youth with American fashions, sports, and movie stars, we do not know the effects of these magazines.

Upper-class families generally have an English newspaper, in addition to *La Presse* and perhaps one or more of the French political or intellectual dailies or weeklies. A few such houses have a Parisian revue of some kind. Nearly all have a good library of French books, both Canadian and from France. Few English books are to be seen in the community—even in the houses of English people.

AMUSEMENTS

The amusement most talked of as affecting the French-Canadian culture is the motion picture. It is generally foreign in origin, in language, and in the life portrayed. Canada depends upon Hollywood for its regular supply of pictures. In the days of silent pictures, language was no problem. French titles were simply inserted for Quebec showings. But with the talking picture came agitation for more French movies. A good many French pictures, however, were not acceptable to Quebec censors and had to be cut or barred. In time a few theaters in Montreal were able to present purely French programs. One small theater showed some of the outstanding pictures for weeks and even months on end. But the neighborhood and small-town theaters could not do this. They continued to show Hollywood pictures most of the time.

In our community there was in 1936 one rather small theater showing English pictures three nights a week and an English and a French picture on the other three nights. It did not run on Sunday. During the next year two new theaters, with a total seating of 1,700, were built and opened. They ran on Sunday, in spite of the outspoken condemnation of the curé. The old theater closed.

One of the two new theaters showed French pictures three days a week and English pictures on the other nights. The other had only a dozen or so French pictures per year.[4] The French pictures, generally

---

[4] French pictures began to be hard to get as soon as the war started.

quite old and inferior, were run on the poor end of the week, from Sunday until Tuesday.

Seventeen hundred theater seats would be very few for an American town of 17,000 surrounded by a well-populated and accessible rural area. The various theater managers, at first doubtful whether the town would support even this many seats, were very optimistic a year later over the marked increase in movie attendance. They unanimously complain of the opposition of the curé to movies in general and especially to Sunday movies. The manager of the original theater complained thus even when his small theater had no competition:

The priest keeps us from making money. That man has cost me $100,000 in the last ten years. We tried a dance hall, but he won't let the people to go to a dance hall. He preaches against the movies. Some of these young people would be better off sitting down in the theater watching a movie of an evening instead of taking their pay checks Saturday noon and going off somewhere to play poker all night. There are lots of bushes around the town, too.

Why, that man even preaches against baseball. I ask you, what harm is there in going to a baseball game after dinner on Sunday and sitting there outdoors until supper time. But no, that fellow doesn't like it. It's funny how in some towns the priests are good fellows, but in others some fellow like this one preaches against everything. You can't get anywhere with them birds.[5]

What happens is that every Saturday and Sunday four or five hundred young people hire cars, get on the train, or any way they can, and go to Three Rivers, Montreal, Sherbrooke, or some place where the priest can't see them. We have lots of people here, but it doesn't do us any good with that fellow. He has preached against us for ten years. What good does it do him to keep the people from having a little innocent fun? The times will change, and the people will change their way of living—sometime. My children won't be as I am; I can bring them up the best I can, but I can't prevent them from having ideas different from mine and from living at a faster pace.

It's only the people right in the town who keep us going. Those villagers, they don't do us any good. They only come to town on Saturday night, and then they just walk around the streets and go to the tavern. Who are those people anyway? They are farmers from all around here. Their farms were poor, and they had too many kids; so they left the farm and came in here to work in the factory. They are like the old peasants in France; every time they get an extra cent, down it goes in the sock. Sometimes when the house isn't full, I leave here and walk through the streets to see where the people are. What are they doing? Nothing. You walk up to St. Jerome village, and what are they doing? Just sitting on the porch or talking to the neighbors. They are even too stingy to put on the light so they can play cards. They came from the farm, and they still think you can go to town only on Saturday night. On Saturday they come home from the factory and put on the "36"; they call it that, it is the only suit they have. Then some of them go out and drink and play cards in a back room. The older ones come to town and walk around. Some of them come to the show. Some of them go to private dances in some house.

[5] The curé does not, in fact, object to Sunday baseball. He stated that he warns people against purely commercial amusements on Sunday.

The two young managers of the new theaters were willing to vent their spleen in much the same manner after they had been in town a while.

Sunday is not a good theater day. It would be better if the curé did not preach against it. He is wrong when he says the gate at the baseball game just pays the costs, which he says makes it not a commercial enterprise and therefore all right on Sunday. The curé objects because he holds the people here close in his fist. I have lived three years in Ontario, and it is different there. But he wants to keep tight hold on them and so he hates films. He thinks it will be a means to *déraciner* the people. Well, this is the only place in the province where Mass costs fifteen cents. I have heard of ten cents, but never fifteen. Think what it costs to take a whole family to Mass. He charges fifteen cents for his show. I don't think that is right. But I go to church all the same.

All the managers also complained of the parsimony of the "farmers" who live in the villages. They are "ignorant" and "tight." Whatever the facts may be about movie attendance, these people who have their livings to make in the business feel both the pressure of the puritanical priest and the unresponsiveness of at least the older rural-bred people.

Yet they testified to a great increase in movie attendance at a time when the town was not growing at a great rate. All say that many people who do not understand English will come to the pictures frequently. We attended several movies, both English and French; the audience was always very largely French. In the English pictures a good deal of the repartee was obviously missed. Westerns, Mickey Mouse, Popeye, and such features are said to be especially liked.

The general air of the moving-picture crowds is chummy. Even in the middle of the main feature young men get up and, leaving their girls behind, go out for a smoke and chat in the vestibule. The seats are held for them until they come back. Even when others are standing, no one takes these seats. Everyone is out for a party; if someone wants to leave his seat for a while, he may do so. A hat or coat left in the seat shows intention to return. This custom indicates that the content of the pictures is not so important as the fact that they make an occasion for a sort of social life. It does not, of course, show that the pictures fail to make any impression on ideas and ways.

Reading matter, the radio, and the motion picture are forms of entertainment or amusement which also portray life and communicate ideas. There are other amusements of which this is not so obviously the case. They may be valued or opposed for their supposed effect on manners and morals or merely because they consume time and money.

A good deal of entertainment goes on inside the household or in informal groups. Previous chapters have given some account of the amusements of the upper social strata of the French people of Canton-ville. Their informal social life has perhaps been slighted. The people of this group have a rich life of family events, visiting, conversation, and the like. It is, on the whole, a quiet life. There is no evidence that it is greatly changed by the presence of a larger population or by the English. Some amusement is had from the rehearsals of amateur or-chestras and theatrical groups, as well as from the public perform-ances. The better-off and more sophisticated people travel frequently to Montreal for concerts and other events of interest. Their world has not been particularly enlarged or changed by recent developments.

But it is to the masses of the population that we address this section. In the outlying villages the informal neighborly visiting and gossip of the country persists. Young men gather about corners, soft-drink places, poolrooms, outdoor bowling alleys, and taverns in the evening. Older men seem generally to stay closer to home, either repairing things, gardening, or merely sitting on one another's porches. On nights when mosquitoes are on the rampage, groups of people of all ages sit in the darkness on their porches amid a haze of smoke from smudges. This sitting without any special activity and without much conversa-tion is perhaps the evening sport of the masses of people in country and town, in Quebec as elsewhere.

But there are organized amusements, both commercial and non-commercial. In the most rustic of the parishes, bean suppers, bingo parties, and home-talent shows are held for the benefit of the parish funds. During our stay a carnival was held in a vacant lot for the benefit of the parish of St. Bernard.

A little traveling carnival was running on the outskirts of St. Bernard in a field. It was advertised in town as for the benefit of the new parish. There were the usual things: a small merry-go-round, circling swings, a couple of gambling wheels, hot-dog stands, baseball-throwing for prizes, a shooting gallery with air guns, and several strength-testing devices, of which the most popular was the one where a blow with a heavy mallet would ring a bell if you were man enough. And—most popular of all— a bingo game. The side shows were not doing very well. One of them advertised a sword-swallower. The signs were badly spelled; several of them were good phonetic renditions of the French of the unlettered elements of Quebec. For instance, the sword-swallower was an "avaleur de sobes," instead of "sabres." Things for sale were "a vande," not "à vendre." A house was a "masson" instead of a "maison." One side show seemed to get more trade than the others. It was a troupe consisting of two Negro girls who did a few disappointing steps to music from three musicians, of whom one was also a Negro. Their show was advertised for people over sixteen years of age only.

The barkers, for the most part dirty women and unshaven men, loud-mouthed as befitted their profession, shouted in worse French than I have ever heard and occasionally in English that was very ungrammatical and strongly accented. (A breed of traveling people, I suspect, who have a language of their own. People of the same type and with the same language make the rounds of the small county fairs in Quebec.) One of the barkers, a young man apparently acquainted with the people in the crowd, wore, a white shirt with the standard red letters "J.O.C." of the Jeunesse ouvrière catholique on the pocket. He, too, was unshaven.

Hitting with the mallet to ring a bell was a popular sport. One lusty workingman (identified for us as a twenty-five-cent-per-hour laborer in the textile mill) paid for one blow but kept on swinging and ringing the bell again and again. The barker vainly tried to stop him and finally gave up. The crowd was much amused; the women went into shrieks of unaffected loud laughter. After this exhibit of his strength, the man's boss (English), who happened to be watching, stepped up and paid twenty-five cents for this assault upon the trembling apparatus. The performer, shy but grinning, took the handful of cheap cigars he had won and wandered off by himself.

The curé sat playing at the bingo game. He was in a genial mood. A bevy of little girls surrounded him and, amid much giggling, tried to show him how to play as he affected ignorance of the procedure. A little, toothless man in a dingy black hat and a white shirt without collar or tie tried to cheat by putting his tokens (grains of corn) on B15 when B5 was called, and complained bitterly when it was not allowed. The bingo players were mostly rather serious about it. They were middle-aged women, heavy-set, many lacking teeth, but all thoroughly and stiffly marceled.

A young vicar was going about as if inspecting the concessions. Later we saw him doing a very good job of throwing baseballs at dummies. A group of women gathered behind him and were loudly amused at his condescension to so lowly a sport. He is, in fact, the son of a farmer who lives only seven miles away.

The merry-go-round and swings were patronized by young couples. The boys held the girls more protectively than was necessary on such mild rides.

The crowd included a lot of young people in town clothes, the boys in sport shirts and narrow suspenders. But there were also a number of men in lumberjacks' red shirts, boots, and coarse breeches reaching halfway from knee to ankle. The latter gloried in their feats of strength. The loud, unaffected, husky wives of the poor, with cheap permanent waves, awkwardly and ineffectually lifted the mallet and, giggling, let it fall with no force at all. Altogether it was a poor crowd, with many really miserable specimens in ragged clothes.

Shortly after ten o'clock the crowd dwindled, and the shows closed. On the next night, Saturday, the crowd was bigger and stayed later. Many children were there; a lot of them were barefoot. The little girls wore ill-cut dresses of drapery satin and other goods, probably remnants from the local mills. It is the custom among the lower classes to take children on visits and to entertainments at night. But this evening there was a special attraction. Early in the evening a Shirley Temple contest was held. Several girls, from about four to nine, dressed and marceled in imitation of the famous child-actress, lined up on a platform to be examined by judges, who kept up a running chatter with the aid of a loud-speaker system. The mothers proudly and anxiously watched. The crowd enjoyed it thoroughly, in a jocular spirit.

Further light on the amusements of the working people may be had from a description of a large rally held by the Jocistes, members of the Jeunesse ouvrière catholique:

The grand study and demonstration Sunday of the Jeunesse ouvrière catholique and the Jeunesse ouvrière catholique féminine ends with a big open meeting in the Arena. I went over at about 9:00 p.m. The Jocistes, in uniform, were seated on chairs on the floor surrounding the platform, which was the one used for wrestling bouts a few nights ago and still fitted up with the ropes. There were said to be 400 of the members present. A miscellaneous crowd of all ages filled the bleachers and side benches in the north half of the Arena. It was distinctly a working-class crowd, the families and friends of the Jocistes. In the front row of chairs facing the platform were eight priests, including the curé of St. Luc's. A loud-speaker arrangement with microphone was set up.

When I entered, the young man whom I had seen acting as barker at the St. Bernard carnival was seated before the microphone, playing jig music on an accordion. The crowd was stamping its feet in time with the music. He got much applause.

After this preliminary, the leader of the Jeunesse ouvrière catholique took the platform in the running, overenergetic manner (half-military, half like a bubbling cheerleader) we so often saw at Nazi rallies in Germany. He used fixed gestures to start and stop applause. He announced the first speaker, the *propagandiste général* of the Jeunesse ouvrière catholique for Canada.

After the speech the leader leaped up again and announced the "Musicians of St. Bernard": a guitarist, an accordion-player, and a fiddler who played with his fiddle on his knee in accepted country-dance style. They played jigs and the American-Negro "Golden Slippers." The crowd loved it.

A speech of the curé was followed by a song written by a Jociste of St. Jerome, sung by the author. It was a popular sentimental tune to which innumerable verses were sung. The Jocistes joined in the choruses. The author and soloist was a thin man of perhaps thirty, who assumed something of a patronizing air toward the crowd, although his thin tenor cracked on the high note in every stanza. He got the respectful hearing French Canadians always give to home talent.

After the song came the surprise of the evening. The author of the song was again called to the platform. He stepped to the microphone and, in the manner of a Major Bowes at his amateur hour, asked the people who had the numbers he would call to come up. Each member of the Jeunesse ouvrière catholique had such a number; and about fifteen—boys and girls—were called up, apparently by chance. Among them was the black-haired handsome show-off of the local skating-rink, of ice-cream parlors, and of all lower-class public gatherings; he dances, does skating tricks, and sings impromptu solos on the slightest provocation. He now came to the platform, pretending great astonishment, dodging about as if about to be hit, and otherwise amusing himself and the crowd.

After they were all on the platform, each was separately called to the microphone and asked his name; then a formal question concerning the Jeunesse ouvrière catholique movement was put. The girls nearly all answered promptly in set phrases in a loud catechism-class voice. Some of the boys did likewise, but several of them did not and eventually went away without the coin which was given for each successful answer. During this catechism test a little man in a raincoat came running up from somewhere and told a couple of "histoires" after having intentionally and ridiculously failed on a couple of questions. (The "histoire" is a regular part of home-talent entertainment. It is a long spun-out comic story, done with some acting and many pauses for laughter. Books of "histoires" are on sale in bookstores and at newsstands.)

Some more speeches were made by priests. This meeting was described by one of the speakers as a demonstration of the growth and strength of the Jeunesse ouvrière catholique and of showing what a jolly lot they are. The members had the air of people who are having their first taste of organization, uniforms, mass singing, and organized cheering—they were a little drunk with it, like college Freshmen who come from small rural high schools. They were honestly enthusiastic but also exceedingly well drilled. They sang when told, applauded and stopped applauding at signals from the leader. Several of the young men who helped in the marshaling and entertainment definitely aped radio announcers. "I now turn the microphone over to M. Dion, our leader," etc.

The Jocistes and the spectators were definitely of the demos, with a rural cast. They loved jig music from a fiddle or an accordion. They stamped their feet to show their pleasure. They smoked, drank pop, and ate *patates frites* during the meeting. One of the uniformed Jocistes was drinking pop from a bottle while the curé was speaking; he was only a few feet from the curé. The crowd talked and laughed a good deal. They changed seats and made remarks to one another. A couple of young fellows (spectators) near me found something funny in all the remarks made (except by the priests). When the Jeunesse ouvrière catholique motto—*joyeux, purs, conquérants*—was repeated for about the tenth time, one of them said: "Joyeux Noel." They nearly died laughing.

As a last, definitive touch of rural folk or of city working classes, they had their children—even small ones—with them, and let them move about, play, or sleep until the close of the meeting late at night. Meanwhile their elders patiently sat through innumerable speeches. It reminded me of the meetings of Polish societies in Chicago, of Mexican dances and celebrations in park field houses near the South Chicago steel mills, of Methodist revival meetings in southern Ohio—the people in no hurry to come and in no hurry to go, patient beyond belief, and with children swarming over them. The crowd was noisy and informal, but profoundly respectful of speeches in general and especially of those of priests and their betters. The Jeunesse ouvrière catholique leaders, whoever they really are, have—either by instinct or by design—figured out their crowd perfectly and tonight gave them just the right kind of entertainment and simple, dogmatic speeches full of the most powerful symbols of French-Canadian society.

At a Labor Day picnic of the Jeunesse ouvrière catholique and their families the crowd was of the same sort. The entertainment consisted of the usual races (three-legged, backwards, hopping, etc.) for children at picnics, a blueberry pie-eating contest, finding a penny in a trough of flour with one's nose and mouth—all the familiar things of simple folk. And it was accompanied by the same slightly show-off acting before a microphone, which was passed from one impresario to another every few minutes. The standard costume for these local impresarios and entertainers is the bowler hat. If the occasion is formal enough, the wearer will be shaven. If it is at a skating-rink or a carnival, he will not be shaven. Several of these young entertainers play their roles all the time, even when loafing of an evening about an ice-cream parlor, or when baiting the "village idiot" for the entertainment of the crowd gathered at the post office to wait for the evening mail.

The standard entertainment of the fraternal organizations and parochial societies is the bingo party or the card party, with a raffle. These are generally accompanied by clowning and other home-talent performances before the microphone. Such parties follow the usual pattern of money-raising entertainment in America. Tickets are sold by the members. Prizes are solicited from merchants and leading citizens, who get therefrom a little advertising. Minor leaders of the organizations marshal and entertain the crowd; the names of the leading people of the town never appear among the active organizers, participants, or prize-winners.

At the entertainments described—the carnival, the lighter parts of the Jeunesse ouvrière catholique demonstration, and the bingo parties of various societies—one sees very much the pattern of entertainment which Americans commonly associate with either Catholic societies or the American Legion. The lottery features, the games of chance for prizes, and the carnival are frequently called "Catholic" by American Protestants. Objection to such features is called "bigotry" by Irish-American Catholics. The truth is probably that Catholics of whatever class would not object to them but that Catholics of the upper classes would not, as they do not in Cantonville, take part in them. Certain features of the entertainment, bingo especially, may be American in origin. But no one complains of the American origin of these features. What is apparently happening is that the rural people who are drawn into such organizations and their entertainments are simply adopting an already present pattern of town lower-class and lower-middle-class behavior. Certain features of it—the parts amenable to fashion—may come from the English-speaking American urban world, but the genre is rather universal and in no way foreign to French Canada.

The more distinctly commercial entertainments gauged for the masses of the people are, in addition to the movies, wrestling and boxing bouts, occasional cheap plays of a very melodramatic kind, and vaudeville programs in the motion-picture theaters. During our visit, the acme of such entertainment was a beauty contest. A traveling theatrical promoter arranged a program of vaudeville acts for several nights in a local theater; at each performance the business of selecting "Mlle Cantonville" proceeded. The winning candidate was the daughter of a carpenter. On Saturday night a gala presentation of "Mlle Cantonville" and the winners of similar contests in other provincial towns was arranged. After the films and the vaudeville, including something intended as a strip-tease, the beauty queen of Cantonville was presented, arrayed in clothing donated by the leading smart shops of the town. The mayor and a few leading citizens were on the stage to congratulate the young lady. After that a party for her was held in the big hotel. Public dances are rare enough, and so many of the gayer people of some social standing were there. The parents of "Mlle Cantonville," awkward and awed, sat through the many dances in which their daughter—very pretty, very tastefully arrayed, and working very industriously on her chewing gum—danced with such partners as were not also too awed. The mayor and his wife sat, stiff, bored, and patient, at the head table until far into the night.

This was a very American thing to do. But the agent who arranged it and all of the participants were French-Canadian. And that is its point; the active agents in introducing what the French élite consider the vulgar features of American city life are invariably not Americans or English Canadians. They are French Canadians, who have their headquarters in Montreal.

A group not present in considerable number in our community are the great urbanized, lower-middle-class masses. In Montreal they are the army of clerical workers, shopgirls, stenographers, etc. One sees them in vacation resorts in the back country in summer. They stay for week ends in smaller hotels advertised to have a *cuisine canadienne* and to be only for Christians. On Saturday nights they gather with great gusto about the piano and sing French-Canadian songs, including "Alouette" with verses and gestures not found in the Camp-Fire Girl version. They also sing risqué Parisian café songs. They dance in close formation, and the boys shout over their shoulders jokes that would not ordinarily be uttered in American mixed company of comparable class. It is against these people and their behavior that much of the castigation of city behavior is directed. To what extent this vulgarity verging on obscenity is present among the French of our community, it is hard to say. One does not hear it among the upper-class people, even in their freest and gayest gatherings—except perhaps in a slightly freer use of the *double entendre* than among English. There are no public dance halls in the community and no public places where young men and women of the lower-white-collar class may drink together. The curé has successfully opposed dance halls. A certain number of semi-clandestine gatherings of such young people occur, and a handful of them appear on the fringes of an occasional public dance arranged mainly for people of somewhat higher standing. Perhaps, as the town element grows, the weight of the curé's influence may not prevent the development of public commercial amusements for this class of people.

In places where there is public provision for their entertainment, they follow American song hits and Parisian café ditties with no apparent preference for either. Sheet music, cheap phonograph records, and broadcasts make both available. In larger cities the cheap French *boîte de nuit* (night club) presents the latest in these things, sung and danced by French-Canadian professional entertainers.

It is difficult, out of this maze, to trace the threads of American influence and to separate them from the French from France and from the things which happen whenever comparable classes of city people develop. Perhaps the fair and tenable statement of the case is that city life in Quebec creates the same classes of people as cities elsewhere in the Western world and that certain of these classes are especially amenable to the fashions of song, dance, and entertainment. In Quebec, further, the fashions are spread through the agency of French Canadians who—taking their inspiration sometimes from New York or Hollywood, sometimes from Paris, sometimes from one another—have their headquarters in Montreal and work out versions of them which can successfully be exploited in the smaller cities. Cantonville is one of the newer of the cities arrived at such size as to be so exploited. And the rustic masses that we saw at the carnival and the Jeunesse ouvrière catholique rallies are evidently still more numerous than the more sophisticated lower-middle class or even working class that one finds in older towns and in Montreal. But even the rustic people are ready to accept urban features—such as the Shirley Temple contest, bingo, and amateur vaudeville—into their rather rural entertainment.

PART III

THE METROPOLIS

CHAPTER XVIII

MONTREAL

TYPICAL though Cantonville is—with due allowance for minor variations—of the smaller centers, Montreal is the port of entry from which English influence and the industrial revolution radiate into the remote corners of the French-Canadian world. This city, where more than 600,000 French Canadians are gathered, has somewhat replaced the older and smaller city of Quebec as the cultural capital of French Canada. While Quebec may still be the unruffled alma mater of the French-Canadian spirit, Montreal is the active and dominating center of the more secular developments of the French-Canadian civilization: of the scientific and commercial branches of learning, of the arts and literature, of the commercial press, of such leadership in business and finance as French Canadians have, and of the newer social movements. All this goes on under the shadow of the skyscrapers from which English Canadians direct the great financial and industrial institutions not merely of the province but of all Canada. The transformation of the Cantonvilles is wrought by the two hands of Montreal—the finer, French one and the stronger, English one.

A number of studies have shown in some detail the places of French and English in the economic structure of Montreal. Jamieson, in the course of a general study of this problem, found that, of the directorates of 83 of the largest corporations with headquarters in Montreal, 768 were held by English persons and only 93 by French. Indicative of the general position of the two ethnic groups was the fact that the three banks with half or a majority of French directors are among the smallest. Their branches are confined mainly to Quebec. The English banks are national in scope and closely entwined with the larger industries.

Analysis of 10,694 Montreal firms rated in the Dun and Bradstreet

Directory showed that those of greatest "estimated pecuniary strength" were nearly all English. Only among those of less than $20,000 "estimated pecuniary strength" were French firms the more numerous. By conservative estimate, at least 86 per cent of all the "estimated pecuniary strength" of the rated firms was that of English firms; over half of the 86 per cent was held by the 200 largest English corporations.[1]

The membership of the board of trade consists largely of English who hold higher positions in large firms, many of which do a national

TABLE 44

NUMBER OF FRENCH AND ENGLISH DIRECTORS OF MONTREAL FIRMS
ENGAGED IN BANKING AND CERTAIN INDUSTRIES, 1935*

INDUSTRY OR BUSINESS	NUMBER OF FIRMS	DIRECTORS	
		English	French
Banks	10	140	26
Transportation and communication	7	73	6
Iron and steel	10	87	7
Nonferrous metals	8	76	5
Milling	6	49	6
Pulp and paper	11	102	10
Electric power	8	68	7
Chemicals	5	48	1
Nonmetallic minerals	13	98	18
Liquor and beverages	5	27	7
Total directorates	83	768†	93†

* Compiled from Stuart M. Jamieson, "French and English in the Institutional Structure of Montreal" (unpublished Master's thesis, McGill University, 1938), Appen. A.
† This total does not eliminate duplication arising through interlocking directorates.

business; the corresponding French organization, the *chambre de commerce*, has a membership composed of representatives of smaller businesses with some minor representatives of bigger concerns. The difference is reflected in a greater concern of the board of trade over national issues affecting business and industry and in the emphasis of the *chambre de commerce* upon local affairs, the rights of smaller business, and of the French Canadian in particular.[2]

Roy assembled data concerning the place of French and English in fourteen major lines of industry. He found that in firms engaged in the

[1] Everett C. Hughes and Margaret L. McDonald, "French and English in the Economic Structure of Montreal," *Canadian Journal of Economics and Political Science*, VII (1941), 493–505.

[2] Data collected by Margaret McDonald.

204   FRENCH CANADA IN TRANSITION

heavier industries, requiring great capital outlay and extensive use of
modern engineering, an overwhelming majority of managers and of
executives of higher rank were English. As in Cantonville's larger industries, it was only at or below the rank of foreman, and in some cases
skilled workman, that the French were more numerous. Only in a few
traditional industries, with smaller plants and operations of the artisan
type, was French management and ownership found to any considerable extent.[3]

DIAGRAM XI*

PERCENTAGE DISTRIBUTION OF ENGLISH AND FRENCH
MERCHANDISING FIRMS BY THEIR ESTIMATED
PECUNIARY STRENGTH†

* Reproduced from Hughes and McDonald, *op. cit.*, p. 499.
† From tabulation of all firms listed and rated in Dun and Bradstreet, *Directory*, March,
1940. Of the firms classified as "Other" (7 per cent of the total), two-thirds belong in Group V.

Unlike Cantonville, Montreal has a large force of English workers in
industry. Roy's study shows that in the iron and steel industries and
in the older textile plants there was a time when practically all the
working force was English. There is still a large proportion of English
among skilled workers. In these industries an actual replacement of
English workers by French has occurred over a long period. At the
time of Roy's work, 43 per cent of the English employees of the industries studied were foremen, clerical help, salesmen, or executives.
Only 11 per cent of the French were in these categories. The English
are a specialized and top-heavy group.

Although the French in Montreal show the same affinity for trade as

[3] William H. Roy, "The French-English Division of Labor in Quebec" (unpublished
Master's thesis, McGill University, 1935).

in Cantonville, wholesaling is largely in English hands. The French
are decidedly more numerous in retail businesses, but the four major
department stores are English. All of them, as well as many other
English retail stores, advertise in the French daily newspapers. French
stores do not, as a rule, bother to advertise in the English press. The
large English retail businesses hire great numbers of French employees
to serve, in their own language, their numerous French customers.
There results an ethnic distribution about like that in industry, with
positions of authority filled mainly by English.

TABLE 45

DISTRIBUTION OF PERCENTAGES OF EMPLOYEES IN SELECTED
MONTREAL MANUFACTURING INDUSTRIES BY OCCU-
PATION AND ETHNIC BACKGROUND, 1934*

OCCUPATION	PERCENTAGES OF INDUSTRIAL EMPLOYEES			
	English	French	Other	Total
Managerial	5.3	0.8	1.2	2.2
Sales force	6.5	1.8	1.6	3.2
Clerical	24.4	5.0	4.2	10.9
Foremen	5.9	2.3	2.0	3.4
Assistant foremen	1.5	0.9	0.9	1.1
Skilled workers	27.8	37.5	27.3	33.9
Semiskilled workers	19.5	36.9	28.3	31.0
Unskilled workers	9.1	14.8	34.5	14.3
Total	100.0	100.0	100.0	100.0

* Roy, *op. cit.*, Appen., p. 32.

Montreal English people sell goods to French people and perform
services for them much more than in Cantonville. In the main, they
do so through the department stores, chain stores, and restaurants—
business units of the newer types developed to a high point in the
United States. The goods and services get to the French customer
mainly from the hands of their own fellows, who are low in the authority hierarchies of the concerns for which they work. For the young
English person of no great training, this means a certain difficulty in
starting in at the bottom, for the bottom is French.

It is also generally true that in Montreal the French are less frequent
in industries and occupations requiring new types of mechanical skill
or higher training in engineering and applied science. Mr. Jamieson
found the French rare in air transport, chemical industries, shipbuild-

ing, manufacture of telephone and telegraph equipment, and in communications industries and services generally.[4]

In the professional occupations a similar difference occurs. The English are far more numerous than chance expectation in engineering, architecture, and accounting. The French are correspondingly few in these professions. Professionals of certain new kinds—librarians, social workers, nurses—are likewise relatively fewer among the French than among the English; the ancient services which these new professions offer continue to be performed for the French largely by nuns and brothers.[5]

TABLE 46

TYPES OF MERCHANDISING FIRMS BY ETHNIC BACKGROUND
IN MONTREAL, 1940*

TYPE OF FIRM	TOTAL NUMBER OF FIRMS	PERCENTAGE			
		Total	English	French	Other
Production........	1,674	100.0	81.2	15.7	3.1
Wholesale.........	888	100.0	67.0	27.5	5.5
Retail............	6,334	100.0	29.8	62.0	8.2
Service...........	1,798	100.0	46.8	46.2	7.0
Total.........	10,694	100.0	43.8	49.2	7.0

* Hughes and McDonald, *op. cit.*, p. 501.

In the traditional professions of medicine and law the difference between the ethnic groups is not so much in the proportional numbers of practitioners as in their mode of practice. Forty-six per cent of the 575 French lawyers practice alone, and 94 per cent in firms of no more than five members; only 28 per cent of the English lawyers practice alone, and 65 per cent in firms of five or less. More than one-third of the English lawyers are in firms of six members or more. Indeed, 45 of the 258 English lawyers are in three firms, each of which includes one or more leading figures who are directors of several of Canada's largest corporations. These data and interviews suggest that corporation law belongs to the English, while the French—and, incidentally, the Jewish—lawyers get their livings from smaller businesses. The French and Jewish lawyers thus adhere more closely to the tradition according to

[4] *Op. cit.*, p. 67. Data from a special tabulation of occupational data for Montreal, prepared by the Dominion Bureau of Statistics from the census of 1931.
[5] *Ibid.*, p. 91.

which each member of the profession has his own clients; the English lawyer in a large firm may, in effect, be an employee of another who has the clients.

In medicine the French are more widely scattered about the city and are specialized in a smaller proportion. Forty-one per cent of all English physicians and 74 per cent of the English specialists have their offices in a dozen blocks in the uptown center of the city. A large proportion practice in two medical buildings, where several doctors may use in common a suite of offices, equipment, and other services. While a considerable proportion (24 per cent) of French physicians are somewhat concentrated along two main thoroughfares, the majority still have office and residence in the same house.[6]

TABLE 47

PERCENTAGE OF MONTREAL LAWYERS OF FRENCH, BRITISH, AND JEWISH EXTRACTION IN FIRMS OF VARIOUS SIZES, 1935*

	NUMBER OF MEMBERS IN FIRMS			
	1 Only	1–5	6–10	11 or More
French (575 members)......	45.6	94.2	5.6	0.2
British (258 members)......	28.0	65.2	17.4	17.4
Jewish (185 members)......	61.1	100.0	....	....

* Compiled from Jamieson, *op. cit.*, p. 141*a*.

English physicians are specialized not only in far greater proportion than their French colleagues of Montreal but in twice that of their colleagues of Toronto and Vancouver, Canada's second and third cities, both of which have a very large proportion of English-speaking population.

The English people of Montreal are more than an ethnic minority in a city. They are, in fact, the metropolitan element of Canada's metropolis. Some among them direct the great economic institutions which operate throughout Canada and beyond the national borders. Their hospitals and medical specialists serve clients from a wide area and train physicians and nurses for a still wider one. English Montreal's hinterland is half a continent. The French of Montreal enter into these nationally dominant institutions in minor and less specialized roles. But the very presence of the numerous French allows the English group to be more specialized and more devoted to control func-

[6] *Ibid.*, p. 107.

tions than they could be if Montreal were a purely English city. Those of the French who are in dominant positions are concentrated in institutions which have for their hinterland, not the continent, but merely the province.

TABLE 48

THE SPECIALIZATION OF PHYSICIANS IN
TORONTO, VANCOUVER, AND
MONTREAL, 1939*

	Specialists (Per Cent)	Members of Specialty Bodies (Per Cent)
Toronto............	16.4	18.2
Vancouver..........	15.0	16.3
Montreal...........	14.5	18.1

* Compiled from the *American Medical Directory, 1939*.

TABLE 49

THE SPECIALIZATION OF PHYSICIANS IN MONTREAL
BY NATIONALITY, 1939*

	Specialists (Per Cent)	Members of Specialty Bodies (Per Cent)	Members of Canadian Medical Association (Per Cent)
French..........	5.9 (18.0) †	2.8	3.3
English.........	30.3 (36.4)	⎫	45.6
Jewish..........	16.9 (25.8)	⎬ 36.6	18.2
Others..........	10.0 (21.4)	⎭	10.0

* Compiled from the official list of registered physicians in Greater Montreal (*American Medical Directory, 1939*).

† The larger percentages, which appear in parentheses, were obtained by adding all listed as specialists in city directories and the general and classified telephone directories. The larger figure probably includes all practitioners who wish to be regarded as specialists, without regard to their affiliation with American and Canadian specialty bodies. We include the larger figure to overcome any bias which might result from failure of French-Canadian specialists to report their specialties and specialty qualifications to the English compilers of the *American Medical Directory*.

Even in matters which concern only their own relatively small population, the English of Montreal have been the more vigorous agents of modern American urban life and institutions. English Protestants set the pace in establishing a federation to conduct a single annual campaign for charities and to co-ordinate the work of the various philan-

thropic agencies. Only within the past decade have the French done
so; even now, many parish priests and social agencies resist the efforts
of the new federation and the introduction of lay professional social
workers. In general, it is safe to say that such new institutions will be
introduced by the English and later adopted, with some modification,
by the French.

These data and other evidence which could be mustered indicate
that French Canadians in the city cling somewhat to their traditional
institutions and occupations. This frequently stated formula does not,
however, fully fit the facts. For urbanity and sophistication are perhaps more characteristic of the French than of the English in Montreal. While there are a few French families of great wealth, it is significant that the members of the Ligue de la Jeunesse féminine are
drawn more from among the daughters of professional men than are
the members of the English Junior League.[7] The French Cercle uni-
versitaire, a club of university men, is a center of cultural and intellectual activity. The English University Club is simply a club of university graduates, third in prestige among exclusive English clubs.
Professional men, intellectuals, and artists have a much greater prestige in Montreal French society than in the English society.

It is probable that the French classical *collège* and the convent play a
large part in maintaining this difference of orientation. It may also be
due to the very fact that for one hundred and fifty years the English,
first as conquerors and later as representatives of the more drastically
capitalistic English and American world, have taken the lead in introducing economic and technological changes. The Jews, under conditions of discrimination in the urban economic world but without a
footing on the land, have developed a commercial ingenuity which has
enabled them to survive and to get ahead. The French Canadians,
with a sure base on the soil, the conviction that they have first rights in
their homeland, and with a set of traditional rural and town institutions, have not aggressively sought new solutions for their economic
problems. Rather they have attempted to consolidate their position in
smaller and older forms of enterprise. And, although it is perhaps a
matter of tradition for them to give a high place to the professions and
to those intellectual pursuits which relate especially to their historic
institutions, one may see in this emphasis at least something of com-
pensation for their lack of pre-eminence in the economic field.

[7] Aileen Ross, "The French and English Social Elites of Montreal" (unpublished
Master's thesis, University of Chicago, 1941), p. 81.

A feature of the French-Canadian mentality is the prevalence of intellectual hobbies. The civil servant or even the businessman may be an amateur historian. The physician of some standing is as likely to be interested in some historical or philosophical phase of medicine as in avid pursuit of some new specialty. The lawyer, the notary, the physician, the civil servant, and the priest have written much of Canada's history and a good deal of French Canada's fiction and poetry. In keeping with this tradition the salon—where literary and artistic chatter and political argument mingle with genteel flirtation and gracious compliment—still flourishes in Montreal.

On the economic side, the French-Canadian city culture has become stabilized about an earlier phase of capitalism. On the intellectual side, it centers less about the sciences and their application than in the rest of North America. The French-Canadian intellectual is a savant rather than an expert. Such an orientation may be typical of a minority constantly threatened by a vigorous and dominant culturally alien force—and especially of a minority which, as the French-Canadians do, feels its identity with one of the great world civilizations.

If one looks at French-Canadian literature, he is impressed by the amount of it which idealizes the past and the rural existence and by the French-Canadian penchant for belles-lettres, criticism, and political journalism. A realistic fiction like that of Sinclair Lewis has not been developed. With a very few recent exceptions, novels are not concerned with the city masses. The critical note appears mainly in essays and articles in the great number of small periodicals and concerns the intellectual world as well as the political position of the French Canadians. Much of it is criticism of the modern economic world and of its concomitants in the culture of the city demos.

The masses of the French Canadians are being swept into the very life which their intellectuals and spiritual leaders decry. French Canadians form the bulk of the laborers in industry; they fill the minor, if more numerous, places in large commercial institutions. Their ultimate employers, if not their immediate superiors, are English. It thus has come about that their employers and their traditional spiritual leaders represent two cultural worlds differently oriented to the major problems of life. Those who have been accustomed to state their values for them and those who guard their sacred symbols and sentiments have little authority over the bread-and-butter activities of the urban French Canadians. The kinds of knowledge and the personal qualities stressed by the intellectual leaders of French Canada do not coincide with those of the economic system in which most urban French Canadians have to work. This is a situation favorable to a certain questioning both of the traditional leadership and of the disturbing new system.

It is also probably significant that the French Canadians are being drawn en masse into the world of extreme industrial capitalism at the very time when that world is already being shaken and when its ideology of laissez faire is being questioned. Quebec's industrial revolution has come late and as a series of changes introduced by culturally alien agents; French Quebec has, in short, been an outpost of the capitalistic industrial world rather than a controlling center. The presence, in the province, of Montreal, an active center of economic change, contradicts this statement geographically but not culturally. The fact that the industrial revolution has come by waves of outside influence may account for the fact that the institutions of French Canada, and especially her educational institutions, have not undergone that transformation which has—in the United States, at least—made them so much the handmaiden of industrial progress.

The American world has developed a system of institutions to cope —how successfully is not in question—with the problems of an industrial civilization. Among these institutions are trade-unions, trade associations, and other forms of interest groups which engage in conflict, bargaining, and lobbying to maintain and improve the place of various estates in the economic and political world. Another set of them are the great philanthropic institutions, with directing boards of financially powerful and socially prominent people and with staffs of lay professional people to deal with the "social problems" of such a civilization. These institutions have entered into the scheme of ambitions placed before modern youth and have supplied them, for good or ill, with life-goals and working careers. The French-Canadian society is only now developing such organs. This may be because of the essentially defensive position of the culture in relation to the more extreme developments of industrialism. But it is also probably the lateness and essential foreignness of the industrial revolution which has left Quebec with an institutional system and a mentality oriented to another and "earlier" economic condition.

CHAPTER XIX

QUEBEC SEEKS A VILLAIN

IT IS the combination of circumstances just described which, I believe, accounts for a certain ambivalence in the expressions of discontent which have swept French Canada in the last few years. The numerous social and political movements of Quebec show, in a peculiar degree, the tendency to condemn the modern economic world while engaged in the very attempt to obtain a better place in it. Attack upon the foreign leaders of business and industry for their alleged discrimination against French Canadians is combined with hints that their own leaders have not adapted, as they presumably should have done, French-Canadian education to the demands of those same business and industrial authorities. Some account of the manifestations of discontent, drawn from newspaper accounts during the 1930's and from interviews and personal observation, will illustrate these points.

In the early days of the great depression French Canadians in and about Montreal were reported to have rioted and attacked foreign-born workmen engaged in public works. Throughout the decade they continued, occasionally by such action and constantly by word, to express strongly the notion that jobs belonged first to French Canadians. In Cantonville a labor agitator interpreted the "closed shop" to mean one closed to all but French Canadians as well as to nonunion workers.

During the latter part of the thirties the National Catholic Labor Syndicates, hitherto promoted without much success as an antidote to the few unions affiliated with the American Federation of Labor, spread rapidly into industries which had not been organized successfully in either the United States or Canada. This happened at the very moment of the upsurge of industrial unionism in the United States. Many strikes and some violence occurred. The American manager of a silk mill in a small town was kidnapped while playing golf, set across the not far distant United States border, and told to stay in his own country. The American manager of an asbestos mill was ridden out of town on a rail. An inkpot was thrown into the face of the English-Canadian president of Canada's largest textile manufacturing com-

pany when he visited a plant where the men were on strike. In Cantonville stones were thrown through the windows of the houses of some
English executives during various strikes. In a neighboring town similar treatment was given the French-Canadian manager of a foundry.

Not all manifestations of the discontent of labor took these elemental
forms. There were many well-organized strikes, conducted to the end
of forcing the employers to negotiate with the syndicates. Even in such
cases, the theme of conflict between French-Canadian worker and
English employer appeared clearly.

The National Catholic Labor Syndicates, whose leaders co-ordinated, if they did not promote, the unrest and collective action of labor, preach the common interest of employer and workman and decry,
in the terms of the papal encyclicals, the development of extreme forms
of industrialization. The situation presented the contradiction of
workmen striking under the aegis of organizations whose doctrine
regards the strike as fundamentally dangerous.

The other important movement of industrial workers developed in
this period is the Jeunesse ouvrière catholique. It is organized on the
parish basis, with divisions for each sex, to which have lately been
added sections for married workers and for pre-working youth. The
principle of organization—by parish, age, sex, and marital condition—
is not adapted to industrial conflict but to the exercise of piety, instruction, recreation, pilgrimages, and demonstrations. The public activities of the Jeunesse ouvrière catholique consist, in fact, of festive parades and demonstrations. The most notorious was the mass demonstration in which more than a hundred couples were married at once
in a Montreal ball park before an audience of thousands of uniformed
Jocistes from all over the province.

In this period numerous smaller movements attested the rise of a
more passionate nationalism among the middle classes of French
Canadians. The nationalistic theme appeared in organizations nominally devoted to economic interests. Leagues of proprietors, chambers
of commerce, junior chambers of commerce (a type of organization
recently borrowed from the English-speaking world), and retail merchants' and professional associations flourished. Their resolutions, designed to promote action to relieve the depression, were often strongly
antiforeign in word and spirit. Political groups, dominated by students and young professional men, attacked, in the same breath, the
evils of capitalism, British imperialists, Jewish plotters, and American
and Canadian financiers, whom they held responsible for the troubles

of French Canada. The villains among their own people were party politicians (*politicailleurs*) and wealthy people who allegedly had sold out to foreigners. Again the cry of discrimination in the economic world carried an undertone of criticism of their own elders for not having so adapted the educational system that young French Canadians could compete equally with English. On the positive side, these political movements proposed economic reorganization which would limit the power of financiers, put Quebec resources back into French hands, and develop small industries. Some talked of a corporative state.

A strong current of anti-Semitism ran through these movements. Chain stores, department stores, high finance, and the burden of mortgages, as well as communism, were blamed on the Jews. Anti-Semitic statements frequently occurred in conjunction with complaint concerning the English and American domination of business and industry. This connection appeared also in certain popular demonstrations, although not in all.

A good many street demonstrations occurred in the period. A group, alleged to be students of the French University of Montreal, marched upon and interrupted a dancing marathon said to be operated by a Jew. Newspapers reported that students of Laval University in the city of Quebec raided houses of prostitution in an access of rage against the demoralizing influences of the modern age. On several occasions Montreal students were reported to have attacked the shops of Jewish news dealers and bookdealers, alleged to be distributors of communist literature and "American obscenity."

The anti-communist phase of these movements reached its peak during the Spanish Civil War. The church took an open stand against the Republicans. In vigorous sermons the people were warned that even minor criticisms of the church at home were the beginnings that might end in the heinous sins of burning churches and murdering priests. When a Spanish priest, alleged by French Canadians to be no longer in good standing, visited Montreal in support of the Republican cause, a crowd, again alleged to be students of the French university, marched to the hall where he was to address an audience of English students. In the resulting disturbances the meeting was called off by the police. For a day or two following, there were reports of street parades with some attacks upon Jewish newsstands and bookshops which were supposed to be communistic. The final act, which seemed to bring the excitement to an end, was the gathering of a crowd of young French men before the office of an English newspaper thought to represent the big businesses of Canada; there the crowd cried: "Down with the English!" "Down with imperialism!"

Two other incidents involving the students of the French University of Montreal may contribute to an understanding of the temper of the period. Students of the law school complained that their instructors were not training them in the modern knowledge required of lawyers. They asked the retirement of some of their teachers. The lectures of one professor were interrupted by the rolling of marbles noisily down the steps of the lecture amphitheater. The other incident was a brief strike of medical students and of the interns in an important French hospital following the appointment of a Jewish student to an internship. Although the faculty and hospital staff roundly condemned the strike, public sympathy seemed on the side of the protesting students. The incident gave occasion for some nationalists to accuse the professors of medicine of failure to make reference to religion in their instruction.

It also happened, during this period, that two important Catholic churches in Montreal, a cathedral in a smaller town, and a Catholic boarding-school for boys in another small city were destroyed by fire. In the burning of the school some forty adolescent boys, sons of small-town, middle-class families, lost their lives. These distressing catastrophes gave rise to accusing rumors, in which the Jews and the communists were the villains. An openly Fascist weekly, *Le Patriote*, which bore the swastika combined with the Christian cross, wondered why synagogues never burned. The school fire was laid, by rumor, first to Jews and communists, then to the slow arrival of the fire department, to the carelessness of the aged night watchman and janitor, and finally to the provincial fire-inspection authorities. A similar sequence of rumor followed the burning of the churches.

These smoldering antagonisms were fanned by the activity of a French-Canadian ex-priest who, as an Anglican missionary in charge of a small parish in a distinctly French section of Montreal, carried on a propaganda of bitter attack against what he alleged was exploitation of the Catholic masses by a wealthy church and clergy. This was simply the usual activity of a renegade priest; carried on in the French language and in a French district, it aroused strong feeling. The sectarian Jehovah's Witnesses added their quota by determined distribution of tracts condemning the church and state as ungodly. This, too, was done in the French language and by French Canadians.

The discontents of the time found expression in a large number of small weekly papers, some of which lasted only a short time. Each had its own "tendency" or emphasis. Some were openly anti-English. A few talked of an independent French-Canadian state. Others wanted their rights within the framework of the Dominion. Some sought public ownership of utilities and abolition of timber grants and power rights to corporations. A few attacked the prevailing educational system for its failure to prepare young people for successful competition with the English in technical and industrial occupations. Some espoused the cause of Social Credit, a movement very strong in the agrarian province of Alberta and designed to break "interest slavery" by manipulation of the currency. Nearly all these periodicals were critical of political parties and party politicians. A very few were openly friendly to the Nazis.

It is not surprising that French Canadians were unusually restless in a period of unemployment and world-wide turmoil and anxiety. Nor should it be concluded that this was a period of much disorder and violence; the French Canadians were, as usual, an orderly and peaceful people. Our interest is rather in the objects upon which the malcontents vented their anger.

The French-Canadian culture, like any other, has its traditional objects of aggression, some internal and some external. No culture can operate without pressure upon individuals, a pressure which leaves some feelings of restriction and resentment. They find expression in small complaints, guardedly stated, against even the more sacred rules and authorities. But it is perhaps commoner to vent feelings of frustration upon objects or persons outside the sacred "we-group."[1]

A minority people has constantly close at hand an alien group upon which to cast its troubles. Canada is doubly blessed by having both England and the United States to blame for her difficulties. French Canada has such blessings too numerous to mention. She has had the American continent into which to spill her excess and misfit people; thus she has not had to absorb her own toxic by-products, as must a completely isolated society. That is a fact of another order. On the psychological level, the booming, disorderly, polyglot American world is an all too convenient scapegoat upon which to cast the aberrations of her own people and culture. Upon the English majority of Canada, upon the imperialism of England, and upon the expanding English-

---

[1] See John Dollard, "Hostility and Fear in Social Life," *Social Forces*, XVII (1938), 15–26.

American capitalistic industrial economy can be and are placed the blame for both the disturbance of the old order in Quebec and the inferior place of French Canadians in the new order. In addition, the immigration of a certain number of Continental Europeans and especially of Jews has provided an internal enemy and disturber completely outside the range of those things which are held dear or are at least respected. The French Canadians have a whole range of "outsiders" in their very midst. Given the mentality of defense against alien pressure and influence bred by a century and a half of minority existence, it is but natural that French-Canadian eyes should see the hand of cultural aliens in all their difficulties. Whether their eyes deceive them does not concern us in this discussion.

Physical attack of workmen upon the persons and property of managers and other executives is an elementary form of industrial conflict, not uncommon among people new to industrial work. It is relatively rare where union tactics have been developed over a long period. The significant point about these manifestations in Quebec is that the persons attacked were usually English. Of course, there are relatively few French managers to attack. But in the minds of the workers, the foreignness of their employers was more than an incident. This is obvious in the setting of one plant manager over the border. One strongly prevailing definition of labor's troubles has been that they are due to the fact that employing corporations and managers are cultural and sometimes political aliens.

The church has sponsored two movements to meet the problems of labor. They are the National Catholic Labor Syndicates and the Jeunesse ouvrière catholique. The active promoters of both are young priests and centrally appointed laymen; through them the church deals directly with the masses of working people without the mediation of those old allies of the church, the middle and upper classes. The latter, the people who are churchwardens and parish leaders, are a little apprehensive both of the emphasis on the laboring class and of the tendency of the church to by-pass the local, middle-class lay leaders.

Observation throughout the period leads me to conclude that the symbolic Jew receives the more bitter of the attacks which the French Canadians would like to make upon the English or perhaps even upon some of their own leaders and institutions. When French Canadians attack the English, they pull their punches. Long association on fairly good terms has led to a good deal of honest mutual respect between the

French and English of Quebec. It is a rare nationalist speech which does not accord the English a rightful place in Canada. The two groups have shared the responsibility of government for a long time. Even though they do not celebrate the same holidays, they both have a strong body of sentiment for Canada. The English are also powerful. Against the Jew, however, attack may proceed without fear either of retaliation or of a bad conscience.

Whether or not this interpretation is correct, many of the accusations made against the Jew in Quebec—with the obvious exception of communist leanings—would be justified in some measure if made against the English. The department stores, chain stores, banks, and large industrial and utility corporations have been introduced and are controlled by Anglo-Saxons. In fact, the Jew in Quebec is the physically present small competitor rather than the hidden wirepuller of high finance and big business. The Jew operates and competes upon the French-Canadian businessman's own level; it is the English who have introduced the new forms of economic enterprise which threaten the French-Canadian way of living and working.

No problem of human behavior is more intriguing than that of discovering why people, when they feel the distress of uncertainty and frustration, lay blame upon one villain rather than another. It is common-enough knowledge that groups of discontented individuals seize upon one tentative explanation of their difficulties after another before they arrive at a stable definition of their situation. A fruitful suggestion is that, in such a case, aggression is displaced upon persons or symbols which lie outside the range of those persons and things which one has been taught to love and respect.[2] To this I would add that people, when so disturbed, apparently engage in exploratory aggression. They seek in their environment objects which their consciences will allow them to attack and which may be effectively associated with the circumstances from which they think they suffer.

A considerable number of French Canadians have for the past decade or more been engaged in just such exploration. It is by no means certain that the eventual definition of their situation has yet emerged. Among the more severely attacked objects have been the Jew, capitalism, and communism. The symbols of democracy have come in for a more moderate drubbing, but one still severe enough to frighten some Canadians. One must remember that the fact of political democracy is much more important to the French Canadian than is the

[2] See *ibid.*, p. 18, for development of the conception of displaced aggression.

word. The word has belonged so definitely to Protestant countries, such as England and the United States, or to anticlerical countries, such as the French Republic, that it has a certain non-Catholic connotation. Certain French-Canadian leaders, both lay and clerical, have said so in no uncertain terms.

But whatever villains are blamed, the circumstances complained of remain mainly those which accompany the development of the modern industrial economy, including the American type of urban life and institutions; their threat to the old French economy, rural and town; and the unsatisfactory place of French Canadians in the newer economic system. It is perhaps the fate of a minority people, no matter what the political system under which it lives, to have major changes introduced by cultural aliens. To the latter, who look upon the divergent merely as the not yet adjusted, the minority seems to be defending an archaic order of things. French Canadians are in the course of making their adjustment to the latest and, thus far, the most revolutionary of changes set going in their midst by their English compatriots. For, unlike the military conquest of the eighteenth century and certain commercial invasions of the past, the industrial revolution of the present moves masses of people from country to city, upsets the equilibrium of the classes, strikes at the very content and aims of education, and threatens a way of life that has, in the past, given comfort and deep satisfaction to its followers.

APPENDIX A

ANALYSIS OF POSITIONS HELD BY NON-FRENCH IN INDUSTRIES OTHER THAN MILL A

Plant	Total Number of Employees	Positions Held by English and Americans
Cotton (weaving)....	600	Only English are the plant manager, the technical adviser, 2 office clerks—first two kept on from American company
Silk (finishing).......	350	Manager and supervising dyer, American. Total of 7 Americans in executive and supervisory jobs
Hosiery.............	300	Manager and 5 others, Americans (executive, supervisory, and maintenance people) Two English Canadians (head dyer and assistant)
Silk (weaving).......	150	Manager, Alsatian Bookkeeper, practical millwright, and cloth inspector, English-Canadian Warping foreman, Polish-American Weaving foreman, New England French-Canadian
Lumber.............	100	Manager, English-Canadian Secretary, English-Canadian
Paper novelties......	60	Manager, American Designer, English A few other non-French (data incomplete)
Rubber heels........	50	Manager, English-Canadian
Pencils.............	40	Manager, Austrian-American
Foundry............	40	
Paper boxes.........	30	

APPENDIX B

DIAGRAM I

PERCENTAGE DISTRIBUTION OF THE FRENCH POPULATION,
RURAL AND URBAN, BY REGIONS, 1931

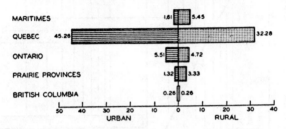

DIAGRAM II

RACIAL ORIGIN OF TOTAL POPULATION OF QUEBEC
1871–1931

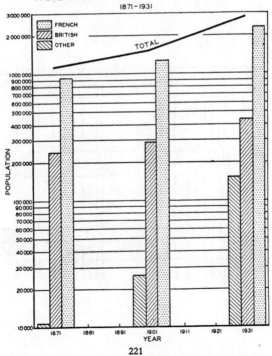

221

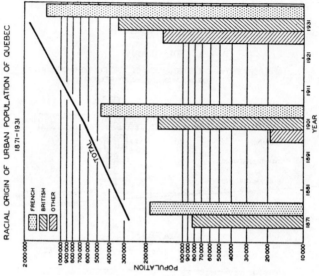

DIAGRAM IV

RACIAL ORIGIN OF URBAN POPULATION OF QUEBEC
1871–1931

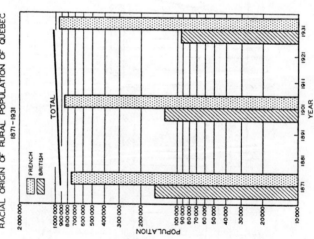

DIAGRAM III

RACIAL ORIGIN OF RURAL POPULATION OF QUEBEC
1871–1931

BIBLIOGRAPHY

Agriculture and the Farm Population. McGill University Social Research Bull. No. 1. Montreal, 1938.

AMERICAN MEDICAL ASSOCIATION. *Directory, 1939.*

AUDIT BUREAU OF CIRCULATION. *Reports, 1935–36.*

BLANCHARD, RAOUL. "Etudes canadiennes, 2ᵉ série. I. La Région du Fleuve St. Laurent entre Québec et Montréal," *Revue de géographie alpine,* XXIV (1936), 1–189.

———. "Etudes canadiennes, 2ᵉ série. II. Les Cantons de l'Est," *ibid.,* XXV (1937), 1–210.

———. "Etudes canadiennes, 2ᵉ série. III. Les Laurentides," *ibid.,* XXVI (1938), 1–183.

———. *L'Est du Canada français.* 2 vols. Montreal, 1935.

DOLLARD, J. "Hostility and Fear in Social Life," *Social Forces,* XVII (1938), 15–26.

DOMINION BUREAU OF STATISTICS. *Canada Year Book, 1940.*

———. *First Census of Canada* (1871), Vol. V.

———. *Second Census of Canada* (1881), Vol. II.

———. *Third Census of Canada* (1891), Vol. IV.

———. *Fifth Census of Canada* (1911), Vols. II and III.

———. *Sixth Census of Canada* (1921), Vol. I.

———. *Seventh Census of Canada* (1931), Vols. I, II, V, VII, and VIII.

———. *The Manufacturing Industries of Canada, 1933.*

———. *The Manufacturing Industries of Canada, 1934.*

———. *The Manufacturing Industries of Canada, 1935: Summary Report* (1938).

———. *The Manufacturing Industries of the Province of Quebec, 1934.*

DUN and BRADSTREET. *Directory* (Chicago), March, 1940.

GÉRIN, LÉON. *Le Type économique et social des canadiens.* Montreal, 1937.

HAYTHORNE, G. V. *Land and Labour, a Social Survey of Agriculture and the Farm Labour Market in Central Canada.* Toronto: Oxford University Press, 1941.

HÉMON, LOUIS. *Maria Chapdelaine.* New York, 1923.

HUGHES, EVERETT C. "Industry and the Rural System in Quebec," *Canadian Journal of Economics and Political Science,* IV (1938), 341–49.

HUGHES, EVERETT C., and McDONALD, MARGARET L. "French and English in the Economic Structure of Montreal," *Canadian Journal of Economics and Political Science,* VII (1941), 493–505.

HURD, W. B. "Population Movements in Canada, 1921–1931, and Their Implications," *Proceedings of the Canadian Political Science Association,* VI (1934), 220–38.

HURD, W. B., and CAMERON, J. B. "Population Movements in Canada, 1921–1931; Some Further Considerations," *Canadian Journal of Economics and Political Science,* I (1935), 222–45.

JAMIESON, STUART M. "French and English in the Institutional Structure of Montreal." M.A. thesis, McGill University, 1938.

LANCTOT, GUSTAVE (ed.). *Les Canadiens français et leurs voisins du sud.* Montreal, 1941.

LEMIEUX, A. O. "Factors in the Growth of the Rural Population in Eastern Canada," *Proceedings of the Canadian Political Science Association*, VI (1934), 196–219.

LUNT, P., and WARNER, W. L. *The Social Life of a Modern Community*. ("Yankee City Series," Vol. I). New Haven, 1941.

MINER, HORACE. *St. Denis, a French-Canadian Parish*. Chicago, 1939.

REDFIELD, ROBERT. *The Folk Culture of Yucatan*. Chicago, 1941.

———. "Folkways and City Ways," in Herring and Weinstock (eds.), *Renascent Mexico*. New York, 1935.

RINGUET (pseud.). *Trente arpents*. Paris, 1939.

ROSS, AILEEN. "The French and English Social Elites of Montreal." M.A. thesis, University of Chicago, 1941.

ROY, WILLIAM H. "The French-English Division of Labor in Quebec." M.A. thesis, McGill University, 1935.

Statistical Year Book. Quebec, 1937.

VINEBERG, SOLOMON. *Provincial and Local Taxation in Canada*. New York, Columbia University, 1912.

INDEX

225

226 FRENCH CANADA IN TRANSITION

Folk, rural, 143
Folk society, 3
Foremen, 54–58
Fraternal orders, 127
Frontiers, 16–21; chronic, 4, 19
Frugality, 179
Frustration, 216, 218
Funerals, 156–58

Gérin, Léon, 4, 5, 7
Gestures, exchange of, 62
Government, 84–91
Grand'messe, 95; *paroissiale*, 93, 98
Groups, interest, 133–38

Habitant, 1, 3, 5, 17, 33, 161, 170
Hémon, Louis, 4
Hierarchy, industrial, 46–64
Hinterland, 208
Holidays, 148
House, rural, 183
Household, 173

Identification, ethnic, 119, 171
Increase, natural, 7, 12
Individualism, 172, 179
Industry, 22–28; distribution of, 25; expansion of, 2, 20; home, 16; locally owned, 47; rural, 23; taxation of, 87, 88, 183; textile, 25
Institutions: communal, 84–91; economic, 84; philanthropic, 211; urban, 208–9
Intellectuals, 210
Intermarriage, 34, 167
Invasion, 19; industrial, 3
Irish, 103

Jamieson, Stuart M., 203
Jeunesse nationale, 89
Jeunesse ouvrière catholique, 100–104, 197–99, 213, 217
Jews, 71, 76, 86, 135, 214, 217–18
Junior League, 161

Kin, 164
Knights of Columbus. *See* Chevaliers de Colomb

Labor, 104
Labor unions, 133
Land, family and, 8
Language, 82; choice of, 82–83; official, 85
Law, 84
Lawyers, 75–76
Le Mieux, A. O., 13

Ligue de la Jeunesse féminine, 161, 209
Literature, French-Canadian, 210
Living, standard of, 68
Lunt, P., 123

Machinery, farm, 6
Magazines, 191–92
Managers, 71; English, 31, 183; hired, 69; origin of, 48
Marginal people, 118–19
Marriage, 185; mixed, 155, 167
Mass, 92–99; English, 120; High, 96; Low, 98
Masses, urbanized, 200
Mentality, French-Canadian, 210
Metropolis, 207
Middle class, 173, 217
Migration, 12, 40, 44
Miner, Horace, 4, 148
Minority, 3, 54, 210, 216, 219
Mobility, 44, 76
Modesty, 187
Motion picture, 192–94
Movements, political, 212, 214, 217
Municipalities, rural, 10

National Catholic Labor Syndicates, 212, 213, 217
Nationalism, 213
Nationalists, 73, 88, 127, 165
New Year's Day, 145
Newspapers, 190–92
Noël, 144
Notary, 75–76

Objectives, family, 62
Occupations, 46; industrial, 22; nonindustrial, 65–83
Order, fraternal, 104
Organizations: charitable, 85–86; parish, 10, 102–5, 122; profane, 103; sports, 130
Orientation, occupational, 63
Origins, ethnic, 46
Ownership of houses, 174–79

Parish, 33, 92–105; city, 105; colonization, 7; and family, 11; old, 7; rural, 9
Pews, 9, 93; auction of, 97; ownership of, 95
Pilgrimages, 104, 143
Politics: local, 86; provincial, 88
Population: Catholic, 43; English, 42, 44; farm, 6, 13; rural, 12–21; turnover of, 17; urban, 12, 26
Position, class, 125, 161
Prejudices, 82